Fodor's
New Zealand

Praise for Fodor's Guides

"Fodor's guides ... are an admirable blend of the cultural and the practical."
— The Washington Post

"Researched by people chosen because they live or have lived in the country, well-written, and with good historical sections ... Obligatory reading for millions of tourists."
— The Independent, London

"Usable, sophisticated restaurant coverage, with an emphasis on good value."
— Andy Birsh, Gourmet restaurant columnist, quoted by Gannett News Service

"Packed with dependable information."
— Atlanta Journal Constitution

"Fodor's always delivers high quality ... thoughtfully presented ... thorough."
— Houston Post

"Valuable because of their comprehensiveness."
— Minneapolis Star-Tribune

Reprinted from Fodor's *Australia & New Zealand '95*

Fodor's Travel Publications, Inc.
New York • Toronto • London • Sydney • Auckland

Fodor's New Zealand

Editor: Marcy Pritchard
Contributors: Steven K. Amsterdam, Terry Durack, Peter Forestal, Echo Garrett, Michael Gebicki, Dawn Lawson, Chips Mackinolty, Bevin McLaughlin, Jacki Passmore, Tracy Patruno, Mary Ellen Schultz, Nancy van Itallie
Creative Director: Fabrizio La Rocca
Cartographer: David Lindroth
Illustrator: Karl Tanner
Cover Photograph: Andrea Pistolesi/Image Bank

Design: Vignelli Associates

Contents

Maps

Foreword

While every care has been taken to ensure the accuracy of the information in this guide, the passage of time will always bring change, and, consequently, the publisher cannot accept responsibility for errors that may occur.

All prices and opening times quoted here are based on information supplied to us at press time. Hours and admission fees may change, however, and the prudent traveler will avoid inconvenience by calling ahead.

Fodor's wants to hear about your travel experiences, both pleasant and unpleasant. When a hotel or restaurant fails to live up to its billing, let us know and we will investigate the complaint and revise our entries where the facts warrant it.

Send your letters to the editors of Fodor's Travel Publications, 201 East 50th Street, New York, NY 10022.

Highlights'95 and Fodor's Choice

Highlights '95

At press time, two new attractions were scheduled to open in New Zealand in late 1994, both on the South Island. The **Christchurch Casino** will be conveniently located on Victoria Street within close walking distance of several of that city's major hotels. The casino, New Zealand's first, will feature 350 coin- and token-operated gaming machines and 30 gaming tables. There will also be an area specifically dedicated to the playing of keno and a wide selection of bars, lounges, and dining areas.

In July 1994, New Zealand's minister of conservation announced the creation of the country's 13th national park, which was to open in November 1994 in the northwest part of the South Island. At over 1 million acres in area, **Kahurangi National Park** will be the country's second largest.

Late December 1993 and early January 1994 saw the opening, below Tamaki Drive in Auckland, of an exciting new family-oriented attraction: **Kelly Tarlton's Underwater World and Antarctic Encounter.** The encounter includes a walk through a lifesize re-creation of Captain Robert Scott's 1911 Antarctic hut and a ride on a vessel called a Snow Cat, which goes through an Antarctic "whiteout" en route to a live penguin colony. The Underwater World is experienced via a moving walkway through an acrylic tunnel under the "ocean," where visitors are surrounded by sharks, stingrays, and giant eels.

Fodor's Choice

No two people will agree on what makes a perfect vacation, but it's fun and helpful to know what others think. We hope you'll have the chance to experience some of Fodor's Choices yourself while visiting New Zealand. For detailed information about each entry, refer to the appropriate chapter in this guidebook.

Dining

Auckland The French Café, *$$$*

Cin Cin on Quay, *$$*

Christchurch Sign of the Takahe, *$$$$*

Espresso 124, *$$*

Wellington Le Petit Lyon, *$$$$*

Brasserie Flipp, *$$$*

City Lodging

Auckland The Regent, *$$$$*

Devonport Villa, *$$*

Christchurch Parkroyal Christchurch, *$$$$*

Riverview Lodge, *$$*

Wellington Parkroyal Wellington, *$$$$*

Country Lodging

Huka Lodge, Lake Taupo, North Island, *$$$$*

Lake Brunner Sporting Lodge, Mitchells, near Greymouth, South Island, *$$$$*

Millbrook Resort, near Queenstown, South Island, *$$$$*

Puka Park Lodge, Coromandel Peninsula, North Island, *$$$$*

California Guest House, Nelson, South Island, *$$$*

Lake Moeraki Wilderness Lodge, South Island, *$$$*

National Park Attractions

Lake Waikaremoana, Urewara National Park, North Island

The Milford Track, Mitre Peak, and Milford Sound, Fiordland National Park, South Island

Mount Cook and Tasman Glacier, Mount Cook National Park, South Island

Special Moments

The Maori choir, St. Faith's Church, Rotorua

Kayaking with the dolphins off Abel Tasman National Park, South Island

Sampling smoked snapper at Nature Smoke, Mapua, South Island

Wildlife Attractions

The gannet colony, Cape Kidnappers, North Island

Cruising with sperm whales off Kaikoura, South Island

The royal albatrosses, Taiaroa Head, South Island

New Zealand

North Cape

Te Kao

Bay of Islands

Whangarei

Hauraki
Gulf

Great Barrier
Island

Te Kopuru

Whangarei

Coromandel
Peninsula

COROMANDEL
FOREST PARK

Auckland

Whangamata

Cape
Runaway

Waiuku

Tauranga

Bay of
Plenty

Port Waikato

Hamilton

Raglan

Rotorua

NORTH ISLAND

North
Taranaki Bight

Lake
Taupo

Taupo

Tasman
Sea

Cape Egmont

Hawke
Bay

Napier

Hastings

ABEL
TASMAN N. P.

Wanganui

Palmerston
North

Cape Farewell

Tasman
Bay

TARARUA FOREST PARK

Upper
Hutt

N.W. Nelson
Forest Park

Nelson

Lower Hutt

Blenheim

Wellington

Cook Strait

Cape Foulwind

Grey R.

Lake Summer
Forest Park

Greymouth

Arthurs
Pass N. P.

Christchurch

WESTLAND
N. P.

Franz Josef

Banks Peninsula

Fox Glacier

MT. COOK
N. P.

Haast

Haast River

SOUTH ISLAND

Mt. Aspiring

Waitaki R.

Southern Alps

Milford
Sound

Lake Wanaka

Queenstown

Oamaru

SOUTH
PACIFIC OCEAN

Lake
Wakatipu

Lake
Te Anau

Te Anau

Lake
Manapouri

Dunedin

FIORDLAND
N. P.

KEY

Rail Lines

Foveaux Strait

Invercargill

Stewart
Island

N

0   200 miles

0   300 km

World Time Zones

Numbers below vertical bands relate each zone to Greenwich Mean Time (0 hrs.).
Local times frequently differ from these general indications,
as indicated by light-face numbers on map.

Introduction

By Michael Gebicki

I first laid eyes on New Zealand in 1967, near the end of an ocean voyage from Los Angeles to Australia. For a long morning, we skirted the New Zealand coastline north of Auckland, slipping past a land of impossibly green hills that seemed to be populated entirely by sheep. When the ship berthed in Auckland, I saw parked along the quay a museum-quality collection of vintage British automobiles, the newest of which was probably 15 years old. The explanation was simple enough: All cars were imported, and imports were taxed at an enormous rate. But to a teenager fresh from the U.S.A., it seemed as though we had entered a time warp. When we took a day tour into the hills, the bus driver kept stopping for chats with other drivers; in those days it seemed possible to know everyone in New Zealand.

Since then, Auckland has caught up with the rest of the world. Its cars, its cellular-phone-toting execs, its waterfront restaurants with sushi and French mineral water all exist, unmistakably, in the modern world. Yet rural New Zealand still belongs to a greener, cleaner, friendlier time. Nostalgia remains a strong suit in New Zealand's deck—second, of course, to the country's splendid scenery. If you travel in search of glamorous shopping, sophisticated nightlife, and gourmet pleasures, it's probably not the place for you. You can find these garnishes, in a minor way, in the cities, but New Zealand's cities are strictly sideshows on the world stage. Gracious, calm, and welcoming they may be, but Auckland, Christchurch, and Wellington are never going to be mistaken for Paris or New York.

New Zealand was a late arrival on the world scene. Its first settlers were Polynesians who reached its shores about AD 850, followed by a second wave of Polynesian migrants in the 14th century. These were not carefree, grass-skirted islanders living in a palmy utopia, but a fierce, martial people who made their homes in hilltop fortresses, where they engaged in an almost continual state of warfare with neighboring tribes. It wasn't until the 1840s that European settlers, primarily from England, arrived in any numbers. Compared with such other immigrant societies as the United States and Australia, New Zealand is overwhelmingly British—in its love of gardens, its architecture, its political system, its food. The Maoris remain an assertive minority of 9%, a dignified, robust people whose art bears witness to a rich culture of legends and dreams. That culture comes dramatically to life in performances of traditional songs and dances, including the *haka*, or war dance, which was calculated to intimidate and demoralize the enemy; little wonder that the national rugby team performs a haka as a prelude to its games.

The New Zealand land mass is divided into two main islands. Most of the country's 3.42 million people live on the North Island, while the South Island has the lion's share of the national parks. (More than one-tenth of the country's total land area has been set aside as parks.) In a country about the size of Colorado—or just slightly larger than Great Britain—nature has assembled active volcanoes, subtropical rain forests, geysers, trout streams (some of the finest on earth), fjords, beaches, glaciers, and some two dozen peaks that soar to more than 3,000 meters (10,000 feet). The country has scenic spectaculars from top to bottom, but while the North Island often resembles a pristine golf course, the South Island is wild, majestic, and exhilarating.

Experiencing these wonders is painless. New Zealand has a well-developed infrastructure of hotels, motels, and tour operators—but the best the country has to offer can't be seen through the windows of a tour bus. A trip here is a hands-on experience: hike, boat, fish, hunt, cycle, raft, and breathe some of the freshest air on earth. And if these adventures sound a little too intrepid for you, the sheer beauty of the landscape and the clarity of the air will give you muscles you never knew you had.

1 Essential Information

Before You Go

Government Tourist Offices

By Michael Gebicki

For information about travel to and within New Zealand, contact the nearest **New Zealand Tourism Board.**

In the U.S.: 501 Santa Monica Blvd., Los Angeles, CA 90401, tel. 800/388–5494.

In Canada: 888 Dansmuir St., Suite 1200, Vancouver, BC V6C 3K4, tel. 800/888–5494.

In the U.K.: New Zealand House, Haymarket, London SW1Y 4TQ, tel. 71/973–0360.

In Australia: Level 8, 35 Pitt St., Sydney 2000, tel. 02/247–3111.

U.S. Government Travel Briefings

The U.S. Department of State's **Overseas Citizens Emergency Center** (Room 4811, Washington, DC 20520; enclose a stamped, self-addressed envelope) issues Consular Information Sheets that detail crime, security, political climate, and health risks, as well as embassy locations, entry requirements, currency regulations, and other routine matters. For the latest information, stop in at any U.S. passport office, consulate, or embassy; call the interactive hot line (tel. 202/647–5225, fax 202/647–3000); or, with your PC's modem, tap into the Bureau of Consular Affairs' computer bulletin board (tel. 202/647–9225).

Tours and Packages

Should you buy your travel arrangements to New Zealand packaged or do it yourself? There are advantages either way. Buying packaged arrangements saves you money, particularly if you can find a program that includes exactly the features you want. You also get a pretty good idea of what your trip will cost from the outset. Generally, you have two options: fully escorted tours and independent packages. Escorted tours are most often via motorcoach, with a tour director in charge. They're ideal if you don't mind having limited free time and traveling with strangers. Your baggage is handled, your time rigorously scheduled, and most meals planned. Such tours are therefore the most hassle-free way to see a destination, as well as generally the least expensive. Independent packages allow plenty of flexibility. They generally include airline travel and hotels, with certain options available, such as sightseeing, car rental, and excursions. Such packages are usually more expensive than escorted tours, but your time is your own.

While you can book directly through tour operators, you will pay no more to go through a travel agent, who will be able to tell you about tours and packages from a number of operators. Whatever program you ultimately choose, be sure to find out exactly what is included: taxes, tips, transfers, meals, baggage handling, ground transportation, entertainment, excursions, sports or recreation (and rental equipment if necessary). Ask about the level of hotel used, its location, the size of its rooms, the kind of bed, and its amenities, such as pool, room service, or programs for children, if they're important to you. Find out the operator's cancellation penalties. Nearly everyone charges them, and the only way to avoid them is to buy trip-cancellation insurance (*see* Trip Insurance, *below*). Also ask about the single supplement, a surcharge assessed to solo travelers. Some operators do not make you pay it if you agree to be matched up with a roommate of the same sex, even if one is not found by departure time. Remember that a program that has features you won't use may not be the most cost-wise choice for you.

Fully Escorted Tours Escorted tours are usually sold in three categories: deluxe, first-class, and tourist or budget class. The most important differences are the price, of course, and the level of accommodations. Some operators specialize in one category, while others offer a range.

Contact **Abercrombie & Kent International** (1520 Kensington Rd., Suite 212, Oak Brook, IL 60521, tel. 708/954–2944 or 800/323–7308), **J & O Holidays** (3131 Camino del Rio N., Suite 1080, San Diego, CA 92108, tel. 800/377–1080, fax 619/283–3131), **Olson Travelworld** (970 W. 190th St., Suite 425, Torrance, CA 90502, tel. 800/421–2255, fax 310/768–0050), **Tauck Tours** (Box 5027, Westport, CT 06881, tel. 800/468–2825, fax 203/221–6828), **Islands in the Sun** (760 W. 16th St., Suite L, Costa Mesa, CA 92627, tel. 714/645–8300 or 800/828–6877, fax 714/548–1654), and **Travcoa** (Box 2630, Newport Beach, CA 92658, tel. 800/992–2003, fax 714/476–2538) in the deluxe category; **Gadabout Tours** (700 E. Tahquitz Canyon Way, Palm Springs, CA 92262, tel. 619/325–5556 or 800/952–5068), **Globus** (5301 S. Federal Circle, Littleton, CO 80123, tel. 800/851–0728, fax 303/798–5441), **Jetabout Quantas Vacations** (300 N. Continental Blvd. Suite 610, El Segundo, CA 90245, tel. 800/641–8772, fax 310/535–1057), and **Sunbeam Tours** (1631 W. Sunflower Ave., Suite C36, Santa Ana, CA 92704, tel. 800/955–1818, fax 714/434–8009) in the first-class category; and Globus' sister company **Cosmos** (at the same number) in the tourist category.

Most itineraries are jam-packed with sightseeing, so you see a lot in a short amount of time (usually one place per day). To judge just how fast-paced the tour is, review the itinerary carefully. If you are in a different hotel each night, you will be getting up early each day to head out, travel to your next destination, do some sightseeing, have dinner, and go to bed; then you'll start all over again. If you want some free time, make sure it's mentioned in the tour brochure; if you want to be escorted to every meal, confirm that any tour you consider does that. Also, when comparing programs, be sure to find out if the motorcoach is air-conditioned and has a restroom on board. Make your selection based on price and stops on the itinerary.

Independent Independent packages, which travel agents call FITs (for for-
Packages eign independent travel), are offered by airlines, tour operators
who may also do escorted programs, and any number of other
companies from large, established firms to small, new entrepreneurs.

Contact **Abercrombie & Kent International** (*see above*), **Aus-
travel** (51 E. 42nd St., Suite 616, New York, NY 10017, tel. 212/
972–6880 or 800/633–3404), **Destination World** (28441 High-
bridge, Suite 510, Rolling Hills Estates, CA 90274, tel. 800/426–
3644, fax 310/544–9387), **Globus** (*see above*), **Islands in the Sun**
(*see above*), **J & O Holidays** (*see above*), **Sunbeam Tours** (*see
above*), **Swain Australia Tours** (6 W. Lancaster Ave., Ardmore,
PA 19003, tel. 800/227–9246, fax 215/896–9592), and **United Vacations** (800/351–4200). **SO/PAC** (tel. 800/551–2012, fax 213/871–
0811) and **Guthreys Pacific** (tel. 800/227–5317, fax 714/960–4678)
offer city packages.

Their programs come in a wide range of prices based on levels of
luxury and options—in addition to hotel and airfare, sightseeing, car rental, transfers, admission to local attractions, and
other extras. Note that when pricing different packages, it
sometimes pays to purchase the same arrangements separately,
as when a rock-bottom promotional airfare is being offered, for
example. Again, base your choice on what's available at your
budget for the destinations you want to visit.

Special- Special-interest programs may be fully escorted or indepen-
Interest dent. Some require a certain amount of expertise, but most are
Travel for the average traveler with an interest and are usually hosted
by experts in the subject matter. When the program is escorted,
it enjoys the advantages and disadvantages of all escorted programs; because your fellow travelers are apt to be passionate or
knowledgeable about the subject, they can prove as enjoyable a
part of your travel experience as the destination itself. The price
range is wide, but the cost is usually higher—sometimes a lot
higher—than for ordinary escorted tours and packages, because of the expert guiding and special activities.

Adventure **Adventure Center** (1311 63rd St., Suite 200, Emeryville, CA
94608, tel. 510/654–1879 or 800/227–8747, fax 510/654–4200),
Mountain Travel/Sobek (6420 Fairmount Ave., El Cerrito, CA
94530, tel. 800/227–2384, fax 510/525–7710), **Backroads Bicycle
Touring** (1516 5th St, Berkeley, CA 91740, tel. 800/462–2848, fax
510/527–1444), **Nature Expeditions International** (474 Wil-
amette, Box 11496, Eugene, OR 97440, tel. 800/869–0639), **Wilderness Travel** (801 Allston Way, Berkeley, CA 94710, tel. 800/
368–2794), and **American Wilderness Experience** (Box 1486,
Boulder, CO 80306, tel. 800/444–0099) offer tours including bicycling, canoeing, fishing, river rafting, sea kayaking, skiing,
trekking, and nature and wildlife expeditions.

Fishing **Rod & Reel Adventures** (3507 Tully Rd., Suite 5, Modesto, CA
95356, tel. 800/423–9731, fax 209/524–1220) and **The Best of New
Zealand Fly Fishing** (2817 Wilshire Blvd., Santa Monica, CA
90403, tel. 800/528–6129) run multi-day fishing trips.

Golf **ITC Golf Tours** (4134 Atlantic Ave., Suite 205, Long Beach, CA 90807, tel. 800/257–4981, fax 310/424–6683) offers customized golf packages to Australia and New Zealand.

Wine Tours **World Travelers, Inc.** (2819 First Ave., Suite 280, Seattle, WA 98121, tel. 800/426–3610, fax 206/441–8862) conducts week-long wine tours of New Zealand with stays in manor houses.

When to Go

New Zealand's climate varies from subtropical in the north to temperate in the south. Its seasons are the reverse of those in North America and Europe. Summers (December–March) are generally warm, with an average of seven to eight hours of sunshine per day throughout the country. Winters (June–September) are mild at lower altitudes on the North Island, but heavy snowfalls are common on the South Island, particularly on the peaks of the Southern Alps. Rain can pour at any time of the year. (Some areas on the west coast of the South Island receive an annual rainfall of more than 100 inches.)

The ideal months for comfortable all-round travel are October–November and February–April, especially for anyone who wants to participate in adventure activities. Avoid the school holidays, when highways may be congested and accommodation is likely to be scarce and more expensive. The summer school holidays (the busiest) fall between mid-December and the end of January; other holiday periods are mid-May to the end of May, early July to mid-July, and late August to mid-September.

Climate The following are average daily maximum and minimum temperatures for major cities in New Zealand.

Auckland	Jan.	74F	23C	May	63F	17C	Sept.	61F	16C
		61	16		52	11		49	9
	Feb.	74F	23C	June	58F	14C	Oct.	63F	17C
		61	16		49	9		52	11
	Mar.	72F	22C	July	56F	13C	Nov.	67F	19C
		59	15		47	8		54	12
	Apr.	67F	19C	Aug.	58F	14C	Dec.	70F	21C
		56	13		47	8		58	14

Christchurch	Jan.	70F	21C	May	56F	13C	Sept.	58F	14C
		54	12		40	4		40	4
	Feb.	70F	21C	June	52F	11C	Oct.	63F	17C
		54	12		36	2		45	7
	Mar.	67F	19C	July	50F	10C	Nov.	67F	19C
		50	10		36	2		47	8
	Apr.	63F	17C	Aug.	52F	11C	Dec.	70F	21C
		45	7		36	2		52	11

Queenstown	Jan.	72F	22C	May	52F	11C	Sept.	56F	13C
		49	9		36	2		38	3
	Feb.	70F	21C	June	47F	8C	Oct.	61F	16C
		50	10		34	1		41	5
	Mar.	67F	19C	July	46F	8C	Nov.	65F	18C
		47	8		34	– 1		45	7
	Apr.	61F	16C	Aug.	50F	10C	Dec.	70F	21C
		43	6		34	1		49	9

Information Sources For current weather conditions for cities in the United States and abroad, plus the local time and helpful travel tips, call the **Weather Channel Connection** (tel. 900/WEATHER or 932–8437; 95¢ per minute) from a touch-tone phone.

Festivals and Seasonal Events

Not surprisingly, sport features heavily in New Zealand's festival calendar. Horse and boat races, triathlons, and fishing competitions are far more prominent than celebrations of the arts. Just about every town holds a yearly agricultural and pastoral ("A&P") show, and these proud displays of local crafts, produce, livestock, and wood-chopping and sheep-shearing prowess provide a memorable look at rural New Zealand. An annual calendar, *New Zealand Special Events*, is available from government tourist offices.

Jan. 1: New Year's Day is a nationwide holiday.

Feb. 1: For the **Auckland Anniversary Day Regatta,** Auckland's birthday party, the "City of Sails" takes to the water.

Feb. 6: Waitangi Day, New Zealand's national day, commemorates the signing of the Treaty of Waitangi between whites and Maoris in 1840. The focus of the nationwide celebration is, naturally enough, the town of Waitangi in the Bay of Islands.

Feb. 11–12: Speights Coast to Coast is the ultimate iron-man challenge—a two-day, 238-kilometer (148-mile) marathon of cycling, running, and kayaking that spans the South Island from west to east. Information: Canterbury Information Centre, corner Worcester Street and Oxford Terrace, tel. 03/79–9629.

Late Feb.–mid-Mar.: New Zealand International Festival of the Arts, a biennial event held in even-numbered years, is the country's premier performing-arts festival, during which many international performers can be seen in Wellington. Information: Wellington City Information Centre, corner Wakefield and Victoria streets, tel. 04/499–4444.

Mar. 2–4: Golden Shears International Shearing Championship is a three-day event that pits men armed with shears against fleecy sheep in the town of Masterton, just north of Wellington. Information: Masterton Visitor Information Centre, 5 Dixon Street, tel. 06/378–7373.

Apr. 2–10: Bluff Oyster Festival celebrates the beginning of the oyster season at this tiny seaport on the southern tip of the South Island. Information: Invercargill Information Centre, 82 Dee Street, tel. 03/218–6091.

Apr. 14–17: The **Easter** holiday weekend lasts from Good Friday through Easter Monday.

Apr. 25: Anzac Day honors the soldiers who fought and died in World War I.

First Monday in June: the Queen's Birthday is celebrated nationwide.

Oct. 23: Labour Day is observed throughout the country.

2nd Week in Nov.: Canterbury Agricultural and Pastoral Show spotlights the farmers and graziers of the rich countryside surrounding Christchurch. Information: Canterbury Information Centre, corner Worcester Street and Oxford Terrace, tel. 03/79-9629.

Dec. 25-26: On **Christmas Day** and **Boxing Day** the country virtually closes down.

What to Pack

Clothing Be prepared for a varied climate. Wet-weather gear and comfortable, sturdy shoes are essential. Dress is fairly casual in most cities, though top resorts and restaurants may require a jacket and tie. A light sweater or jacket will suffice for evenings in the autumn, but winter demands a heavier coat—a raincoat with a zip-out wool lining is ideal. Comfortable walking shoes are a must. You should have a pair of running shoes or the equivalent if you're planning to trek, and rubber-sole sandals or canvas shoes are needed for walking on reef coral.

Miscellaneous An extra pair of glasses, contact lenses, or prescription sunglasses is always a good idea. Stores carry the same cosmetic products as back home, so you don't need to carry extra supplies. If you have a health problem that may require you to purchase a prescription drug, take enough to last the duration of the trip, and be sure to pack it in your carry-on luggage. And don't forget to pack a list of the addresses of offices that supply refunds for lost or stolen traveler's checks.

Electricity The electrical current in New Zealand is 230 volts, 50 cycles alternating current (AC); the United States runs on 110-volt, 60-cycle AC current. Unlike wall outlets in the United States, which accept plugs with two flat prongs, outlets in New Zealand take a slanted three-prong plug.

Adapters, To use U.S.-made electric appliances abroad, you'll need an *Converters,* adapter plug. Unless the appliance is dual-voltage and made for *Transformers* travel, you'll also need a converter. Hotels sometimes have 110-volt outlets marked "For Shavers Only" near the sink; don't use them for a high-wattage appliance like a blow-dryer. If you're traveling with an older laptop computer, carry a transformer. New laptop computers are autosensing, operating equally well on 110 or 220 volts, so you need only the appropriate adapter plug. For a copy of the free brochure "Foreign Electricity is No Deep Dark Secret," send a stamped, self-addressed envelope to adapter-converter manufacturer **Franzus Company** (Customer Service, Dept. B50, Murtha Industrial Park, Box 142, Beacon Falls, CT 06403, tel. 203/723-6664).

Luggage Free airline baggage allowances depend on the airline, the *Regulations* route, and the class of your ticket. In general, on domestic flights and on international flights between the United States and foreign destinations, you are entitled to check two bags—neither exceeding 62 inches, or 158 centimeters (length + width + height), or weighing more than 70 pounds (32 kilograms). A third piece may be brought aboard as a carryon; its total dimensions are generally limited to less than 45 inches (114 centimeters), so it will fit easily under the seat in front of you or in the overhead compartment. In the United States, the Federal Aviation Administration (FAA) gives airlines broad latitude for carry-on allowances and tailors limits to different aircraft and operational conditions. Charges for excess, oversize, or overweight pieces will therefore vary.

If you are flying between two foreign destinations, note that baggage allowances may be determined not by number of pieces, but by weight; you'll generally be allowed 88 pounds (40 kilograms) of luggage in first class, 66 pounds (30 kilograms) in business class, and 44 pounds (20 kilograms) in economy. If your flight between two cities abroad *connects* with your transatlantic or transpacific flight, the piece method still applies.

Safeguarding Your Luggage Before leaving home, itemize your bags' contents and their worth so you'll be prepared if they somehow go astray. To minimize that risk, tag them inside and out with your name, address, and phone number. (If you use your home address, cover it so that potential thieves can't see it.) At check-in, make sure that the tag attached by baggage handlers bears the correct three-letter code for your destination. If your bags do not arrive with you, or if you detect damage, do not leave the airport until you've filed a written report with the airline.

Taking Money Abroad

Traveler's Checks Traveler's checks are preferable in metropolitan centers, although you'll need cash in rural areas and small towns. The most widely recognized are **American Express, Citicorp, Diners Club, Thomas Cook,** and **Visa.** Both American Express and Thomas Cook issue checks that can be countersigned and used by you or your traveling companion. Typically the issuing company or the bank at which you make your purchase charges 1% to 3% of the checks' face value as a fee. Some foreign banks charge as much as 20% of the face value as the fee for cashing traveler's checks in a foreign currency. Buy a few checks in small denominations to cash toward the end of your trip, so you won't be left with excess foreign currency. Record the numbers of checks as you spend them, and keep this list separate from the checks.

You can also buy traveler's checks in New Zealand dollars—a good idea if the U.S. dollar is falling and you want to lock in the current rate.

Currency Exchange Banks offer the most favorable exchange rates. If you use currency exchange booths at airports, rail and bus stations, hotels, stores, and privately run exchange firms, you'll typically get less favorable rates, but you may find the hours more convenient.

You can get good rates and avoid long lines at airport currency-exchange booths by getting a small amount of currency at **Thomas Cook Currency Services** (630 Fifth Ave., New York, NY 10111, tel. 212/757–6915 or 800/223–7373 for locations in major metropolitan areas throughout the U.S.) or **Ruesch International** (tel. 800/424–2923 for locations) before you depart.

Getting Money from Home

Cash Machines Many automated-teller machines (ATMs) are tied to such international networks as **Cirrus** and **Plus.** You can use your bank card at ATMs away from home to withdraw money from an account and get cash advances on a credit-card account if your card has been programmed with a personal identification number, or PIN. Check in advance on limits on withdrawals and cash advances within specified periods. Ask whether your bank-card or credit-card PIN number will need to be reprogrammed for use in the area you'll be visiting, because only four-digit numbers are commonly used overseas. Note that on cash advances, interest is charged from the day that the money is withdrawn, without the usual grace period. Although transaction fees for ATM withdrawals abroad will probably be higher than fees for withdrawals at home, Cirrus and Plus exchange rates tend to be good. At press time, Cirrus was coming on-line in New Zealand; Discover cards, however, are still accepted only in the United States.

Wiring Money You don't have to be a cardholder to send or receive a **MoneyGram from American Express** for up to $10,000. Go to a MoneyGram agent in retail and convenience stores and American Express travel offices, and pay up to $1,000 with a credit card and anything over that in cash. You are allowed a free long-distance call to give the transaction code to your intended recipient, who needs only present identification and the reference number to the nearest MoneyGram agent to pick up the cash. MoneyGram agents are in more than 70 countries (call 800/926–9400 for locations). Fees range from 3% to 10%, depending on the amount and method of payment.

You can also use **Western Union.** To wire money, take either cash or a cashier's check to the nearest office or call and use your MasterCard or Visa. Money sent from the United States or Canada will be available for pickup at agent locations in New Zealand within minutes. Once the money is in the system, it can be picked up at any of 22,000 locations (call 800/325–6000 for the one nearest you).

Currency

New Zealand's unit of currency is the dollar, divided into 100 cents. Bills are in $100, $50, $10, and $5 denominations. Coins are $2, $1, 50¢, 20¢, 10¢, and 5¢. At press time, the rate of exchange was NZ$1.85 to the U.S. dollar, NZ$1.41 to the Canadian dollar, NZ$2.78 to the pound sterling, and NZ$1.25 to the

Australian dollar. Prices quoted throughout are in New Zealand dollars.

What It Will Cost

For most travelers, New Zealand is not an expensive destination. The cost of meals, accommodation, and travel is slightly higher than in the United States but considerably less than in Western Europe. At about $1 per liter—equal to about US$2.10 per gallon—premium-grade gasoline is expensive by North American standards, but not by European ones.

Inflation, which reached a peak of almost 20% in the late 1980s, has now been reduced to less than 5%. Prices are expected to remain stable as the government pursues strict monetarist policies and continues to allow free market forces to determine costs.

Taxes A goods and services tax (GST) of 12.5% is levied throughout New Zealand. It's usually incorporated into the cost of an item, but in hotels and some restaurants it is added to the bill.

Visitors exiting the country must pay a departure tax of $20.

Sample Costs Cup of coffee: $2.50
Glass of beer in a bar: $2.50–$4
Take-out ham sandwich or meat pie: $2.50
Hamburger in a café: $4
Room-service sandwich in a hotel: $12
A 2-kilometer (1¼-mile) taxi ride: $5

Passports and Visas

If your passport is lost or stolen abroad, report it immediately to the nearest embassy or consulate and to the local police. If you can provide the information contained in the passport, the consular officer will usually be able to issue you a new passport. For this reason, it is a good idea to keep a photocopy of the data page of your passport separate from your money and traveler's checks. Also leave a photocopy with a relative or friend at home.

U.S. Citizens All U.S. citizens, even infants, need a valid passport to enter New Zealand for stays of up to 90 days. You can pick up new and renewal application forms at any of the 13 U.S. Passport Agency offices and at some post offices and courthouses. Although passports are usually mailed within four weeks of your application's receipt, allow five weeks or more from April through summer. Call the Department of State Office of Passport Services' information line (tel. 202/647–0518) for fees, documentation requirements, and other details.

Canadian Citizens Canadian citizens need a valid passport to enter New Zealand for stays of up to 90 days. Application forms are available at 23 regional passport offices as well as post offices and travel agencies. You must appear in person whether you're applying for a first-time or a subsequent passport. Children under 16 may be included on a parent's passport but must have their own passport if they will be traveling alone. Passports are valid for five years and are usually mailed within two weeks of an application's receipt. For fees, documentation requirements, and other information in English or French, call the passport office (tel. 514/283–2152 or 800/567–6868).

U.K. Citizens Citizens of the United Kingdom need a valid passport to enter New Zealand. Applications for new and renewal passports are available from main post offices as well as at the six passport offices, located in Belfast, Glasgow, Liverpool, London, Newport, and Peterborough. You may apply in person at all passport offices or by mail to all except the London office. Children under 16 may travel on an accompanying parent's passport. All passports are valid for 10 years. Allow a month for processing.

Customs and Duties

On Arrival New Zealand has stringent regulations governing the import of weapons, foodstuffs, and certain plant and animal material. Anti-drug laws are strict and penalties severe. In addition to personal effects, nonresidents over 17 years of age may bring in, duty-free, 200 cigarettes or 250 grams of tobacco or 50 cigars, 4.5 liters of wine, one bottle containing not more than 1,125 milliliters of spirits or liqueur, and personal purchases and gifts up to the value of US \$380 (NZ\$700).

Returning Home
U.S. Customs Provided you've been out of the country for at least 48 hours and haven't already used the exemption, or any part of it, in the past 30 days, you may bring home \$400 worth of foreign goods duty-free. So can each member of your family, regardless of age; and your exemptions may be pooled, so one of you can bring in more if another brings in less. A flat 10% duty applies to the next \$1,000 of goods; above \$1,400, the rate varies with the merchandise. (If the 48-hour or 30-day limits apply, your duty-free allowance drops to \$25, which may not be pooled.) Please note that these are the *general* rules, applicable to most countries, including New Zealand.

Travelers 21 or older may bring back 1 liter of alcohol duty-free, provided the beverage laws of the state through which they reenter the United States allow it. In addition, 100 non-Cuban cigars and 200 cigarettes are allowed, regardless of your age. Antiques and works of art more than 100 years old are duty-free.

Gifts valued at less than \$50 may be mailed to the United States duty-free, with a limit of one package per day per addressee (do not send alcohol or tobacco products, nor perfume valued at more than \$5); mark the package "Unsolicited Gift" and include the nature of the gift and its retail value on the outside of the package.

For a copy of "Know Before You Go," a free brochure detailing what you may and may not bring back to the United States, rates of duty, and other pointers, contact the **U.S. Customs Service** (Box 7407, Washington, DC 20044, tel. 202/927–6724).

Canadian Once per calendar year, when you've been out of Canada for at
Customs least seven days, you may bring in C$300 worth of goods duty-
free. If you've been away less than seven days but more than 48
hours, the duty-free exemption drops to C$100 but can be
claimed any number of times (as can a C$20 duty-free exemption
for absences of 24 hours or more). You cannot combine the yearly
and 48-hour exemptions, use the C$300 exemption only partially
(to save the balance for a later trip), or pool exemptions with
family members. Goods claimed under the C$300 exemption
may follow you by mail; those claimed under the lesser exemptions must accompany you on your return.

Alcohol and tobacco products may be included in the yearly and
48-hour exemptions but not in the 24-hour exemption. If you
meet the age requirements of the province through which you
reenter Canada, you may bring in, duty-free, 1.14 liters (40 im-
perial ounces) of wine or liquor *or* two dozen 12-ounce cans or
bottles of beer or ale. If you are 16 or older, you may bring in,
duty-free, 200 cigarettes, 50 cigars or cigarillos, and 400 tobacco
sticks or 400 grams of manufactured tobacco. Alcohol and tobacco must accompany you on your return.

An unlimited number of gifts valued up to C$60 each may be
mailed to Canada duty-free. These do not count as part of your
exemption. Label the package "Unsolicited Gift—Value under
$60." Alcohol and tobacco are excluded.

For more information, including details of duties on items that
exceed your duty-free limit, ask the **Revenue Canada Customs
and Excise Department** (Connaught Bldg., MacKenzie Ave., Ottawa, Ontario, K1A OL5, tel. 613/957–0275) for a copy of the
free brochure "I Declare/Je Déclare."

U.K. Customs From countries outside the EU such as New Zealand, you may
import duty-free 200 cigarettes, 100 cigarillos, 50 cigars, or 250
grams of tobacco; 1 liter of spirits or 2 liters of fortified or sparkling wine; 2 liters of still table wine; 60 milliliters of perfume;
250 milliliters of toilet water; plus £36 worth of other goods, including gifts and souvenirs.

For further information or a copy of "A Guide for Travellers,"
which details standard customs procedures as well as what you
may bring into the United Kingdom from abroad, contact **HM
Customs and Excise** (Dorset House, Stamford St., London SE1
9PY, tel. 0171/928–3344).

Traveling with Cameras, Camcorders, and Laptops

About Film If your camera is new or if you haven't used it for a while, shoot
and Cameras and develop a few rolls of film before leaving home. Store film in
a cool, dry place—never in the car's glove compartment or on the
shelf under the rear window.

Airport security X-rays generally aren't harmful to film with
ISO below 400. To protect your film, carry it with you in a clear
plastic bag and ask for a hand inspection. Such requests are hon-
ored at U.S. airports but are at the discretion of the inspector

abroad. Don't depend on a lead-lined bag to protect film in checked luggage—the airline may increase the radiation to see what's inside. Call the **Kodak Information Center** (tel. 800/242–2424) for details.

About Camcorders Before your trip, put camcorders through their paces: shoot some practice tape, invest in a skylight filter to protect the lens, and check the batteries. Most newer camcorders are equipped with batteries that can be recharged with a universal or world-wide AC adapter charger (or multivoltage converter) usable whether the voltage is 110 or 220. All that's needed is the appropriate plug.

About Videotape Videotape is not damaged by X-rays, but it may be harmed by the magnetic field of a walk-through metal detector, so ask for a hand-check. Airport security personnel may ask you to turn on your camcorder to prove that it's not an explosive device, so make sure the battery is charged. Note that rather than the National Television System Committee video standard (NTSC) used in the United States and Canada, New Zealand uses PAL technology. You will not be able to view North American tapes on TV sets down under, nor view movies bought there with your home VCR. Blank tapes bought in New Zealand can be used for NTSC camcorder taping, but they are pricey.

About Laptops Security X-rays do not harm hard-disk or floppy-disk storage, but you may request a hand-check, at which point you may be asked to turn on the computer to prove that it is indeed what it appears to be. (Check your battery before departure.) Most airlines allow you to use your laptop aloft except during takeoff and landing (so as not to interfere with navigation equipment). For international travel, register your foreign-made laptop with U.S. Customs as you leave the country. If your laptop is U.S.-made, call the consulate of the country you'll be visiting to find out whether it should be registered with customs upon arrival. Before departure, find out about repair facilities at your destination, and don't forget any transformer or adapter plug you may need (*see* Electricity, *above*).

Language

The Maori language is still spoken by many New Zealanders of Polynesian descent, but English is the everyday language for all races. A number of Maori words have found their way into common usage, most noticeably in place-names, which often refer to peculiar features of the local geography or food supply. The Maori word for New Zealand, *Aotearoa*, means "land of the long white cloud." The South Island town of Kaikoura is famous for its crayfish—and the word means "to eat crayfish." *Whangapiro*, the Maori name for the Government Gardens in Rotorua, means "an evil-smelling place"; if you visit the town, you'll find out why. A Polynesian noun you'll sometimes come across in Maori churches is *tapu*—"sacred"—which has entered the English language as *taboo*. Another Maori word you will frequently encounter is *pakeha*, which means you, the non-Maori.

The Maori greeting is *kia ora*, which can also mean "goodbye," "good health," or "good luck."

A Personal Kiwi-Yankee Dictionary, by Louis S. Leland, Jr., is an amusing and informative guide to New Zealand idioms.

Staying Healthy

Nutrition and general health standards in New Zealand are high, and it would be hard to find a more pristine natural environment. There are no venomous snakes, and the only poisonous spider, the katipo, is a rarity. One surprising health hazard is the water. While the country's alpine lakes might look like backdrops for mineral-water ads, some on the South Island harbor a tiny organism that can cause "duck itch," a temporary but intense skin irritation. The organism is found only on the shallow lake margins, so the chances of infection are greatly reduced if you stick to deeper water. Some streams are infected by giardia, a water-borne protozoal parasite that can cause gastrointestinal disorders, including acute diarrhea. Giardia is most likely to occur when streams pass through an area inhabited by mammals (such as cattle or possums). There is no risk of infection if you drink from streams above the tree line.

One New Zealander you will come to loathe is the tiny black sandfly, common to the western half of the South Island, which inflicts a painful bite that can itch for several days. Insect repellents are readily available throughout New Zealand.

Insurance

Every visitor to New Zealand is covered by the government's Accident Compensation scheme. Under this scheme, anyone who is injured in an accident is entitled to claim compensation, irrespective of fault. Benefits include most medical and hospital expenses and lump-sum payments for physical disability, but not loss of earnings outside New Zealand. (New Zealand law prohibits any injured party from bringing legal action for damages in New Zealand courts.)

For U.S. Residents Most tour operators, travel agents, and insurance agents sell specialized health-and-accident, flight, trip-cancellation, and luggage insurance as well as comprehensive policies with some or all of these features. But before you make any purchase, review your existing health and homeowner policies to find out whether they cover expenses incurred while traveling.

Health-and-Accident Insurance Specific policy provisions of supplemental health-and-accident insurance for travelers include reimbursement of $1,000 to $150,000 worth of medical and/or dental expenses caused by an accident or illness during a trip. The personal-accident, or death-and-dismemberment, provision pays a lump sum to your beneficiaries if you die or to you if you lose a limb or your eyesight; the lump sum awarded can range from $15,000 to $500,000. The medical-assistance provision may reimburse you for the cost of referrals, evacuation, or repatriation and other services, or it may automatically enroll you as a member of a particular medical-assistance company.

Flight Insurance Often bought on a last-minute impulse at the airport, flight insurance pays a lump sum when a plane crashes either to a beneficiary if the insured dies, or sometimes to a surviving passenger who loses eyesight or a limb. Like most impulse buys, flight insurance is expensive and basically unnecessary. It supplements the airlines' coverage described in the limits-of-liability paragraphs on your ticket. Charging an airline ticket to a major credit card often automatically entitles you to coverage and may also cover travel by bus, train, and ship.

Baggage Insurance In the event of loss, damage, or theft on international flights, airlines limit their liability to $20 per kilogram for checked baggage (roughly about $640 per 70-pound bag) and $400 per passenger for unchecked baggage. On domestic flights, the ceiling is $1,250 per passenger. Excess-valuation insurance can be bought directly from the airline at check-in for about $10 per $1,000 worth of coverage. However, you cannot buy it at any price for the rather extensive list of excluded items shown on your airline ticket.

Trip Insurance **Trip-cancellation-and-interruption insurance** protects you in the event you are unable to undertake or finish your trip, especially if your airline ticket, cruise, or package tour does not allow changes or cancellations. The amount of coverage you purchase should equal the amount of your travel costs that you'd be liable for if you, a traveling companion, or a family member fell ill and were forced to stay home; also include the nondiscounted, one-way airline ticket you would need to buy if you had to return home early. Read the fine print carefully, especially sections defining "family member" and "preexisting medical conditions." **Default** or **bankruptcy insurance** protects you against a supplier's failure to deliver. Such policies often do not cover default by a travel agency, tour operator, airline, or cruise line if you bought your tour and the coverage directly from the firm in question. Tours packaged by one of the 33 members of the **United States Tour Operators Association** (USTOA, 211 E. 51st St., Suite 12B, New York, NY 10022; tel. 212/750–7371), which requires members to maintain $1 million each in an account to reimburse clients in case of default, are likely to present the fewest difficulties. Even better, pay for travel arrangements with a major credit card, so that you can refuse to pay the bill if services have not been rendered—and let the card company fight your battles.

Comprehensive Policies Companies supplying comprehensive policies with some or all of the above features include **Access America, Inc.** (Box 90315, Richmond, VA 23230, tel. 800/284–8300); **Carefree Travel Insurance** (Box 310, 120 Mineola Blvd., Mineola, NY 11501, tel. 516/294–0220 or 800/323–3149); **Tele-Trip** (Mutual of Omaha Plaza, Box 31762, Omaha, NE 68131, tel. 800/228–9792); **The Travelers Companies** (1 Tower Sq., Hartford, CT 06183, tel. 203/277–0111 or 800/243–3174); **Travel Guard International** (1145 Clark St., Stevens Point, WI 54481, tel. 715/345–0505 or 800/782–5151);

and **Wallach and Company, Inc.** (107 W. Federal St., Box 480, Middleburg, VA 22117, tel. 703/687–3166 or 800/237–6615).

U.K. Residents Most tour operators, travel agents, and insurance agents sell specialized policies covering accident, medical expenses, personal liability, trip cancellation, and loss or theft of personal property. Some policies include coverage for delayed departure and legal expenses, winter-sports, accidents, or motoring abroad. You can also purchase an annual travel-insurance policy valid for every trip you make during the year in which it's purchased (usually only trips of less than 90 days). Before you leave, make sure you will be covered if you have a preexisting medical condition or are pregnant; your insurers may not pay for routine or continuing treatment, or may require a note from your doctor certifying your fitness to travel.

For advice by phone or a free booklet, "Holiday Insurance," that sets out what to expect from a holiday-insurance policy and gives price guidelines, contact the **Association of British Insurers** (51 Gresham St., London EC2V 7HQ, tel. 0171/600–3333; 30 Gordon St., Glasgow G1 3PU, tel. 0141/226–3905; Scottish Provincial Bldg., Donegall Sq. W, Belfast BT1 6JE, tel. 01232/249176; call for other locations).

Car Rentals

All the major car rental car companies are represented in New Zealand, including **Alamo** (tel. 800/327–9633); **Avis** (tel. 800/331–1212); **Budget** (tel. 800/527–0700); **Eurodollar Rent a Car, Ltd.** (tel. 800/800–4000); **Hertz** (tel. 800/654–3131, 800/263-0600 in Canada); **National** (tel. 800/227–7368); and **Thrifty** (tel. 800/367–2277). **Koala Tours** (tel. 800/535–0316) also handles car rentals, but these must be made through travel agents. Visitors are advised to make a reservation in advance.

Requirements Usually, you must be over 21 to rent a car (some rental companies require a driver to be 25) and some restrictions may apply to drivers over 60 years of age. Most companies will accept your driver's license from home, but some may require an International Driver's Permit, available from the American Automobile Association (AAA) and the Canadian Automobile Association (CAA).

The cost (including compulsory insurance) for a small vehicle such as a Toyota Corolla is about $75 per day with unlimited mileage; for a Ford Fairmont, $95 per day. Local operators will rent to you for about one-third less, but you have to return the car to the pick-up point, and the minimum hire period is usually four days.

The cost of a two-berth camper van varies from $100 to $185 per day, depending on the season; a six-berth camper runs $140 to $240 per day. The minimum hire period is usually six days. There are more than 400 motor camps, with communal bathroom and laundry facilities, grocery stores, and power sites, scattered the length and breadth of New Zealand; a van site at one of these goes for $6–$12 per night.

Extra Charges Picking up the car in one city and leaving it in another may entail substantial drop-off charges or one-way service fees. The cost of a collision or loss damage waiver (*see below*) can be high, also. Automatic transmissions and air-conditioning are not universally available abroad; ask for them when you book if you want them, and check the cost before you commit yourself to the rental. Fill the tank just before you turn in the vehicle to avoid being charged for refueling at what you'll swear is the most expensive pump in town.

Cutting Costs Major international companies have programs that discount their standard rates by 15%–30% if you make the reservation before departure (anywhere from 24 hours to 14 days), rent for a minimum number of days (typically three or four), and prepay the rental. Ask about these advance-purchase plans when you call for information. More economical rentals may come as part of fly/drive or other packages, including bare-bones deals that combine only the rental plus an airline ticket (*see* Tours and Packages, *above*).

Several companies operate as wholesalers—they don't own their own fleets but they rent in bulk from those that do and offer advantageous rates to their customers. Rentals through such companies must be arranged and paid for before you leave the United States. Among them are **Auto Europe** (Box 1097, Camden, ME 04843, tel. 207/236–8235 or 800/223–5555, 800/458–9503 in Canada), which rents cars in the United States, Europe, Australia, New Zealand, and other regions, and **Foremost Euro-Car** (5430 Van Nuys Blvd., Suite 306, Van Nuys, CA 91401, tel. 818/786–1960 or 800/272–3299), which rents in Europe as well as New Zealand. You won't see these wholesalers' deals advertised; they're even better in summer, when business travel is down. Always ask whether the prices are guaranteed in U.S. dollars or foreign currency and if unlimited mileage is available. Find out about any required deposits, cancellation penalties, and drop-off charges, and confirm the cost of the collision damage waiver.

Insurance and Collision Damage Waiver Until recently, standard rental contracts included liability coverage (for damage to public property, injury to pedestrians, and so on) and coverage for the car against fire, theft, and collision damage with a deductible. Due to law changes in some states and rising liability costs, several car rental agencies have reduced the type of coverage they offer. Before you rent a car, find out exactly what coverage, if any, is provided by your personal auto insurer. Don't assume that you are covered. If you do want insurance from the rental company, secondary coverage may be the only type offered. You may already have secondary coverage if you charge the rental to a credit card. Only Diners Club (tel. 800/234–6377) provides primary coverage in the United States and worldwide.

Rail and Bus Passes

Travelers can purchase an **InterCity Travelpass** good for unlimited travel on trains, buses, and InterIsland ferries. The pass allows 8 days of travel within a 21-day period ($425), 15 days of travel within 36 days ($530), or 22 days of travel within 56 days ($650). Children aged 4 to 14 pay 67% of the adult fare. The **4 in 1 New Zealand Travelpass,** which is available for purchase outside New Zealand only, includes one flight sector on Ansett New Zealand between assigned city pairs. The flight may be at any time after the date of issue of the Travelpass and up to seven days after expiry of the Travelpass. The pass entitles the visitor to 8 days of travel in 21 days ($616), 15 days of travel in 35 days ($721), or 22 days of travel in 56 days ($841). Children aged 4 to 14 travel at 67% of the adult fare. An additional two flight sectors may be purchased at $191 per sector. For Youth Hostel Association members, the **InterCity Youth Hostel Travel Card** ($75 for 14 days, $99 for 28 days) gives a 50% discount on most train services, all InterCity coach services, and on the InterIsland ferries. Students with an International Student Identity Card (ISIC) get a 20% discount (*see* Student and Youth Travel, *below*). Contact InterCity Travel Centres (tel. 09/358–4085 in Auckland, 03/379–9020 in Christchurch, 04/472–5111 in Wellington) for ticket information. In the United States, contact ATS Tours (tel. 818/841–1030) or Austravel Inc. (tel. 800/633–3404).

Valid for travel in both Australia and New Zealand, the **Down Under Pass** is offered by Australian Coachlines and Mt. Cook Line. The passes range from 9 to 45 days, to be used within prescribed time allotments that allow for a 10-day break in travel between the two countries. The passes are priced from $467 to $1,475.

Student and Youth Travel

In addition to Hostelling International (*see below*), a network of low-cost, independent backpacker hostels operates in New Zealand. They can be found in nearly every city and tourist spot, and they offer clean dormitory-style accommodations and self-catering kitchens, with no membership required. To find out about these hostels, contact **Budget Backpackers Hostels NZ, Ltd.** (Rainbow Lodge, 99 Titiraupenga St., Taupo, tel. 074/8–5754 or Downtown Backpackers, 208 Kilgore St., Christchurch, tel. 03/366–9720).

Travel Agencies **Council Travel Services (CTS),** a subsidiary of the nonprofit Council on International Educational Exchange (CIEE) specializes in low-cost travel arrangements abroad for students and is the exclusive U.S. agent for several discount cards. Also newly available from CTS are domestic air passes for bargain travel within the United States. CIEE's twice-yearly *Student Travels* magazine is available at the CTS office at CIEE headquarters (205 E. 42nd St., 16th Floor, New York, NY 10017, tel. 212/661–1450); in Boston (tel. 617/266–1926), Miami (tel. 305/670–9261), and Los Angeles (tel. 310/208–3551); and at 43 branches in college towns nationwide (free in person, $1 by mail). **Campus Connections** (1100 E. Marlton Pike, Cherry Hill, NJ 08034, tel. 800/428–3235) specializes in discounted accommodations and airline fares for students. The **Educational Travel Centre** (438 N. Frances St., Madison, WI 53703, tel. 608/256–5551) offers low-cost domestic and international airline tickets, mostly for flights departing from Chicago, as well as rail passes. Other travel agencies catering to students include **TMI Student Travel** (1146 Pleasant St., Watertown, MA 02172, tel. 800/245–3672) and **Travel Cuts** (187 College St., Toronto, Ontario M5T 1P7, tel. 416/979–2406).

Discount For discounts on transportation and on museum and attractions
Cards admissions, buy the **International Student Identity Card** (ISIC) if you're a bona fide student, or the **International Youth Card** (IYC) if you're under 26. In the United States the ISIC and IYC cards cost $16 each and include basic travel accident and sickness coverage. Apply to **CIEE** (*see address above*, tel. 212/661–1414; the application is in *Student Travels*). In Canada the cards are available for $15 each from **Travel Cuts** (*see above*). In the United Kingdom they cost £5 and £4 respectively at student unions and student travel companies, including Council Travel's London office (28A Poland St., London W1V 3DB, tel. 0171/437–7767).

Hostelling A **Hostelling International** (HI) membership card is the key to more than 6,000 hostels in 70 countries; the sex-segregated, dormitory-style sleeping quarters, including some for families, go for $7 to $20 a night per person. Membership is available in the United States through **Hostelling International American Youth Hostels** (HIAYH, 733 15th St. NW, Washington, DC 20005, tel. 202/783–6161), the American link in the worldwide chain, and costs $25 for adults 18–54, $10 for those under 18, $15 for those 55 and over, and $35 for families. Volume 2 of the two-volume *Guide to Budget Accommodation*, which can be purchased from HIAYH and the other HI member organizations, lists hostels in Asia, Australia, and New Zealand as well as in Canada and the United States ($13.95 including postage). HI membership is available in Canada through **Hostelling International–Canada** (205 Catherine St., Suite 400, Ottawa, Ontario K2P 1C3, tel. 613/748–5638) for $26.75, and in the United Kingdom through the **Youth Hostel Association of England and Wales** (Trevelyan House, 8 St. Stephen's Hill, St. Albans, Hertfordshire AL1 2DY, tel. 01727/55215) for £9.

Traveling with Children

Publications *Family Travel Times,* published 10 times a year by **Travel With**
Newsletter **Your Children** (TWYCH, 45 W. 18th St., 7th Floor Tower, New York, NY 10011, tel. 212/206–0688; annual subscription $55), covers destinations, types of vacations, and modes of travel.

Books *Traveling with Children—And Enjoying It,* by Arlene K. Butler ($11.95 plus $3 shipping; Globe Pequot Press, Box 833, Old

Saybrook, CT 06475, tel. 800/243–0495, or 800/962–0973 in CT) helps you plan your trip with children, from toddlers to teens.

Tour **Grandtravel** (6900 Wisconsin Ave., Suite 706, Chevy Chase, MD
Operators 20815, tel. 800/247–7651) offers tours for people traveling with their grandchildren. The catalogue, as charmingly written and illustrated as a children's book, positively invites armchair traveling with lap-sitters aboard. **Rascals in Paradise** (650 5th St., Suite 505, San Francisco, CA 94107, tel. 800/872–7225) specializes in adventurous, exotic, and fun-filled vacations for families to carefully screened resorts and hotels around the world.

Getting On international flights, the fare for infants under two not occu-
There pying a seat is generally 10% of the accompanying adult's fare;
Air Fares children ages 2 to 11 usually pay half to two-thirds of the adult fare. On domestic flights, children under two not occupying a seat travel free, and older children currently travel on the "lowest applicable" adult fare.

Baggage In general, infants paying 10% of the adult fare are allowed one carry-on bag, not to exceed 70 pounds or 45 inches (length + width + height), and a collapsible stroller; check with the airline before departure because you may be allowed less if the flight is full. The adult baggage allowance applies for children paying half or more of the adult fare.

Safety Seats The FAA recommends the use of safety seats aloft and details approved models in the free leaflet **"Child/Infant Safety Seats Recommended for Use in Aircraft"** (available from the Federal Aviation Administration, APA–200, 800 Independence Ave. SW, Washington, DC 20591, tel. 202/267–3479). Airline policy varies. U.S. carriers allow FAA-approved models bearing a sticker declaring their FAA approval. Because these seats are strapped into a regular passenger seat, they may require that parents buy a ticket even for an infant under two who would otherwise ride free. Foreign carriers may not allow infant seats, may charge the child's rather than the infant's fare for their use, or may require you to hold your baby during takeoff and landing, thus defeating the seat's purpose.

Facilities Aloft Some airlines provide other facilities and services for children, such as children's meals and freestanding bassinets (to those with seats at the bulkhead, where there's enough legroom). Make your request when reserving. The annual February/ March issue of *Family Travel Times* gives details of the children's services of dozens of airlines (*see above*). "Kids and Teens in Flight" (free from the U.S. Department of Transportation, tel. 202/366–2220) offers tips for children flying alone.

Dining New Zealanders are genuinely fond of and considerate toward children, and their own children are included in most of their parents' social activities. Children are welcome in all restaurants throughout the country. However, they are rarely seen in those restaurants that appear in Fodor's very expensive ($$$$) and expensive ($$$) price categories. These restaurants may not have high chairs, nor might they be prepared to make special children's meals. Major cities and important tourist centers have McDonald's and Kentucky Fried Chicken outlets.

Lodging In hotels in New Zealand, roll-away beds are usually free, and children under 12 sharing a hotel room with adults either stay free or receive a discount rate. The **Hyatt** (tel. 800/233–1234) in Auckland allows children under 18 to stay free when sharing a room with parents.

Home Stays Home hosting provides an ideal opportunity for visitors to stay with a local family, either in town or on a working farm. For information on home and farm stays, *see* Lodging in Staying in New Zealand, *below.* Also see that section for information on home exchange and apartment rentals.

Baby-sitting Most hotels and resorts have baby-sitters available through the
Services concierge or front desk, at a charge of around $10 to $15 per hour. Baby-sitting services are also listed in the yellow pages of city telephone directories.

In New Zealand, strollers and bassinets can be rented from the **Royal New Zealand Plunket Society** (472 George St., Dunedin North, tel. 03/477–0110). Most car-rental agencies provide "cocoons" for newborns as well as child safety seats.

Hints for Travelers with Disabilities

New Zealand is at the forefront in providing facilities for people with disabilities. Contact the **Royal New Zealand Plunket Society** (472 George St., Dunedin North, tel. 03/477–0110).

Lodging In New Zealand, all accommodations are required by law to provide at least one room with facilities for people with disabilities. The **New Zealand Tourism Board** publishes *Access: A Guide for the Less Mobile Traveller*, listing accommodations, attractions, restaurants, and thermal pools with special facilities.

Getting On Air New Zealand, wheelchairs for in-flight mobility are stan-
Around dard equipment; seat-belt extensions, quadriplegic harnesses,
By Air and padded leg rests are also available. Ask for the company's brochure "Air Travel for People with Disabilities."

By Train Passengers on mainline passenger trains in New Zealand can request collapsible wheelchairs to negotiate the narrow interior corridors. However, compact toilet areas and platform access problems make long-distance train travel difficult.

By Taxi Companies in New Zealand have recently introduced vans equipped with hoists and floor clamps, but these should be booked several hours in advance if possible; contact the Plunket Society (*see above*) for more information.

Car Rental Only **Budget** (tel. 800/527–0700 in the U.S. and Canada) offers cars fitted with hand controls, but these are limited. **Hertz** (tel. 800/654–3131 in the U.S. and 800/263–0600 in Canada) will fit hand-held controls onto standard cars in some cities.

Organizations Several organizations provide travel information for people with disabilities, usually for a membership fee, and some publish newsletters and bulletins. Among them are the **Information Center for Individuals with Disabilities** (Fort Point Pl., 27–43 Wormwood St., Boston, MA 02210, tel. 617/727–5540, or 800/462–5015 in MA; TTY tel. 617/345–9743); **Mobility International USA** (Box 10767, Eugene, OR 97440, tel. and TTY 503/343–1284, fax 503/343–6812), the U.S. branch of an international organization based in Britain (*see below*) and present in 30 countries; **MossRehab Hospital Travel Information Service** (tel. 215/456–9603, TDD tel. 215/456–9602); the **Travel Industry and Disabled Exchange** (TIDE, 5435 Donna Ave., Tarzana, CA 91356, tel. 818/368–5648); and **Travelin' Talk** (Box 3534, Clarksville, TN 37043, tel. 615/552–6670, fax 615/552–1182).

In the United Kingdom Main sources include the **Royal Association for Disability and Rehabilitation** (RADAR, 25 Mortimer St., London W1N 8AB, tel. 0171/637–5400), which publishes travel information for people with disabilities in Britain, and **Mobility International** (228 Borough High St., London SE1 1JX, tel. 0171/403–5688), the headquarters of an international membership organization that serves as a clearinghouse of travel information for people with disabilities.

Travel Agency **Flying Wheels Travel** (143 W. Bridge St., Box 382, Owatonna, MN 55060, tel. 507/451–5005 or 800/535–6790) is a travel agency specializing in domestic and worldwide cruises, tours, and independent travel itineraries for people with mobility impairments.

Publications Two free publications are available from the Consumer Information Center (Pueblo, CO 81009): "New Horizons for the Air Traveler with a Disability," a U.S. Department of Transportation booklet describing changes resulting from the 1986 Air Carrier Access Act and those still to come from the 1990 Americans with Disabilities Act (include Dept. 608Y in the address), and the Airport Operators Council's *Access Travel: Airports* (Dept. 5804), which describes facilities and services for people with disabilities at more than 500 airports worldwide.

Travelin' Talk Directory (*see* Organizations, *above*) was published in 1993. This 500-page resource book ($35) is packed with information for travelers with disabilities. **Twin Peaks Press** (Box 129, Vancouver, WA 98666, tel. 206/694–2462 or 800/637–2256) publishes the *Directory of Travel Agencies for the Disabled* ($19.95), listing more than 370 agencies worldwide, and *Wheelchair Vagabond* ($14.95), a collection of personal travel tips. Add $2 per book for shipping.

Hints for Older Travelers

Organizations The **American Association of Retired Persons** (AARP, 601 E St. NW, Washington, DC 20049, tel. 202/434–2277) provides independent travelers who are members of AARP (open to those age 50 or older; $8 per person or couple annually) with the Purchase Privilege Program. This program offers discounts on lodging, car rentals, and sightseeing and arranges group tours, cruises, and apartment living through **AARP Travel Experience from**

American Express (400 Pinnacle Way, Suite 450, Norcross, GA 30071, tel. 800/927–0111 or 800/745–4567).

Two other organizations offer discounts on lodgings, car rentals, and other travel products, along with such nontravel perks as magazines and newsletters: the **National Council of Senior Citizens** (1331 F St. NW, Washington, DC 20004, tel. 202/347–8800, $12 annual membership fee) and **Mature Outlook** (6001 N. Clark St., Chicago, IL 60660, tel. 800/336–6330, $9.95 annually).

For reduced rates, mention your senior-citizen identification card when booking your accommodations, not when checking out. At restaurants, show your card before you're seated; discounts may be limited to certain menus, days, or hours. If you are renting a car, ask about promotional rates that might improve on your senior-citizen discount.

Educational Travel The nonprofit **Elderhostel** (75 Federal St., 3rd Floor, Boston, MA 02110, tel. 617/426–7788) has offered inexpensive study programs for people age 60 and older since 1975. Held at more than 1,800 educational institutions, courses cover everything from marine science to Greek myths to cowboy poetry. Participants usually attend lectures in the morning, then spend the afternoon sightseeing or on field trips; they live in dorms on the host campuses. Fees for two- to three-week international trips—including room, board, and transportation from the United States—range from $1,800 to $4,500.

Tour Operators **Saga International Holidays** (222 Berkeley St., Boston, MA 02116, tel. 800/343–0273), which specializes in group travel for people over 60, offers a selection of variously priced tours and cruises covering five continents. If you want to take your grandchildren, look into Grandtravel (*see* Traveling with Children, *above*).

Hints for Gay and Lesbian Travelers

Organizations The **International Gay Travel Association** (Box 4974, Key West, FL 33041, tel. 800/448–8550), which has 700 members, provides names of travel agents and tour operators who specialize in gay travel. The **Gay & Lesbian Visitors Center of New York Inc.** (135 W. 20th St., 3rd Floor, New York, NY 10011, tel. 800/395–2315; $100 annually) mails a monthly newsletter, valuable coupons, and more to its members.

Tour Operators and Travel Agencies The dominant travel agency in the market is **Above and Beyond** (3568 Sacramento St., San Francisco, CA 94118, tel. 800/397–2681). Tour operator **Olympus Vacations** (8424 Santa Monica Blvd., Suite 721, West Hollywood, CA 90069, tel. 310/657–2220) offers all-gay-or-lesbian resort holidays. **Skylink Women's Travel** (746 Ashland Ave., Santa Monica, CA 90405, tel. 800/225–5759) handles individual travel for lesbians and conducts two international and five domestic group trips annually.

Publications The premier international travel magazine for gays and lesbians is **Our World** (1104 N. Nova Rd., Suite 251, Daytona Beach, FL 32117, tel. 904/441–5367; $35 for 10 issues). **Out & About** (tel. 800/929–2268; $49 for 10 issues) is a 16-page monthly newsletter with extensive information on resorts, hotels, and airlines that are gay-friendly.

Further Reading

History *The Oxford Illustrated History of New Zealand*, edited by Keith Sinclair, provides a comprehensive but highly readable account of the country's social, political, cultural, and economic evolution from the earliest days of settlement to 1989. *The Colonial New Zealand Wars*, by Tim Ryan and Bill Parham, is a vivid history of the Maori-British battles. Lavishly illustrated with photographs of colonial infantry and drawings of Maori hill forts, flags, and weapons, the book makes far more compelling reading than the dry military history suggested by the title. J. C. Beaglehole's *The Discovery of New Zealand* is an authoritative and scholarly analysis of the voyages of discovery, from the first Polynesians to the Europeans of the late 18th century.

Fiction New Zealand's best-known novelist is Katherine Mansfield (1888–1923), whose early stories were set in and around the city of Wellington, her birthplace. The most celebrated work of fiction to come from New Zealand in recent years is Keri Hulme's *The Bone People*, winner of the Booker McConnell Prize in 1985. Set on the isolated west coast of the South Island, this challenging, vital novel weaves Polynesian myth with Christian symbolism and the powerful sense of place that characterizes modern Maori writing. Another important contemporary writer is Janet Frame, who made an impact on the literary scene with the publication of *The Carpathians* in 1985.

Specialized Guidebooks Strictly for wine buffs, *The Wines and Vineyards of New Zealand*, by Michael Cooper, is an exhaustive evaluation in words and pictures of every vineyard in the country. For travelers who plan to make hiking a major component of their vacations, *Tramping in New Zealand*, published by Lonely Planet, is an invaluable guide.

Illustrated Books *Salute to New Zealand*, edited by Sandra Coney, is a coffee-table book that intersperses lavish photographs with chapters by some of the country's finest contemporary writers. *Wild New Zealand*, published by Reader's Digest, is a pictorial account of the country's landscape, flora, and fauna, supplemented by an informative text with such a wealth of detail that it turns the sensory experience of the landscape into a cerebral one.

Arriving and Departing

From North America by Plane

Flights are either nonstop, direct, or connecting. A **nonstop** flight requires no change of plane and makes no stops. A **direct** flight stops at least once and can involve a change of plane, although the flight number remains the same; if the first leg is late, the second waits. This is not the case with a **connecting** flight, which involves a different plane and a different flight number.

Airlines Currently, the following airlines serve New Zealand from the United States and Canada: Australia's national airline, **Qantas** (tel. 800/227–4500 in the U.S. and in Canada); **Air New Zealand** (tel. 800/262–1234 in the U.S., 800/663–5494 in Canada); **United** (tel. 800/538–2929 in the U.S.); **Canadian Airlines International** (tel. 800/665–1177 in Canada, 800/426–7000 in the U.S.); and **Northwest** (tel. 800/447–4747 in the U.S. and Canada).

Flights leave from Los Angeles, San Francisco, Honolulu, New York, Toronto, and Vancouver. Air New Zealand is the only carrier with direct flights from North America to Christchurch as well as Auckland.

Flying Times Flying time from New York to Auckland (via Los Angeles) is about 19 hours; from Los Angeles or San Francisco to Auckland (nonstop), about 13 hours. These are actual air hours and do not include ground time.

Cutting Flight Costs The Sunday travel section of most newspapers is a good source of deals. When booking, particularly through an unfamiliar company, call the Better Business Bureau or Consumer Protection Bureau to find out whether any complaints have been registered against the company, pay with a credit card if you can, and consider trip-cancellation and default insurance (*see* Insurance in Before You Go, *above*).

Promotional Airfares Less expensive fares, called promotional or discount fares, are round-trip and involve restrictions, which vary according to the route and season. You must usually buy the ticket—commonly called an APEX (advance purchase excursion) when it's for international travel—in advance (seven, 14, or 21 days is usual), although some of the major airlines have added no-frills, cheap flights to compete with new bargain airlines on certain routes.

With the major airlines the cheaper fares generally require minimum and maximum stays (for instance, over a Saturday night or at least seven and no more than 30 days). Airlines generally allow some return date changes for a $25 to $50 fee, but most low-fare tickets are nonrefundable. Only a death in the family would prompt the airline to return any of your money if you cancel a nonrefundable ticket. However, you can apply an unused nonrefundable ticket toward a new ticket, again with a small fee. The lowest fare is subject to availability, and only a small percentage of the plane's total seats will be sold at that price.

Contact the U.S. Department of Transportation's **Office of Consumer Affairs** (I–25, Washington, DC 20590, tel. 202/366–2220) for a copy of "Fly-Rights: A Guide to Air Travel in the U.S." Randy Petersen's *Official Frequent Flyer Guidebook* ($14.99 plus $3 shipping; 4715-C Town Center Dr., Colorado Springs, CO 80916, tel. 800/487–8893) yields valuable hints on getting the most for your air travel dollars.

Consolidators Consolidators or bulk-fare operators—"bucket shops"—buy blocks of seats on scheduled flights that airlines anticipate they won't be able to sell. They pay wholesale prices, add a markup, and resell the seats to travel agents or directly to the public at prices that still undercut the airline's promotional or discount fares. Their prices are higher than a charter ticket but lower than an APEX ticket and usually are without the advance-purchase restriction. Moreover, some consolidators will sometimes allow you to return your ticket; carefully read the fine print detailing penalties for changes and cancellations. If you doubt the reliability of a company, call the airline once you've made your booking and confirm that you do, indeed, have a reservation on the flight.

Charter Charters usually have the lowest fares and the most restric-
Flights tions. Departures are limited and seldom on time, and you can lose all or most of your money if you cancel. (The closer to departure you cancel, the more you lose, although sometimes you will be charged only a small fee if you supply a substitute passenger.) The charterer may legally cancel the flight for any reason up to 10 days before departure; within 10 days of departure, the flight may be canceled only if it is physically impossible to operate it. The charterer may also revise the itinerary or increase the price after you have bought the ticket, but if the new arrangement constitutes a "major change," you have the right to a refund. Before buying a charter ticket, read the fine print for the company's refund policy and details on major changes. Money for charter flights is usually paid into a bank escrow account, the name of which should be on the contract. If you don't pay by credit card, make your check payable to the escrow account (unless you're dealing with a travel agent, in which case, the agent's check should be payable to the escrow account). The U.S. Department of Transportation's **Office of Consumer Affairs** (I–25, Washington, DC 20590, tel. 202/366–2220) can answer questions on charters and send you its "Plane Talk: Public Charter Flights" information sheet.

Charter operators may offer flights alone or with ground arrangements that constitute a charter package. Typically you must book charters through your travel agent. One good source is **Charterlink** (988 Sing Sing Rd., Horseheads, NY 14845, tel. 800/221–1802), a no-fee charter broker that operates 24 hours a day.

Discount Travel clubs offer members unsold space on airplanes, cruise
Travel Clubs ships, and package tours for as much as 50% below regular prices. Membership may include a regular bulletin or access to a toll-free hot line giving details of available trips departing from

three or four days to several months in the future. Most also offer 50% discounts off hotel rack rates, but double-check with the hotel to make sure it isn't offering a better promotional rate independent of the club. Clubs include **Discount Travel International** (114 Forrest Ave., Suite 203, Narberth, PA 19072, tel. 215/668–7184; $45 annually, single or family), **Entertainment Travel Editions** (Box 1014 Trumbull, CT 06611, tel. 800/445–4137; $28–$48 annually), **Great American Traveler** (Box 27965, Salt Lake City, UT 84127, tel. 800/548–2812; $29.95 annually), **Moment's Notice Discount Travel Club** (425 Madison Ave., New York, NY 10017, tel. 212/486–0503; $45 annually, single or family), **Privilege Card** (3391 Peachtree Rd. NE, Suite 110, Atlanta, GA 30326, tel. 800/236–9732; annually $49.95 domestic, $74.95 international), **Travelers Advantage** (CUC Travel Service, 49 Music Sq. W, Nashville, TN 37203, tel. 800/548–1116; $49 annually, single or family), and **Worldwide Discount Travel Club** (1674 Meridian Ave., Miami Beach, FL 33139, tel. 305/534–2082; annually $50 family, $40 single).

Publications The newsletter *Travel Smart* (40 Beechdale Rd., Dobbs Ferry, NY 10522, tel. 800/327–3633; $44 annually) has a wealth of travel deals in each monthly issue.

Enjoying the Flight Fly at night if you're able to sleep on a plane. Because the air aloft is dry, drink plenty of beverages while on board; remember that drinking alcohol contributes to jet lag, as do heavy meals. Sleepers usually prefer window seats to curl up against; restless passengers ask to be on the aisle. Bulkhead seats, in the front row of each cabin, have more legroom, but since there's no seat ahead, trays attach awkwardly to the arms of your seat, and you must stow all possessions overhead. Bulkhead seats are usually reserved for people with disabilities, the elderly, and people traveling with babies.

Smoking Smoking is banned on all of New Zealand's domestic flights. The ban also applies to domestic segments of international flights aboard U.S. and foreign carriers. On U.S. carriers flying to New Zealand and other destinations abroad, a seat in a no-smoking section must be provided for every passenger who requests one, and the section must be enlarged to accommodate such passengers if necessary as long as they have complied with the airline's deadline for check-in and seat assignment. If smoking bothers you, request a seat far from the smoking section.

From the United Kingdom by Plane

British Airways (tel. 0181/897–4000), **Cathay Pacific** (tel. 0171/930–7878), **Japan Airlines (JAL;** tel. 0171/408–1000), **Qantas** (tel. 0181/846–1466), and **Singapore Airlines** (tel. 0181/747–0007) operate between London and Auckland via Asia. **Air New Zealand** (tel. 0171/930–3434) and **United** (tel. 0181/990–9900) operate between London and Auckland via the United States. The flying time from London to Auckland is about 24 hours via either route.

Cutting
Flight Costs
A round-trip ticket from London to Auckland can cost more than £3,000. Fortunately, a number of specialist travel companies, such as **Trailfinders** (tel. 0171/938–3366) and **Travel Cuts** (tel. 0171/255–2082), offer significant reductions on scheduled fares, plus advice on stopovers and additional services, especially from Trailfinders, which specializes in discounted round-the-world airfares. Book several months in advance, especially for peak periods. Check the advertisements in *Time Out* magazine for further information.

Staying in New Zealand

Geography

New Zealand consists of three main islands: North Island (44,197 square miles), South Island (58,170 square miles), and Stewart Island (676 square miles). If it were stretched out along the west coast of the United States, the country would extend from Los Angeles to Seattle. No point is more than 70 miles from the sea, and owing to the hilly nature of the country, rivers tend to be short, swift, and broad. More than 70% of the total population of 3.36 million lives on the North Island, where industry and government are concentrated. The South Island is dominated by the Southern Alps, a spine of mountains running almost two-thirds the length of the island close to the west coast.

Getting Around

By Plane The major domestic airlines are **Air New Zealand** (tel. 09/379–3510) and **Ansett New Zealand** (tel. 09/37–6950). Both compete on intercity trunk routes, while a third carrier, **Mount Cook Airline** (tel. toll-free 0800/800–737) services the country's resort areas. Economy-price air travel is expensive compared with the cost of bus or train travel; however, multi-trip tickets offer a substantial saving. Ansett New Zealand has a **New Zealand Airpass** entitling you to fly between three and eight sectors (i.e., point-to-point flights) at an adult fare that runs from $435 for a three-sector pass to $1,100 for an eight-sector pass. Children under 12 pay two-thirds the adult fare. The pass is valid for the duration of your stay in New Zealand and should be purchased prior to arrival to avoid New Zealand sales tax. You can fly one sector on Ansett New Zealand between designated city pairs as part of the 4 in 1 InterCity New Zealand Travelpass (*see* Rail and Bus Passes in Before You Go, *above*) and can add up to two sectors for an additional fare. Air New Zealand and Mount Cook offer similar discount tickets, available through travel agents.

Smoking Smoking is not allowed on any flight within New Zealand.

By Train New Zealand's railroad system operates under the **InterCity** (tel. 09/358–4085) banner. Trains usually cost the same as buses and are marginally quicker, but they run far less frequently. The country's most notable rail journey is the **TranzAlpine Express**, a scenic spectacular across the mountainous spine of the

South Island between Greymouth and Christchurch (*see* Arriving and Departing by Train for Marlborough, Nelson, and the West Coast in Chapter 5).

By Bus New Zealand is served by an extensive bus network, and for many travelers, buses offer the optimal combination of cost and convenience. The main bus line is **InterCity** (tel. 09/358–4085), which also operates the railroad system. The other major operator on the North Island is **Newmans** (tel. 09/309–9738), and on the South Island **Mount Cook Landline** (tel. 03/379–0690 in Christchurch or toll-free 0800/800–737). The **InterCity Travelpass** allows unlimited travel on all InterCity buses and trains and on the InterIslander ferries that link the North and South Islands (*see* Rail and Bus Passes in Before You Go, *above*).

By Car A valid American, Canadian, or British license allows you to drive in New Zealand, and nothing beats the freedom and mobility of a car for exploring. Even for those nervous about traveling on the "wrong" side of the road, driving here is relatively easy. Roads are well maintained and generally uncrowded, though signposting, even on major highways, is often poor. The speed limit is 100 kilometers per hour (62 mph) on the open road and 50 kph (31 mph) in towns and cities. A circular sign with the letters "LSZ" (Limited Speed Zone) means there is no speed limit—speed should be governed by prevailing road conditions.

If you drive in rural New Zealand, you will encounter one-lane bridges. These must be crossed with caution. A yellow sign on the left will usually warn that you are approaching a one-lane bridge, and another sign will tell you whether you have the right-of-way. A rectangular blue sign means you have the right-of-way; a circular sign with a red border means you must pull over to the left and wait to cross until oncoming traffic has passed. Even when you have the right-of-way, slow down and take care. Some one-lane bridges on the South Island are used by trains as well as cars; trains always have the right-of-way.

Telephones

Most pay phones now accept **PhoneCards** rather than coins. These plastic cards, available in denominations of $5, $10, $20, or $50, are sold at shops displaying the green PhoneCard symbol. To use a PhoneCard, lift the receiver, put the card in the slot in the front of the phone, and dial. The cost of the call is automatically deducted from your card; the display on the telephone tells you how much credit you have left at the end of the call.

Local Calls A local call from a public phone costs 20¢ per minute.

International Calls International calls may be dialed direct. The country code for the United States and Canada is 1, and the code for New Zealand is 64. For international directory assistance, dial 0172. For the international operator, dial 0170. AT&T, MCI, and Sprint each have services that allow you to contact an operator in the United States directly, thus circumventing some pricey hotel surcharges. Place your calling-card or collect calls by dialing the

New Zealand access number for one of the following: **AT&T USADirect** (tel. 000–911), **MCI Call USA** (tel. 000–912), or **Sprint Express** (tel. 000–999). Similar toll-free numbers exist for other countries: UK, tel. 000–944; Canada, tel. 000–919; Australia, tel. 000–961.

Mail

Postage Rates Post offices are open weekdays 9–5. The cost of mailing a letter within New Zealand is 45¢ standard post, 80¢ fast post. Sending a standard-size letter by air mail costs $1.50 to North America, $1.80 to Europe, and $1 to Australia. Aerogrammes and postcards are $1 to any overseas destination.

Receiving Mail Mail will be held for collection for one month at the central post office in any town or city if it is addressed to you "c/o Poste Restante, CPO," followed by the name of the town. This service is free.

Tipping

Tipping is not widely practiced in New Zealand. Only in the better city restaurants will you be expected to show your appreciation for good service with a 10% tip.

Opening and Closing Times

Banks are open weekdays 9–4:30, but trading in foreign currencies ceases at 3. Shops are generally open Monday–Thursday 9–5:30, Friday 9–9, and Saturday 9–noon.

Shopping

New Zealand produces several unique souvenirs, but don't expect to find many bargains. Sheepskins and quality woolens are widely available. Bowls hewn from native timbers and polished to a lustrous finish are distinctive souvenirs, but a fine example will cost several hundred dollars. Greenstone, a type of jade once prized by the Maoris, is now used for ornaments and jewelry—especially the figurine known as a *tiki*, which is often worn as a pendant. The two major areas for crafts are the Coromandel Peninsula, close to Auckland, and the environs of Nelson, at the northern tip of the South Island. The Parnell area of Auckland and the Galleria in Christchurch Arts Centre are the places to shop for souvenirs. In Nelson, Craft Habitat brings together some of the finest local arts and crafts under one roof.

Sports and the Outdoors

Bicycling Despite its precipitous topography, New Zealand offers superb biking. A temperate climate, excellent roads with relatively little traffic, and scenic variety make cycling a delight for anyone who is reasonably fit and has the time to travel slowly. The most common problem for cyclists is buckled wheel rims: Narrow, lightweight alloy rims won't stand up long to the rigors of the road. A wide-rimmed hybrid or a mountain bike with road tires is a better bet for extensive touring.

If two-wheel touring sounds appealing but pedaling a heavily laden bicycle doesn't, consider a guided cycle tour. The tours last from two to 18 days; bikes are supplied, and your gear is loaded on a bus or trailer that follows the riders. (You have the option of busing in the "sag wagon" when your legs give out.) Contact **New Zealand Pedaltours** (Box 49–039, Auckland, tel. 09/302–0968) or **Unravel Tours** (Square Edge Bldg., Palmerston North, tel. 06/356–5500).

Boating and Sailing The country's premier cruising regions are the Bay of Islands and Marlborough Sounds, near the northern tips of the North and South Islands respectively. Both areas offer sheltered waters, marvelous scenery, and secluded beaches. Of the two, the Bay of Islands enjoys warmer summer temperatures, while Marlborough Sounds has a wild, untamed quality. Both are well supplied with operators offering either bare-boat or skippered charters and a range of vessels from small motor cruisers to sleek Beneteau yachts. For more information, contact **Rainbow Yacht Charters** (Box 8327, Symonds St., Auckland, tel. 09/78–0719) or **Charterlink** (Box 246, Picton, tel. 03/573–6591).

Fishing Considering that they were introduced from California little more than a hundred years ago, the explosion in New Zealand's **trout** population has been phenomenal. The average summer rainbow trout taken from Lake Tarawera, near Rotorua, weighs 5 pounds, and 8- to 10-pound fish are not unusual. In the lakes of the North Island, fingerlings often reach a weight of 4 pounds nine months after they are released. Trout do not reach maturity until they grow to 14 inches, and in fact all trout below that length must be returned to the water.

Trout fishing has a distinctly different flavor on the two islands. In the Rotorua-Taupo region of the North Island, the main quarry is rainbow trout, which are usually taken from the lakes with a wet fly or spinners. Trolling is also popular and productive. On the South Island, where brown trout predominate, the streams offer outstanding dry-fly fishing. It's best in the Nelson region and in the Southern Lakes district, at the top and bottom end of the South Island respectively. On both islands, anglers who can afford to indulge their passion are well catered to. Several specialist lodges provide guides and transport to wilderness streams that are sometimes accessible only by helicopter. The trout season lasts from October through April in most areas, though Lakes Taupo and Rotorua are open all year.

Salmon are found in the rivers that drain the eastern slopes of the Southern Alps, especially those that reach the sea between Christchurch and Dunedin. Anglers are usually transported by jetboat up these shallow rivers to the pools where the salmon rest on their spawning run. The salmon season, which runs from October to April, is at its peak from January to March.

Fishing licenses are available from fishing-tackle and sports shops on a daily, weekly, monthly, or seasonal basis. The cost ranges from $10.50 for a single day to $53 for the season, and each is valid for the entire country, with the exception of Lake Taupo, for which a separate license is required. For anyone who plans to fish extensively, the best buy is a tourist fishing license—available from Visitor Information Centres in all the major cities—which, for $56.26, permits fishing anywhere in New Zealand for one month.

The seas off the east coast of the North Island are among the world's finest **big-game fishing** waters. The quarry is mako, hammerhead, tiger shark, and marlin—especially striped marlin, which average around 250 pounds. For light tackle fishing, bonito and skipjack tuna and kahawai (sea trout) offer excellent sport. Many anglers maintain that kahawai are better fighters, pound for pound, than freshwater trout. The bases for big-game fishing are the towns of Pahia and Russell, which have a number of established charter operators. The season runs from January to April, although smaller game fishing is good all year. No fishing license is required for big-game fishing.

Wherever they fish, and whatever they fish for, anglers will profit immensely from the services of a local guide. On Lake Taupo or Rotorua, a boat with a guide plus all equipment will cost around $130 for two hours. On the South Island, a top fishing guide who can supply all equipment and a four-wheel drive vehicle will charge about $400 per day for two people. In the Bay of Islands region, an evening fishing trip aboard a small boat can cost as little as $35. For a big-game fishing boat, expect to pay between $600 and $1,000 per day.

For more information and brochures on fishing in New Zealand, contact **Simon Dickie Adventures** (Box 682, Taupo, tel. 07/378–9680); **Lake Brunner Lodge** (Mitchells, R. D. 1 Kumara 7871, Westlands, tel. 03/738–0163); or **Bay of Islands Sportfishing Ltd.** (Box 48, Russell, tel. 09/403–7008).

Golf Golf is played all year; winter is the major season. Most of New Zealand's 400 courses welcome visitors. Greens fees range from $5 at country courses to $40 at the exclusive city courses. Many have clubs for hire, and the better urban courses offer resident professionals and golf carts for hire. For more information, contact the Executive Director, **NZ Golf Association,** Box 11–842, Wellington.

Hiking If you want to see the very best the country has to offer, put on a pair of walking boots and head for the hills. Range upon range of mountains; deep, ice-carved valleys; wilderness areas that have never been farmed, logged, or grazed; and a first-class network of marked trails and tramping huts are just some of the reasons that hiking is a national addiction.

The traditional way to hike in New Zealand is freedom walking. Freedom walkers carry their own provisions, sleeping bags, food, and cooking gear and sleep in basic huts. A more refined alternative—usually available only on the more popular trails—

is the guided walk, on which you trek with just a light day pack, guides do the cooking, and you sleep in heated lodges. If you prefer your wilderness served with hot showers and an eiderdown on your bed, the guided walk is for you.

There are almost 900 **back country huts** in New Zealand; they provide basic shelter but few frills. Huts are usually placed about four hours apart, although in isolated areas it can take a full day to get from one hut to the next. They are graded 1 to 4, and the cost varies from nothing to $14 per person per night. Category 1 huts (the $14 ones) have cooking equipment and fuel, bunks or sleeping platforms with mattresses, toilets, washing facilities, and a supply of water. At the other end of the scale, Category 4 huts (the free ones) are simple shelters without bunks or other facilities. Payment is by coupons, available in books from Department of Conservation offices. If you plan to make extensive use of huts, an annual pass giving access to all Category 2 and 3 huts for one year is available for $58.

The most popular walks are located in the Southern Alps, where the postcard views of mountains, wild rivers, mossy beech forests, and fjords issue a challenge to the legs that is hard to resist. The trekking season in the mountains usually lasts from October to mid-April. The best-known of all New Zealand's trails is the **Milford Track,** a four-day walk through breathtaking scenery to the edge of Milford Sound. Its main drawback is its popularity. This is the only track in New Zealand on which numbers are controlled: You are required to obtain a permit and to begin walking on the day specified (to ensure that the overnight huts along the track don't become impossibly crowded). If you plan to walk the Milford in December or January, book at least six months in advance; at other times, three months is usually sufficient. (If you arrive without a booking, there are sometimes last-minute cancellations, and parties of one or two can often be accommodated.) The Milford Track is closed from the end of April to early September. Bookings, either as a freedom walker or on a guided walk, can be made by contacting the THC Milford Track Office (THC Te Anau Resort Hotel, Box 185, Te Anau, tel. 03/249–7411).

While the Milford gets the lion's share of publicity, many other walks offer a similar—some would say better—combination of scenery and exercise. The **Routeburn Track** is a three-day walk that rises through beech forests, traverses a mountain face across a high pass, and descends through a glacial valley. The **Kepler** and the **Hollyford** are both exceptional, and the **Abel Tasman,** at the northern end of the South Island, is a spectacular three-to-four-day coastal track that can be walked year-round.

Clothing and footwear are major considerations. Even at the height of summer the weather can change quickly, and hikers must be prepared—especially for the rainstorms that regularly drench the Southern Alps. (The Milford Sound region, with its average annual rainfall of 160 inches, is one of the wettest places on earth.) The most cost-effective rain gear you can buy is the U.S. Army poncho. For more information, contact Routeburn

Walk Ltd. (Box 185, Te Anau, tel. 03/249–7411) or Abel Tasman National Park Enterprises (Old Cedarman House, Main Rd., Riwaka, Motueka R. D. 3, tel. 03/528–7801).

Hunting New Zealand offers superb hunting. Faced with an abundance of food and a complete lack of predators, wild animals such as the deer that were introduced last century have multiplied to such numbers that they're considered pests, and an open season applies to many species. Sika stag are found in the beech forests of the North Island, and red stag are common to the forests of both islands. Higher altitudes of the Southern Alps are inhabited by the prized tahr and chamois.

Hunters can choose between "fair chase" hunts, for which they pay a minimum daily fee for a minimum number of days, and "ranch" hunts, in which the owner controls the game and the fee is charged per trophy. Ammunition is widely available for all common calibers. If you plan to bring a firearm into the country, you must present it on arrival to the police, who will issue you a license. March and April are the prime months for hunting most deer, May and June for tahr and chamois.

Except for national parks, forest parks, scenic reserves, and conservation areas, no hunting permit is necessary for deer; however, special conditions apply in some areas. When required, a permit can be obtained from Department of Conservation offices and from the visitor centers located in all national parks. A hunting guide is essential, not only for success but also for safety. For more information, contact **New Zealand Hunting and Fishing Consultants** (210–212 Lake Terr., Taupo. tel. 07/378–7070); **Mid Southern Tracks** (Box 2, Lake Tekapo, tel. 03/680–6774); or **Wildsouth** (Box 199, Mosgiel, tel. 03/489–7322).

Skiing New Zealand has 27 peaks that top the 10,000-foot mark, and the June–October ski season is the reason many skiers head "down under" when the snow melts in the northern hemisphere. On the South Island, the site of most of the country's 13 commercial skifields, the outstanding areas are **Treble Cone and Cardrona,** served by the town of Wanaka, and **Coronet Peak and the Remarkables,** close to Queenstown. The North Island has only two commercial skifields, **Whakapapa and Turoa,** both near Lake Taupo on the slopes of Mount Ruapehu. Lift prices average about $40 per day.

What the New Zealand skifields lack is sophistication. By international standards they are comparatively small, and the slopes lack the extensive interlocking lift systems that are a feature of European skiing. There is no such thing as snowfield accommodations: Skiers must stay in one of the nearby subalpine towns.

Heliskiing is very popular. Harris Mountains Heliski, the second largest heliski operation in the world, gives access from the town of Wanaka to more than 200 runs on more than 100 peaks accessible to skiers by no other means. The ultimate heliski adventure is the 13-kilometer (8½-mile) run down the Tasman Glacier, available from Glentanner Park, near Mount Cook Village.

Beaches

The list of great New Zealand beaches is almost endless. There are no private beaches, no risks from pollution; the greatest danger is sunburn. Most New Zealanders prefer the beaches along the east coast of the North Island, where the combination of gentle seas and balmy summers is a powerful attraction in the January holidays. During the summer months, popular beaches close to the cities and in major holiday areas are patrolled by lifeguards. Swim with caution on unpatrolled beaches.

Dining

Auckland, Wellington, and Christchurch offer cosmopolitan dining, but, apart from a few expensive sporting lodges, most country cooking still gets its recipes from the meat-and-two-veg school of English cuisine. The country's greatest culinary asset is its raw materials. The lamb and the New Zealand crayfish, often known as spiny or rock lobster, are delicious, and the succulent, white-shelled Bluff oysters, available from March to about July, are rated highly by gourmets. Watch for orange roughy, a delicate white-fleshed fish that is at its best with a light sauce. Venison is widely available, and many chefs are preparing exciting dishes based on cervena, a leaner, lighter style of farmed venison.

A New Zealand specialty is the *hangi*, the Maori feast of steamed meat and vegetables. Several hotels in Rotorua offer a hangi, usually combined with an evening of Maori song and dance. (These days it's unlikely that the food will be cooked by steaming it in the traditional hot earth oven.)

The difference in price between a reasonable meal and a very good one is often not great. Even bistro-style restaurants charge $12–$16 for a dish of pasta, and a main course at the French Café in Auckland—one of the country's finest restaurants—costs about $25. For cheap lunches, the standard takeaways are meat pies and fish and chips. Most country pubs serve inexpensive cooked lunches and sometimes a selection of salads. In season, stock up on fruit from the roadside stalls that are scattered throughout the country's fruitgrowing areas.

New Zealand wines can be excellent, but there are few bargains. Hawke's Bay and Marlborough are the premier winegrowing regions. Some restaurants are not licensed to serve alcohol, but diners are welcome to bring their own; check when reserving a table.

Prices   Dining prices given in this guidebook are per person, excluding drinks, service, and general sales tax (12.5%). Highly recommended restaurants are indicated by a star ★.

Category	Cost
$$$$	over $45
$$$	$35–$45
$$	$25–$35
$	under $25

Lodging

The New Zealand Tourism Board (*see* Government Tourist Offices in Before You Go, *above*) publishes an annual *Where to Stay* directory listing more than 1,000 properties.

Motels   Motels are by far the most common accommodations, and most offer comfortable rooms for $60–$90 per night. Some motels have two-bedroom suites for families. All motel rooms come equipped with tea- and coffee-making facilities, many have toasters or electric frying pans, and full kitchen facilities are not uncommon.

Home and Farm Stays   If you want more than just a bed for the night, farm stays and home stays are a great way to get to know the land and its people. Farm-stay guests can generally expect to share meals with the family and share in the farmwork if they feel inclined. For two people, the average cost is $90–$150 per night, including all meals. Home stays, the urban equivalent of farm stays, are less expensive. For a list, contact **New Zealand Farm Holidays Ltd.** (Box 256, Silverdale, Auckland, tel. 09/307–2024) or **Homestay Ltd. Farmstay Ltd.** (Box 25–115, Auckland, tel. 09/55–5980).

Home Exchange   You can find a house, apartment, or other vacation property to exchange for your own by becoming a member of a home-exchange organization, which then sends you its annual directories listing available exchanges and includes your own listing in at least one of them. Arrangements for the actual exchange are made by the two parties to it, not by the organization. For more information contact the **International Home Exchange Association** (IHEA, 41 Sutter St., Suite 1090, San Francisco, CA 94104, tel. 800/788–2489). Another principal clearinghouse is **Home-Link International** (Box 650, Key West, FL 33041, tel. 800/638–3841), which has thousands of foreign and domestic listings and publishes four annual directories plus updates; the $50 membership includes your listing in one book. **Intervac International Home Exchange** (Box 590504, San Francisco, CA 94159, tel. 415/435–3497) is the oldest organization, with thousands of foreign and domestic homes for exchange in its three annual directories; membership is $62, or $72 if you want to receive the directories but remain unlisted. **Loan-a-Home** (2 Park La., Apt. 6E, Mount Vernon, NY 10552, tel. 914/664–7640) specializes in long-term exchanges; there is no charge to list your home, but the directories cost $35 or $45 depending on the number you receive.

Apartment and Villa Rentals If you want a home base that's roomy enough for a family and comes with cooking facilities, a furnished rental may be the solution. It's generally cost-wise, too, although not always—some rentals are luxury properties (economical only when your party is large). Home-exchange directories do list rentals—often second homes owned by prospective house swappers—and there are services that can not only look for a house or apartment for you (even a castle if that's your fancy) but also handle the paperwork. Some send an illustrated catalogue and others send photographs of specific properties, sometimes at a charge; up-front registration fees may apply.

Among the companies are **Europa-Let** (92 N. Main St., Ashland, OR 97520, tel. 800/462–4486), **Property Rentals International** (1 Park West Circle, Suite 108, Midlothian, VA 23113, tel. 800/220–3332), **Rent a Home International** (7200 34th Ave. NW, Seattle, WA 98117, tel. 206/789–9377 or 800/488–7368), and **Villas International** (605 Market St., Suite 510, San Francisco, CA 94105, tel. 415/281–0910 or 800/221–2260).

Tourist Cabins and Flats The least expensive accommodations are the tourist cabins and flats in most of New Zealand's 400 motor camps. Tourist cabins offer basic accommodation and shared cooking, laundry, and bathroom facilities. Bedding and towels are not provided. A notch higher up the comfort scale, tourist flats usually provide bedding, fully equipped kitchens, and private bathrooms. Overnight tariffs run about $6–$20 for cabins and $25–$70 for flats.

Sporting Lodges At the other end of the price scale, a number of luxury sporting lodges offer the best of country life plus fine dining and superb accommodations. Fishing is a specialty at most, but there is usually a range of outdoor activities for nonanglers. Tariffs run about $350–$800 per day for two people; meals are generally included.

Prices Lodging prices given in this guidebook are for a standard double room, excluding general sales tax (12.5%). Highly recommended lodgings are indicated by a star ★.

Category	Cost
$$$$	over $200
$$$	$125–$200
$$	$80–$125
$	under $80

Credit Cards

The following credit card abbreviations are used: AE, American Express; DC, Diner's Club; MC, MasterCard; V, Visa.

Great Itineraries

New Zealand is an experience to be savored, not rushed, but if a one-week visit is all you can manage, this itinerary will introduce you to the main attractions of both islands.

Length 7 days

The Main Route **Day 1:** Arrive in Auckland and explore the city. Take an evening ferry ride across the harbor to Devonport.
Day 2: Travel to the Waitomo Caves; tour the Glow-worm Cave and hike the Waitomo Walkway, then continue to Rotorua.
Day 3: Take the Waimangu Round Trip day tour, finish off with a soak in the Polynesian Pools, then take in a Maori hangi.
Day 4: Catch the morning flight to Mount Cook. Hike along the Hooker Valley and watch the sun set over the Southern Alps.
Day 5: Take an early morning scenic flight around the Southern Alps with a glacier landing; then travel to Queenstown. Explore Arrowtown.
Day 6: Join a day tour to Milford Sound with a midday cruise, returning to Queenstown in the evening.
Day 7: Fly to Christchurch and explore the city center. Spend your last afternoon shopping for souvenirs in the Galleria.

Information *See* Chapters 3, 4, and 5.

Experiencing New Zealand

For anyone who wants to hike, canoe, fish, and explore some of the less well-known attractions, 10 days on each island is a practical minimum. This tour includes the main cities as well as the country's natural splendors, with emphasis on wildlife.

Length 20 days

The Main Route **Day 1:** Arrive in and explore Auckland. Take an evening ferry to Devonport and dine on the waterfront.
Day 2: Travel north to the Bay of Islands. Explore the Treaty House, and cross by ferry to spend the night in Russell.
Day 3: Explore Russell and take a catmaran trip out to Cape Brett, followed by an evening fishing trip.
Day 4: Travel to the Coromandel Peninsula via Auckland.
Day 5: Explore the seascapes and wilderness of the Coromandel Peninsula, preferably on a half-day tour with Doug Johansen. Travel to Rotorua in the late afternoon.
Day 6: Take the Waimangu Round Trip day tour. End with a mineral bath, and spend the evening at a Maori hangi.
Day 7: Travel to Taupo and view the thermal infernos along the way. Spend the evening on a sightseeing cruise of the lake, or trawling in champion trout territory.
Day 8: Travel to Napier and explore the city's art deco architecture and the surrounding wineries.

Day 9: Travel to Wellington and explore the national capital.

Day 10: Cross to the South Island by ferry, then travel to Nelson along the edge of the Marlborough Sounds.

Day 11: Join a one-day guided cruise along the coastline of the Abel Tasman National Park, with a flight back at the end.

Day 12: Travel to the west coast glacier country and spend the night at Franz Josef.

Day 13: Take an early scenic flight across the glaciers and Mount Cook, the highest peak in the country, or join a glacier-walking party. Travel on to Lake Moeraki Lodge and spend the evening canoeing on the lake.

Day 14: Join a beach tour from Lake Moeraki Lodge to see the penguins and seals; travel to Queenstown in the afternoon.

Day 15: Explore Queenstown and Arrowtown, go bungy jumping or trail riding, or take the Dart River jetboat safari.

Day 16: Join a one-day tour to Milford Sound, traveling through the spectacular wilderness of Fiordland National Park, followed by a cruise on the sound.

Day 17: Drive to Dunedin and visit the royal albatross colony at Taiaroa Head.

Day 18: Travel to Christchurch and spend the afternoon on a walking tour of the city.

Day 19: Travel to Kaikoura and join a whale-watching expedition. Return to Christchurch in the evening.

Day 20: Explore Akaroa and return to Christchurch for souvenir and duty-free shopping.

Information *See* Chapters 3, 4, and 5.

South Island Adventure Tour

This action-packed tour takes place against some of the finest natural backdrops in the country. It begins with a biking tour across the Southern Alps to the rugged west coast, travels south to Fiordland National Park for a hike on the Milford Track, and ends with a kayaking and camping trip along the edge of Abel Tasman National Park. While this might sound demanding, both the biking and the Milford Track are guided tours requiring only a moderate level of fitness.

Length 21 days

The Main Route **Day 1:** Arrive at Christchurch. Take a walking tour of the city and stock up on any necessary provisions.

Days 2–10: Join a nine-day Pedaltours Southern Comfort cycling tour, traveling to Queenstown via Arthur's Pass and the west coast glaciers. This tour concludes with a scenic flight to Milford Sound and a cruise.

Day 11: Travel to Te Anau and spend the afternoon preparing for the Milford Track, "the finest walk in the world."

Days 12–15: Walk the Milford Track.

Day 16: Return to Queenstown and spend the rest of the day exploring the surroundings—or bungee jumping, jet boating, or trying any of the other heart-stopping thrills in the area.

Day 17: Take the early morning flight to Mount Cook. Walk the Hooker Valley and watch the sun set.

Day 18: Fly to Nelson and spend the night in the town.

Days 19–21: Travel to Marahau, hire a kayak, and spend two days along the coastline of the Abel Tasman National Park.

Information *See* Chapter 5.

2 Portraits of New Zealand

New Zealand at a Glance: A Chronology

c. AD 750 The first Polynesians arrive, settling mainly in the South Island, where the moa, a flightless bird and an important food source, is concentrated.

950 Kupe, the Polynesian voyager, names the country Aotearoa, "land of the long white cloud." He returns to his native Hawaiki, believed to be present-day French Polynesia.

1300s A population explosion in Hawaiki triggers a wave of immigrants who quickly displace the archaic moa hunters.

1642 Abel Tasman of the Dutch East India Company becomes the first European to sight the land—he names his discovery Nieuw Zeeland. But after several of his crew are killed by Maoris, he sails away without landing.

1769 Captain James Cook becomes the first European to set foot on New Zealand. He takes possession in the name of the British crown.

1790s Sealers, whalers, and timber cutters arrive, plundering the natural wealth and introducing the Maoris to the musket, liquor, and influenza.

1814 The Reverend Samuel Marsden establishes the first mission station, but 11 years will pass before the first convert is made.

1832 James Busby is appointed British Resident, charged with protecting the Maori people and fostering British trade.

1840 Captain William Hobson, representing the crown, and Maori chiefs sign the Treaty of Waitangi. In return for the peaceful possession of their land and the rights and privileges of British citizens, the chiefs recognize British sovereignty.

1840–1841 The New Zealand Company, an association of British entrepreneurs, establishes settlements at Wanganui, New Plymouth, Nelson, and Wellington.

1852 The British parliament passes the New Zealand Constitution Act, establishing limited self-government.

1861 Gold is discovered in the river valleys of central Otago, west of Dunedin.

1860–1872 Maori grievances over loss of land trigger the Land Wars of the North Island. The Maoris win some notable victories, but lack of unity ensures their ultimate defeat. Vast tracts of ancestral land are confiscated from rebel tribes.

1882 The first refrigerated cargo is dispatched to England, giving the country a new source of prosperity—the sheep. A century later, there will be 20 sheep for every New Zealander.

1893 Under the Liberal government, New Zealand becomes the first country to give women the vote.

1914 New Zealand enters World War I.

1931 The Hawke's Bay earthquake kills 258 and levels the city of Napier.

1939 New Zealand enters World War II.

1950 New Zealand troops sail for Korea.

1965 Despite public disquiet, troops are sent to Vietnam.

1973 Britain joins the European Economic Community, and the loss of this traditional export market is reflected in a crippling balance-of-payments deficit two years later.

1981 Violent antigovernment demonstrations erupt during a tour by a South African rugby team.

1985 The Greenpeace ship *Rainbow Warrior* is sunk by a mine in Auckland Harbour and a crewman is killed. Two of the French secret service agents responsible are arrested, jailed, and, shortly afterward, transferred to French custody—from which they are soon released.

Sir Paul Reeves is sworn in as the first Maori Governor-General. The newly elected Labour government of David Lange begins a process of drastic economic reform that includes dismembering the traditional welfare state. The resulting social unrest worsens when unemployment tops 10%.

Relations with the United States sour when the government bans visits by ships carrying nuclear weapons. The U.S. government responds by ejecting New Zealand from the ANZUS alliance.

1989 David Lange resigns as prime minister.

1990 The National Party replaces the Labour Party in government.

From *Return to Paradise*

By James A.
Michener

New Zealand is probably the most beautiful country on earth. The official school history says that when Richard John Sedon, the great Prime Minister, died, "he passed on to a better place even than God's Own Country."

The New Zealander finds it difficult to believe that there could be a better land than his, either on earth or in heaven. He is always ready to boast of four national distinctions. "We have a land of unmatched beauty. (True) We have demonstrated that two races of different color can inhabit one land in peace and honor. (True) We showed the world how to pass social legislation for the good of all. (True) And today we enjoy the highest standard of living known by any nation. (False)"

As regards the first claim, the natural beauty of New Zealand is difficult to believe. Its two islands, no larger than Colorado, combine all types of alluring scenery, all kinds of climates. Consider what you could see in one day's travel.

At the northern tip of North Island you find a dazzling tropical beach sixty miles long. (New Zealanders call it Ninety Mile Beach.) It ends in a cluster of handsome islands around which sport immense marlin and swordfish. Farther south are prehistoric sub-tropical forests with towering kauri pines that took 1500 years to mature. In the center of North Island is a brooding desert surmounted by three majestic volcanoes, one or the other of which seems always to be active, spouting lava ash by day and beacon fires at night. At Rotorua the wonders of Yellowstone Park are challenged, for here geysers play, mud pools bubble and hot waters tumble down over colored terraces.

On the west coast you will see Mount Egmont, rising in beauty, the perfect snow-capped cone of a dead volcano, cloud wreathed and pointed like Fujiyama. But in New Zealand you always say, "Fujiyama looks a lot like Mount Egmont."

Now you leave the North Island and fly south across Cook Strait, where vast mountains sank into the sea until only their tips remained aloft. Here earth and ocean mingle in astonishing beauty, varied, twisted, glowing in the sunlight.

Ahead lies South Island, where the real beauty of New Zealand is found. Here Mount Cook rises more than 12,000 feet, perpetually glaciated, with huge fingers of ice reaching almost into the sea. Nearby are the Southern Alps, immense rows of jagged peaks beneath which nestle dozens of wonderful lakes, each serving as a mirror for some great range of mountains.

On the coast, near the glaciers, you find dramatic evidence of New Zealand's turbulent geological history. During millions of years this land rose and fell repeatedly. When it lay under the sea, sand covered it. When it was thrust upward, limestone deposits collected. Finally the resulting rocks were forced high into the air, where howling winds eroded the sandstone layers and left tall rounded pillars of limestone wafers piled one upon the other, appropriately called The Pancakes. And then, since New Zealand scenery is completely prodigal in its wonders, the hungry Tasman Sea ate huge caverns beneath The Pancakes into which tides roar, bursting upward through crevices and shooting thin strands of spray high into the air.

Farther south lies Milford Sound, first and finest of the fjords. Cutting deep inland, it is enclosed by brooding and majestic peaks. High waterfalls plunge from mountain plateaus directly into its waters, and jagged bays probe into dark forests. At the head of one such indentation Sutherland Falls leaps nearly 2,000 feet down into a solemn glen, one of the superb waterfalls of the world. Almost inaccessible, it is reached by means of a difficult trail labeled on maps "The World's Finest Walk." Along ten casual miles I counted forty sheer granite cliffs, each at least 800 feet high, three of them dropping precipitously for more than a thousand feet. I also saw at least 200 waterfalls, some of them hundreds of feet high. One unnamed one—there are so many wonders in this part of New Zealand that they are not even recorded—fell 300 feet and then leaped backward, borne aloft on surging currents of air. Another zigzagged eight times to get down a cliff face. A third fell some hundred feet, then dashed upon a huge projecting boulder which split the fall and threw each half high into the air, so that the falling plumes looked like two Grecian horses plunging into battle. At no point in the ten miles did I fail to see at least three waterfalls. Frequently more than ten were visible. And this was in the dry season!

In the same ten miles there were other spectacular phenomena so far unnamed: a cataract that had gnawed its way sixty feet through solid rock, leaving at the land's surface a gorge only 36 inches across; a tiny lake of perfect ultramarine; a balanced boulder bigger than a cathedral; a walled valley hidden in circles of granite cliff. And often above me flamed that most brilliant tree, the pohutukawa, at the end of whose branches grow massive clusters of scarlet flowers, so that sometimes the forest seemed to be on fire.

On even the best maps the land south of Milford Sound is marked UNEXPLORED. New Zealand has dozens of fjords still to be opened to travel. It has hundreds of natural wonders still to be discovered. One who knows the region said, "For the rest of this century my country could open up each year some new spectacle that would astonish the eye."

Proof of this came dramatically in 1949. New Zealand is geologically a recent land and has few animals that resemble those found elsewhere. It does, however, have some that are unique. Among those still living is the kiwi, a long-billed, flightless bird that has become the national symbol. (New Zealand fighting men are Kiwis.) Now almost extinct, the kiwi is famous for two qualities: it feeds by stomping its feet over worm holes to imitate rain, thus luring the hors d'oeuvre into position; and it lays an egg of ridiculous size. If a hen were to do comparatively as well, chicken eggs would be 14 inches long and would weigh three pounds each!

The most famous of New Zealand's extinct creatures was the moa, a gigantic bird that towered above the heads of men who liked its rich meat so much they exterminated it about 150 years ago. (There's a great fight on about this, some scholars maintaining that moas were never seen after 1350.) Another of the extinct birds was the notornis, a beautiful turkey-like creature with blue-green feathers and a brilliant red toucan-like bill. The last one was seen in 1898, a previous specimen having been eaten by shipwrecked sailors some years before.

Then in 1949 some explorers in the wild southern valleys came upon a family of notornis that had miraculously survived. Cautious investigators probed the area and discovered perhaps fifty of the handsome fowl. A surge of excitement swept across the scientific world and other expeditions were hastily outfitted. Warned the Government: "It is ridiculous to call these excursions moa hunts. No moa could possibly be alive in New Zealand." But the scientists point out that there used to be a dwarf moa and in most bars you can get even money that sooner or later a moa is going to turn up in those southern valleys marked UN-EXPLORED.

3 Auckland and the North

By Michael Gebicki

Auckland, with a population of more than 800,000, is the largest city in New Zealand and the country's major gateway. It's the only city in the nation large enough to have a traffic problem (though one most international cities would envy), and your first impressions will probably be of calm, cleanliness, and a fertility that extends into the heart of the city. The drive from the airport will take you past the tall cones of extinct volcanoes, where grass as green and smooth as a billiards table is cropped by four-footed lawnmowers known as sheep.

Chances are that along the way you'll pass knots of cyclists and joggers. Aucklanders, like all New Zealanders, are addicted to the outdoors. There are some 70,000 powerboats and sailing craft in the Greater Auckland area—about one for every four households. Within an hour's drive of the city center are 102 beaches. Yet the city has not been kind to its greatest asset, Waitemata Harbour—a Maori name meaning "Sea of Sparkling Waters." Where there should be harborfront parks edged with palm trees and gardens, there are dockyards and warehouses instead.

Auckland is not an easy city to explore: It sprawls across its isthmus, with the Pacific Ocean on one side and the Tasman Sea on the other. If you arrive at the end of a long flight and time is limited, the best introduction to the city is the commuter ferry that crosses the harbor to Devonport, where you can soak up the atmosphere in a leisurely stroll.

Beyond Auckland, the Bay of Islands, to the north, is an area that's both beautiful and—as the place where modern New Zealand came into being with the signing of the Treaty of Waitangi in 1840—historic. Finally, off in a different direction, we outline a drive around the rugged and exhilarating Coramandel Peninsula.

Auckland

Important Addresses and Numbers

Tourist Information **Auckland Visitor Information Centre.** *Aotea Sq., Queen and Myers Sts., tel. 09/366–6888. Open weekdays 8:30–5:30, weekends 9–5.*

Published every Thursday, **Auckland Tourist Times** is a free newspaper with the latest information on tours, exhibitions, and shopping. The paper is available from hotels and from the Visitor Information Centre.

Consulates **U.S. Consulate.** *General Assurance Bldg., Shortland and O'Connell Sts., tel. 09/303–2724. Open weekdays 8–4:30.*

British Consulate. *Fay Richwhite Bldg., 151 Queen St., tel. 09/303–2971. Open weekdays 9:30–12:20.*

Canadian Consulate. *Jetset Centre, 48 Emily Pl., tel. 09/309–8516. Open weekdays 8:30–4:30.*

Australian Consulate. *Union House, 32–38 Quay St., tel. 09/ 303–2429. Open weekdays 8:30–4:45.*

Emergencies Dial 111 for **fire, police,** or **ambulance** services.

Hospital **Auckland Hospital.** *Park Rd., Grafton, tel. 09/379–7440. Open daily 24 hrs.*

Doctors **Auckland Accident and Emergency Clinic.** *122 Remuera Rd., tel. 09/524–5943 or 09/524–7906. Open daily 24 hrs.*

Dentists For emergency dental services, phone **St. John's Ambulance** and ask for the nearest dentist on duty. *Tel. 09/579–9099. Open daily 24 hrs.*

Where to Change Money The Bank of New Zealand branch inside the international terminal of Auckland International Airport is open for all arriving and departing flights. There are several currency-exchange agencies at the lower end of Queen Street, between Victoria and Customs streets, offering the same rate as the banks (weekdays 9–5, Sat. 9–1; closed Sun.). Foreign currency may also be exchanged daily 8–4 at the cashier's office above Celebrity Walk, at the Drake Street entrance of Victoria Park Market (tel. 09/ 309–6911). Automatic teller machines can be found throughout the city center. A 24-hour exchange machine outside the Downtown Airline Terminal on Quay Street will change notes of any major currency into New Zealand dollars, but the rate is significantly less than that offered by banks.

Late-night Pharmacy **The Late-night Pharmacy.** *60 Broadway, tel. 09/520–6634. Open weekdays 5:30 PM–7 AM, weekends 9 AM–7 AM.*

Travel Agencies **American Express Travel Service.** *101 Queen St., tel. 09/379– 8243.*
Thomas Cook. *107 Queen St., tel. 09/379–3924.*

Arriving and Departing by Plane

Airport **Auckland International Airport** lies 21 kilometers (13 miles) southwest of the city center. The **Visitor Information Centre** inside the terminal provides free maps and brochures as well as a booking service for tours and accommodations (open 5 AM–2 AM). Avis, Budget, and Hertz have offices inside the international terminal. A free **Interterminal Bus** links the international and domestic terminals, with frequent departures in each direction 6 AM–10 PM. Alternatively, the walk between the two terminals takes about 10 minutes along the signposted walkway. Luggage for flights aboard the two major domestic airlines, Air New Zealand and Ansett New Zealand, can be checked in at the international terminal.

Airlines Major international carriers serving Auckland include **British Airways** (tel. 09/367–7500), **Canadian Airlines International** (tel. 09/309–0735), **Qantas Airways** (tel. 09/379–0306), and **United Airlines** (tel. 09/379–3800).

Domestic carriers with services to Auckland are **Air New Zealand** (tel. 09/379–3510), **Air Nelson** (tel. 09/379–3510), **Ansett**

New Zealand (tel. 09/302–2146), and **Mount Cook Airlines** (tel. 09/309–5395).

Airport to City Center The journey between the airport and the city center takes about 30 minutes.

By Bus **Johnston's Shuttle Express** (tel. 09/256–0333) operates a minibus service between the airport and any address in the city center. The cost is $12 for a single traveler, $9 per person for two traveling together. The service meets all incoming flights.

The **Airbus** (tel. 09/275–9396) leaves the international terminal every 20 minutes between 6:20 AM and 8:20 PM. The fixed route between the airport and the Downtown Airline Terminal, on the corner of Quay Street and Albert Road, includes a stop at the railway station and, on request, at any bus stop, hotel, or motel along the way. Returning from the city, the bus leaves the Downtown Airline Terminal at 20-minute intervals between 6:20 AM and 9 PM. *Cost: $9 adults, $3 children 5–14.*

By Taxi The fare to the city is between $30 and $35.

By Limousine **Gateway Limousines and Tours** (tel. 09/528–9198) operates Ford LTD limousines between the airport and the city. The cost is approximately $60.

Arriving and Departing by Car, Train, and Bus

By Car By the standards of most cities, Auckland's traffic is light, parking space is inexpensive and readily available, and highways pass close to the heart of the city. On the other hand, unless your accommodation is some distance from the city, there's no real advantage in having a car of your own.

By Train The terminal for all InterCity train services is **Auckland Central Railway Station** (tel. 09/358–4085) on Beach Road, about 1½ kilometers (1 mile) east of the city center. A booking office is located inside the Auckland Visitor Information Centre at Aotea Square, 299 Queen Street.

By Bus The terminal for **InterCity Coaches** (tel. 09/358–4085) is the Auckland Central Railway Station (*see above*). **Newmans Coaches** (tel. 09/309–9738) arrive and depart from the Downtown Airline Terminal, on the corner of Quay and Albert streets.

Getting Around

By Bus Auckland's public bus system, the **Yellow Bus Company**, operates Monday–Saturday 6 AM–11:30 PM, Sunday 9 AM–5 PM. The main terminal for public buses is the **Municipal Transport Station,** between Commerce Street and Britomart Place near the Central Post Office. The bus network is divided into zones; fares are calculated according the number of zones traveled. For travel within the inner city, the fare is 40¢ for adults, 20¢ for children 5–15. **BusAbout passes,** which allow unlimited travel on all buses after 9 AM daily, are available from bus drivers for $8 adults, $4

children. For timetables, bus routes, fares, and lost property, stop
by the **Bus Place,** on the corner of Hobson and Victoria streets
(weekdays 8:15–5), or call **Buz A Bus** (tel. 09/366–6400, Mon.–
Sat. 7–7).

By Taxi Taxis can be hailed in the street but are more readily available
from the cab ranks located throughout the city. Rates differ depending on which company you use, but the fare and flag fall are
listed on the driver's door. Most taxis will accept American Express, Diners Club, MasterCard, or Visa cards. **Alert Taxis** (tel.
09/309–2000), **Auckland Cooperative Taxi Service** (tel. 09/300–
3000), and **Eastern Taxis** (tel. 09/527–7077) are reliable operators with radio-controlled fleets.

Guided Tours

Orientation The most economical introduction to Auckland is the **United Airlines Explorer Bus** (tel. 09/360–0033). The blue-and-silver double-decker bus travels in a circuit, stopping at six of the city's
major attractions; passengers can leave at any stop and reboard
any following Explorer bus. The buses depart from the Downtown Airline Terminal every hour between 11 and 4 daily; tickets
are available from the driver. *Fares: $10 adults, $5 children
5–15.*

Scenic Tours (tel. 09/634–0189) operates a three-hour *City Highlights* guided bus tour, which takes in the main attractions in the
city and Parnell and the view from the lookout on Mount Eden.
Tours leave at 9:30 and 2, and tickets are $32 adults, $16 children
5–14, $5 children 2–4. The **Gray Line** (tel. 09/358–5868) operates
a Morning Highlights tour, which includes admission to Kelly
Tarlton's Underwater World (*see* What to See and Do with Children, *below*). This tour departs daily from the Downtown Airline Terminal on Quay Street at 9 AM and costs $42 adults, $21
children 5–14.

Special- The **Antipodean Explorer** (tel. 09/302–2400) offers a minibus
Interest tour of the wineries, coast, and native forests of the Waitakere
Tours Ranges west of Auckland, including a visit to a gannet colony. It
costs $55 and departs daily at 9:30 AM from the Downtown Airline
Terminal.

Boat Tours Various companies offer cruises of Waitemata Harbor; one of the
best and least expensive is the **Devonport commuter ferry.** The
ferry terminal is located on the harbor side of the Ferry Building
on Quay Street, near the corner of Albert Street. Ferries depart
Monday–Thursday 6:15 AM–11 PM, Friday and Saturday 6:15
AM–1 AM, and Sunday 7 AM–11 PM. *Round-trip tickets: $7 adults,
$3.50 children 5–15.*

The **Pride of Auckland Company** (tel. 09/373–4557) operates
lunch and dinner sailing cruises on the inner harbor, departing
at 12:30 and 6 from the wharf opposite the Downtown Airline
Terminal on the corner of Quay and Albert streets. *Tickets: $35
lunch, $75 dinner.*

Fullers Cruise Centre (tel. 09/377–1771) offers a variety of cruises of the harbor and to the islands of the Hauraki Gulf. The two-hour coffee cruise ($22 adults, $11 children 4–14) departs daily at 9:30, 11:30, 1:30, and 3:30. The Supercat cruise ($50 adults, $25 children) to Great Barrier Island, the most distant of the Hauraki Gulf Islands, is a popular day trip for Aucklanders. The cruise departs Tuesday, Thursday, and weekends at 9.

Exploring Auckland

Numbers in the margin correspond to points of interest on the Auckland map.

1 This walk begins at the **Civic Theatre** on the corner of Queen and Wellesley streets, one block down Queen Street from the Visitor Information Centre. This extravagant art nouveau movie theater was the talk of the town when it opened in 1929, but just nine months later the owner, Thomas O'Brien, went bust and fled, taking with him the week's revenues and an usherette. During World War II a cabaret show in the basement was popular with Allied servicemen in transit to the battlefields of the Pacific. One of the entertainers, Freda Stark, is said to have appeared regularly wearing nothing more than a coat of gold paint.

2 Walk up Wellesley Street toward the white building with the clock on top. This is the **Auckland City Art Gallery,** which houses the country's finest collection of contemporary art as well as paintings of New Zealand dating back to the time of Captain Cook. Watch for works by Frances Hodgkins, New Zealand's best-known artist. *Cnr. Kitchener St. and Wellesley St. E, tel. 09/379–2020. Admission free. Open 10–4:30.*

3 Turn into Kitchener Street, walk past the fountain, and climb the stone stairs on the right. At the top is **Albert Park,** 15 acres of formal gardens, fountains, and statue-studded lawns. The park is built on the site of a garrison that was intended to protect the settlement from the neighboring Maori tribes. There are still remnants of its stone walls (with rifle slits) behind the university buildings on the eastern side of the park.

4 Leave the park and cross onto Alfred Street. Continue downhill and at the bottom cross Stanley Street and take the red path that climbs into the **Auckland Domain.** This rolling, 340-acre park is a favorite leisure space for Aucklanders. The hillside you are climbing is the side of an extinct volcano, Pukekawa, and the track is part of the Coast to Coast Walkway, a 13-kilometer (8-mile) track that spans the isthmus between the Pacific Ocean on the east and the Tasman Sea on the west.

5 At the top of the path, off to the left, is the sprawling gray **Auckland Institute and Museum.** The museum is known especially for its Maori artifacts, the largest and finest collection of its kind. The portraits of Maori chiefs by C. F. Goldie are splendid character studies of a fiercely martial people. Other collections in the museum are dedicated to natural history, geology, military history, and a reconstructed streetscape of early Auckland.

Auckland

KEY

AE American Express Office

ℹ️ Tourist Information

— Rail Lines

Waitemata Harbour

Auckland Domain, tel. 09/309–0443. Admission free. Open daily 10–5.

Leave the museum by the front door, pausing for a fine view of Waitemata Harbour with Rangitoto Island to the right. Turn left and walk down toward the twin domed buildings. These are **❻** the greenhouses of the **Wintergardens,** housing an exotic collection of tropical plants and palms. The wisteria-covered loggia surrounding the sunken courtyard is a shady spot for a rest on a warm day. *Auckland Domain. Admission free. Open daily 10–4.*

Return to the museum, walk past the entrance and on to the back of the building, and follow the road down the hill past the Parnell Lawn Tennis Club. Continue as this road becomes Maunsell Road, turn left into Parnell Road, and turn right at **❼** Ayr Street. Behind a white picket fence on the left is **Ewelme Cottage,** built by the Reverend Vicesimus Lush and inhabited by his descendants for more than a century. The house is constructed of kauri, a resilient timber highly prized by the Maoris for their war canoes. With the arrival of Europeans, kauri became the basic building material for the new settlement, and the kauri forests were rapidly depleted. All kauris are now protected by law, but only a few majestic examples of mature ones remain in the forests. Ewelme Cottage contains much of the original furniture and personal effects of the Lush family. *14 Ayr St., tel. 09/379–0202. Admission: $2.50 adults, 50¢ children 5–15. Open daily 10:30–noon and 1–4:30.*

Return to Parnell Road and turn right. The splendid white **❽** church on the right is the Anglican **Cathedral Church of St. Mary,** built in 1886 and regarded as one of the world's finest examples of a Gothic wooden church. This is one of a number of churches built by Bishop Selwyn, an early Anglican missionary bishop. The craftsmanship inside the church is remarkable, but just as remarkable is the story of the church's relocation. St. Mary's originally stood on the other side of Parnell Road, but in 1982 the entire structure was jacked up, placed on a bed of steel girders, put on rollers, and hauled across to the other side. Photographs inside show the progress of the work. The church now forms part of the Cathedral of the Holy Trinity. *Parnell Rd. and St. Stephen's Ave. Open daily 8–6.*

Just below the intersection of St. Stephen's Avenue, the streetscape suddenly changes character. This is the beginning **❾** of **Parnell Village,** an avenue of pretty Victorian timber villas that have been transformed into antiques shops, designer boutiques, street cafés, and restaurants. Parnell Village is the creation of Les Harvey, who saw the potential of the quaint but run-down shops and houses and almost single-handedly snatched them from the jaws of the developers' bulldozers by buying them, renovating them, and leasing them out. Harvey's vision has paid handsome dividends, and today this village of trim pink-and-white timber facades is a delightful part of the city. At night its restaurants, pubs, and discos attract

Auckland's smart set. Parnell is also one of the few places in Auckland where the shops are open Sunday.

Time Out   At the heart of Parnell Village, **Konditorei Boss** is a pleasant and inexpensive sidewalk café selling open sandwiches, soups, salads, and a wicked but irresistible collection of cakes. There is no table service; walk inside and make your selection from the counter. *305 Parnell Rd., Parnell, tel. 09/377–8953. Open daily 8–5.*

Find the United Airlines Explorer Bus stop, about 50 yards above Konditorei Boss, and take the next bus to the Downtown Airline Terminal ($1 adults, 50¢ children 5–15). Explorer buses depart this stop at 11:45 and then at one-hour intervals until 4:45.

⑩ At the terminal, cross Quay Street to the imposing **Ferry Building** and purchase a ferry ticket for Devonport ($7 adults, $3.50 children 5–15 round-trip). Ferries leave for Devonport weekdays on the hour between 10 and 3, and at half-hour intervals during the morning and evening commuter periods; on Saturday they leave every hour from 6:15 AM until 1 AM, on Sunday from 7 AM to 11 PM.

⑪ The 20-minute ride to Devonport across **Waitemata Harbour** provides one of the finest views of Auckland. The first harbor ferry service began with whaleboats in 1854. Later in the century the Devonport Steam Ferry Co. began operations, and ferries scuttled back and forth across the harbor until the Harbour Bridge opened in 1959. The bridge now carries the bulk of the commuter traffic, but the ferry still has a small, devoted clientele.

From the Devonport wharf, cross Marine Square and walk along
⑫ **Victoria Road.** Devonport, the first settlement on the north side of the harbor, was originally known as Flagstaff, after the signal station on the summit of Mount Victoria. Later the area drew some of the city's wealthiest traders, who built their homes where they could watch their sailing ships arriving with cargoes from Europe. These days the village of Devonport has a relaxed, seaside atmosphere, despite its proximity to the city.

Walk away from the harbor along Victoria Road, past the shops and cafés that line this pleasant avenue. At the end of the street,
⑬ bear right into Kerr Street and turn left to climb **Mount Victoria.** Don't be put off by the name—this is more molehill than mountain. Long before the era of European settlement, this ancient volcano was the site of a Maori *pa*, a fortified village of the local Kawerau tribe. On the northern and eastern flanks of the hill you can still see traces of the terraces that palisades of sharpened stakes once protected.

Return to the ferry terminal via Victoria Road. On weekdays, ferries leave for the city every hour on the half hour between 9:30 and 2:30, and every half hour during the morning and evening commuter periods. On weekends, ferries leave Devonport at 6:30 AM, then every hour on the half hour until 9:30 PM. The last boat leaves Devonport at 11:30 PM Monday–Thursday, 12:30 AM on Friday and Saturday, and 10:30 PM on Sunday.

Auckland for Free

On weekdays during the spring and summer months, **Aotea Square** becomes the venue for a series of free outdoor performances by groups ranging from classical string quartets to jazz artists to Pacific Islander dance companies. The one-hour performances generally begin at 12:30. For recorded "what's on" information, phone the **Aotea Centre Hotline** (tel. 09/309–2678). *BNZ Foyer, Aotea Sq., Queen St. near Myers St.*

What to See and Do with Children

Hobson Wharf. New Zealand's rich seafaring heritage is celebrated at the National Maritime Museum, housed in a new marina complex on Auckland Harbour. Exhibits include Polynesian outrigger canoes, a brigantine, a scow, a steam crane ship, and examples of the sleek sailboats that can still be seen racing in the harbor. The museum also hosts workshops, where traditional boatbuilding, sailmaking, and rigging skills are kept alive. The pride of the museum is the *KZ1*, the 133-foot racing sloop built for the America's Cup challenge in 1988. *Eastern Viaduct, Quay St., tel. 09/358–3010. Admission: $9 adults, $4 children 5–17, $18 family. Open Oct.–Easter Mon.–Thurs. 10–6, Fri.–Sun. 10–9; Easter–Sept. daily 10–5.*

Kelly Tarlton's Underwater World and Antarctic Encounter. The creation of New Zealand's most celebrated undersea explorer and treasure hunter, this harborside marine park offers visitors a fish-eye view of the sea without getting wet. The main attraction is a submerged transparent tunnel, 120 yards long, where a slow-moving walkway makes a circuit while moray eels and lobsters peer from rock caverns and sharks and stingrays glide overhead. The second part of the complex is Antarctic Encounter, opened in early 1994. Visitors enter through a replica of Scott's Hut at McMurdo Sound, then circle around a deep-freeze environment aboard a heated snow cat that winds through a penguin colony and an aquarium exhibiting marine life of the polar sea. The ride emerges at Scott Base 2000 for a glimpse of the next century's antarctic research and exploration. *Orakei Wharf, Tamaki Dr., tel. 09/528–0603. Admission: $16 adults, $8 children 4–11.*

Museum of Transport and Technology. This fascinating collection of aircraft, telephones, cameras, locomotives, steam engines, and farming equipment is a tribute to Kiwi ingenuity. One of the most intriguing exhibits is the remains of an aircraft built by Robert Pearse, who made a successful powered flight barely three months after the Wright brothers first took to the skies. The flight ended inauspiciously when his plane crashed into a hedge, but Pearse, considered a wild eccentric by his farming neighbors, is recognized today as a mechanical genius. *Great North Rd., Western Springs, tel. 09/846–0199. Admis-*

sion: $8.50 adults, $4.50 children 5–15. Open weekdays 9–5, weekends 10–5.

Off the Beaten Track

On Friday and Saturday after 7 PM, the regular Devonport ferry is replaced by the **MV *Kestrel,*** a turn-of-the-century ferry restored to its brassy splendor and fitted out with a bar and a jazz band ($7 adults, $3.50 children 5–15). For a night to remember, leave the ferry at Devonport, dine at the Torpedo Bay Bar and Brasserie above the ferry terminal, then take an evening stroll through the historic streets.

Shopping

Shopping Districts Auckland's main shopping precinct for clothes, outdoor gear, duty-free goods, greenstone jewelry, and souvenirs is **Queen Street. Ponsonby,** about 1½ kilometers (1 mile) west of the city center, is known for its antiques shops and fashion boutiques.

Department Stores **Smith and Caughey Ltd.** is Auckland's only department store. *253–261 Queen St., tel. 09/377–4770. Open Mon.–Thurs. 9–5, Fri. 9–9, Sat. 9–1.*

Street Markets **Victoria Park Market** is Auckland's main bazaar—2½ acres of clothing, footwear, sportswear, furniture, souvenirs, and crafts at knockdown prices. It's housed in the city's former garbage incinerator. The International Foodhall has a range of inexpensive dishes from Thai to Texan. *Cnr. Victoria and Wellesley Sts., tel. 09/309–6911. Open Mon.–Sat. 9–7, Sun. 10–7.*

Specialty Stores
Books **Whitcoulls** is a general bookshop with a good selection of New Zealand titles. *186 Queen St., tel. 09/377–8329. Open Mon.–Thurs. 9–5:30, Fri. 9–9, Sat. 9–noon.*

Clothes **Action Downunder** is part of a nationwide chain of stores selling high-quality outdoor clothing for men and women. *75 Queen St., tel. 09/309–0241. Open Mon.–Thurs. 9–5:30, Fri. 9–9, Sat. 9–4, Sun. 11–5.*
Wool 'n' Trends has a high-quality selection of knitted woolen garments and woven hangings. *85 Victoria Rd., Devonport, tel. 09/445–2226. Open Oct.–Mar., daily 9–6; closed Sun. Apr.–Sept.*

Souvenirs **He Kohinga** specializes in high-quality Maori art, including carved greenstone and wooden bowls and flutes made from native totara. *259 Parnell Rd., tel. 09/366–4585. Open Mon.–Sat. 10–5:30, Sun. 11–4.*
Wild Places sells posters, T-shirts, books, and cards on the themes of whales, rain forests, and native birds. All proceeds go to conservation projects in New Zealand and the Pacific. *28 Lorne St., tel. 09/358–0795. Open Mon.–Thurs. 9–5:30, Fri. 9–9, Sat. 9–noon.*

Sports and Hiking **Kathmandu** sells quality New Zealand–made clothing and equipment for the outdoor enthusiast. *350 Queen St., tel. 09/*

309–4615. Open Mon.–Thurs. 9–5:30, Fri. 9–9., Sat. 9–2, Sun. 10–2.

Infomaps, published by the Department of Survey and Land Information, are essential equipment for wilderness walkers. The complete range is available from the department's office. *6th Floor, AA Centre, cnr. Albert and Victoria Sts., tel. 09/377–1899. Open weekdays 8–4.*

Sports and the Outdoors

Biking Auckland is a pleasant and relaxed city for two-wheeled exploring, especially around its waterfront. **Penny Farthing Cycle Shop** hires out mountain bikes for $25 per day or $140 per week. *Cnr. Symonds St. and Khyber Pass Rd., tel. 09/379–2524. Open Sept.–Apr., Mon.–Thurs. 8:30–5:30, Fri. 8:30 AM–9 PM, weekends 9:30–3 (closed Sun. May–Aug.).*

Golf **Chamberlain Park Golf Course** is an 18-hole public course in a parkland setting a five-minute drive from the city. Clubs and golf carts can be hired from the club shop. *Linwood Ave., Western Springs, tel. 09/846–6758.*

Titirangi Golf Course, a 15-minute drive south of the city, is one of the country's finest 18-hole courses. Nonmembers are welcome to play provided they contact the professional in advance and show evidence of membership at an overseas golf club. Clubs and golf carts can be hired; the greens fee is $50. *Links Rd., New Lynn, tel. 09/827–5749.*

Jogging Auckland's favorite running track is **Tamaki Drive,** a 10-kilometer (6-mile) route that heads east from the city along the southern shoreline of Waitemata Harbour and ends at St. Heliers Bay. Close to the city, the **Auckland Domain** (*see* Exploring Auckland, *above*) is popular with executive lunchtime joggers.

Spectator Sports **Eden Park** is the city's major stadium for sporting events. For information on current events, *Auckland Alive* is a quarterly guide available from the Visitor Information Centre. Tickets can be booked through Bass New Zealand (tel. 09/307–5000).

Swimming **The Tepid Baths,** located near the heart of Auckland, has a large indoor swimming pool, a spa pool, saunas, and a steam room. *102 Customs St. W, tel. 09/379–4794. Admission: $5.50 adults, $3 children under 15; swimming pool only, $3.50 adults, $1.50 children under 15. Open weekdays 6 AM–10 PM, weekends 7–7.*

Tennis **Auckland Tennis Inc.** offers a choice of 12 hard courts, either indoors or outdoors, a half mile east of the city center. *48 Stanley St., tel. 09/373–3623. Cost: $18 per hr outdoors, $30 per hr indoors. Open 11–7.*

Beaches

Auckland's beaches are commonly categorized by area—East, West, or North. The ones closest to the city are the east coast beaches along Tamaki Drive, which are well protected and safe

for children. **Judge's Bay** and **Mission Bay** are particularly recommended for their settings. The best swimming is at high tide.
The west coast beaches are popular in the summer, but the sea is
often rough, and sudden rips and holes can trap the unwary. The
most popular of these is **Piha,** some 40 kilometers (25 miles) from
Auckland, which has pounding surf as well as a sheltered lagoon
dominated by the reclining mass of Lion Rock. **Whatipu,** south of
Piha, is a broad sweep of sand offering safe bathing behind the
sand bar that guards Manukau Harbour; **Bethells,** to the north,
is exposed and often subject to heavy surf. Across Waitemata
Harbour from the city, a chain of magnificent beaches stretches
north as far as the Whangaparaoa Peninsula, 40 kilometers (25
miles) from Auckland. In the Hauraki Gulf, the island of
Waiheke is ringed by a number of splendid small beaches.

Dining

$$$$ **Varick's.** Varick Neilsen's converted two-story terrace house is
still the first choice for many Aucklanders looking for a warm atmosphere and innovative food. The fried spicy tuatara fritters
with mushrooms, lemon oil, and balsamic vinegar and the eel fillets with caramelized onions, garlic, and a red-wine *jus* are two
of the first-course choices on a varied and imaginative menu.
Main courses include roast venison cutlets with grilled vegetables and risotto, and grilled beef tournedos with a sweet pepper
and black bean sauce. Varick's attracts a sophisticated, dressy
clientele. *70 Jervois Rd., Herne Bay, tel. 09/376–2049. Reservations advised. Jacket required. AE, DC, MC, V. No lunch Mon.,
Tues., Sat. Closed Sun.*

$$$ **The Brasserie.** Auckland's Regent hotel has replaced its fine din-
ing room with a bright, breezy, less formal dining room that's
right for all seasons. Wild rice and shrimp chowder, crayfish
tempura with mustard-seed sauce and potato cake, barbecued
salmon steak with red caviar, and grilled lamb loin with *rösti* po-
tatoes (hash browns) and spinach are offered on a menu that is
essentially Mediterranean, with a fashionable tilt toward the
Orient. Service is regally Regent. *Albert St., tel. 03/309–8888.
Reservations not required. Dress: casual. AE, DC, MC, V.*

$$$ **The French Café.** Prices have crept up to match the reputation of
★ this modestly elegant city-fringe restaurant, whose menu
draws from a variety of Mediterranean cuisines. A first-course
salad of bocconcini, olives, tomatoes, and basil, and a main
course of sautéed breast of chicken stuffed with sheep-milk
cheese and prosciutto are representative of the summer menu.
The restaurant has a brasserie-style dining room looking out
onto the street and a more formal restaurant at the rear. On
warm evenings you can sit in the courtyard. *210B Symonds St.,
tel. 09/377–1911. Reservations advised. Jacket required. AE,
DC, MC, V. Closed Sun.*

$$$ **Harbourside Seafood Bar and Grill.** Overlooking the water from
the upper level of the restored ferry building, this vast, modish,
seafood restaurant is the perfect choice for warm-weather din-
ing. Some of the finest New Zealand fish and shellfish, including
orange roughy, salmon, and snapper, appear on a menu with a

Auckland Dining and Lodging

N

0 — 500 yards
0 — 500 meters

Waitemata Harbour

KEY

AE American Express Office

i Tourist Information

— Rail Lines

Harner St.
Brigham St.
Jellicoe St.
Beaumont St.
Madden St.
Fanshawe St.
Princes Wharf
Queens Wharf
Kings Wharf
Tooley St.
Quay St.

Customs St. E
Beach Rd.
Anzac Ave.

AUCKLAND CITY

VICTORIA PARK

Nelson St.
Hobson St.
Albert St.
Queen St.
Victoria St. E.
Wellesley St. West
Cook St.
Kitchener St.

Visitor Information Centre

Aotea Sq.
Mayoral Dr.
Greys Ave.
Queen St.
Symonds St.

MYERS PARK

Karangahape Rd.

ALBERT PARK

Waterloo Quad.
Stanley St.

Railway Station
The Strand

CARLAW PARK

AUCKLAND DOMAIN

Garfield St.
Parnell Rd.
PARNELL
St. Georges Bay Rd.
RESERVE
St. Stephen's Ave.

NEWTON
Newton Rd.

EDEN TERRACE
New North Rd.
Mt. Eden Rd.
Nugent St.

Auckland Hamilton Motorway

Grafton Rd.
Park Rd.
GRAFTON
Carlton Gore Rd.
Khyber Pass Rd.

Tilaki St.
Parnell Rd.
RESERVE
NEWMARKET BORO
Broadway

Dining

The Brasserie, **7**
Cin Cin on Quay, **5**
Death by Chocolate, **12**
The French Café, **18**
Harbourside Seafood Bar and Grill, **5**
Iguacu, **16**

Rick's Café Americain, **8**
Saint's Waterfront Brasserie, **3**
Torpedo Bay Bar and Brasserie, **1**
Tuatara, **9**
Varick's, **10**
Vinnie's, **11**

Lodging

Albion Hotel, **13**
Ascott Parnell, **17**
Centra, **14**
Devonport Villa, **2**
Florida Motel, **4**
Hotel du Vin, **19**
Pan Pacific, **15**
Parkroyal, **6**
The Regent, **7**

fashionably Mediterranean accent. Lobster fresh from the tank is a house specialty and the reason the restaurant is a favorite with Japanese tourists. Non–fish eaters have their choice of venison, lamb, and poultry. On warm nights, book ahead and request a table outside on the deck. *Auckland Ferry Bldg., 99 Quay St., tel. 09/307–0486. Reservations advised. Dress: casual. AE, DC, MC, V.*

$$$ Saint's Waterfront Brasserie. On any warm weekend, this stylish brasserie, a 15-minute drive from the city, is the perfect place to enjoy the city of sails sunny side up. The extensive lunch menu is mostly derived from French and Italian cooking, and includes soups, salads, open sandwiches, pasta, fish, beef, lamb, and sweetbreads. The dinner menu is a more substantial variation on the same theme. The weekend brunch menu offers healthy combinations of fresh fruit plates with yogurt, bagels, croissants, fruit whips, and muesli. The gray carpet and white tablecloths under glass create a smart, clean atmosphere, accented by art deco motifs. Big concertina doors frame an impressive sea view dominated by the cone of Rangitoto. *425 Tamaki Dr., St. Heliers, tel. 09/575–5210. Reservations advised on weekends. Dress: casual but neat. AE, DC, MC, V.*

$$$ Vinnie's. The decor—white tablecloths, black chairs, and a gunmetal-gray carpet—borders on austere, but there is nothing restrained about the gutsy French-Italian provincial cooking at this shopfront restaurant in suburban Herne Bay. Carpaccio of salmon with vanilla and olive oil, figs wrapped in prosciutto and flavored with melted mascarpone, lamb shanks cooked in red wine and rosemary with roasted garlic, and braised ox tongue with baby leeks are typical selections from a menu that also includes many imaginative game dishes. *166 Jervois Rd., Herne Bay, tel. 09/376–5597. Reservations advised. Dress: casual. AE, DC, MC, V. No lunch. Closed Sun.*

$$ Cin Cin on Quay. This busy, bold, waterfront oyster bar and
★   brasserie is an appealing combination to Auckland's 20-to-30-somethings, who come as much to let their hair down as for the menu. The food varies from pizzas made in the wood-fired oven to bar snacks such as sweet-potato fries with chili-spiced sour cream, to exotic main courses such as Thai-style seafood cooked in a clay pot. The aqua-and-amber decor and the music are anything but subtle. New Zealand wines are well represented on the extensive wine list, and a wide range of domestic and imported beers is available. The site right next to the Devonport ferry terminal is a bonus for anyone with time to kill before the next ferry. *Auckland Ferry Bldg., 99 Quay St., tel. 09/307–6966. Reservations advised. Dress: casual. AE, DC, MC, V.*

$$ Iguacu. At the leading edge of restaurant chic in Auckland, this restaurant is big, funky, and different. Flares blaze at the front, and dappled red ocher walls, enormous mirrors in Mexican metalwork frames, a big glass ceiling, and a pair of chandeliers made from copper tubing create a polished if culturally cacophonous atmosphere. The menu, like the decor, grazes the galaxy, with dishes such as Cajun-blackened kingfish with jambalaya rice, chicken curry with dahl and fried rice, teriyaki roast venison, and Polish sausage with sauerkraut; however it fails to leave an imprint with any distinctive cuisine of its own. *269 Parnell Rd., Parnell, tel. 09/309–4124. Reservations not required. Dress: casual. AE, DC, MC, V.*

$$ Rick's Café Americain. Owned by an American named Rick, this casual bistro in the Victoria Park Markets is aimed at a young market, but the chrome-and-neon decor, spirited service, reasonable prices, and subdued rock and funky jazz give it a wide appeal. Burgers, spare ribs, steaks, and pasta are staples on the menu, but there are several exotic surprises, such as tandoori lamb satay, wild mushroom ragout, and a vegetarian pie with spinach and feta cheese. Rick's is open daily for breakfast. In Parnell, **Rick's Blue Falcon** has an identical menu. *Victoria Park Market, tel. 09/309–9074. No reservations. Dress: casual. AE, DC, MC, V. Rick's Blue Falcon: 27 Falcon St., Parnell, tel. 09/ 309–0854.*

$$ Torpedo Bay Bar and Brasserie. Overlooking the harbor from the new Devonport ferry terminal, Auckland's breeziest restaurant has exceptional views. The two dozen dishes on the summer menu include pizzas, pasta, salads, and main courses such as baked salmon, chicken breast with scallops, panfried pork medallions, and baked venison. The art deco–inspired interior is pleasant but a long second to the deck; it's essential to book ahead to ensure an outside table. *Devonport Wharf, tel. 09/445– 9770. Reservations advised. Dress: casual but neat. AE, DC, MC, V.*

$$ Tuatara. Although it takes its name from a local reptile, there is nothing sluggish about Auckland's hippest bistro. The menu is a capable but unambitious roundup of current crowd pleasers, with a choice of salads, focaccia, an antipasto plate, pasta, fish and shellfish, and main courses such as grilled chicken breast with sweet peppers, sun-dried tomatoes, and baby potatoes. Ambience is consciously understated: bare wooden floors, cream-color walls, chunky tables, a big wooden bar in the middle, medium-volume reggae music, and folding glass doors that allow the inevitably crowded tables to spill out onto Ponsonby Road. *198 Ponsonby Rd., Ponsonby, tel. 09/360–0098. No reservations. Dress: casual but neat. AE, DC, MC, V.*

$ ★ Death by Chocolate. This dessert-only restaurant is strictly for chocoholics. Butterscotch pecan ice cream with fresh cream, chocolate flakes in a chocolate-covered waffle cone, chocolate scallop shells with melon and summer berries dusted with caster sugar, and ice cream studded with caramel balls and served with hot fudge sauce are typical of the gooey delights. *42 Jervois Rd., Ponsonby, tel. 09/360–2828. Reservations not required. Dress: casual but neat. AE, DC, MC, V. No lunch.*

Lodging

$$$$ ★ Hotel du Vin. There can be no finer introduction to New Zealand than to head south from the Auckland International Airport to this smart, luxurious hotel, set on the floor of a valley and surrounded by native forests and the grapevines of the de Redcliffe Estate. Standard rooms are palatial, and the rooms built in 1987 were upgraded in 1994, but request one of the newer rooms at the far end of the resort. The decor is crisp and modern, and the central restaurant and reception areas glow with honey-color wood and rough stone fireplaces. The restaurant has an excellent reputation, though prices are high. The hotel is 40 miles from Auckland, a 45-minute drive from both Auckland airport and the city via the motorway. *Lyons Rd., Mangatawhiri Valley, tel. 09/233–6314, fax 09/233–6215. 46 rooms with bath. Facilities: bar, restaurant, heated indoor pool, spa, gym, tennis courts, bicycles, winery. AE, DC, MC, V.*

$$$$ Pan Pacific. When this atrium-style hotel opened early in 1990, it became the most glamorous member of the city's five-star elite. Guest rooms are spacious and elegantly furnished, and the bathrooms are particularly well equipped. The best views are from the rooms that overlook the parklands and the harbor to the east. Polished granite and warm, earthy tones have been used liberally throughout the hotel. A favorite with business travelers, it is located close to the Aotea Centre and the business and shopping districts. *Mayoral Dr., tel. 09/366–3000, fax 09/366–0121. 286 rooms with bath. Facilities: 2 bars, 2 restaurants, 24-hr coffee shop, tennis court. AE, DC, MC, V.*

$$$$ Parkroyal. This was Auckland's premier hotel for almost two decades after it was built in the late '60s, but its age is difficult to ignore. The hotel is scrupulously maintained and constantly upgraded, but no amount of tender loving care can overcome the slightly cramped rooms and, by today's standards, limited natural lighting. On the positive side, it has a comforting clublike atmosphere, and its location at the lower end of Queen Street, close to the ferry terminal, is one of the best of any city hotel. *8 Customs St., tel. 09/377–8920, fax 09/307–3739. 188 rooms with bath. Facilities: 4 bars, 2 restaurants. AE, DC, MC, V.*

$$$$ The Regent. This mid-city hotel brought a dash of style to Auck-
★ land when it opened in the mid-'80s, and despite some energetic competitors, its service, sophistication, and attention to detail keep it on top. Standard rooms are large and furnished extensively with natural fabrics and native timbers. The marble bathrooms are luxuriously appointed. Due to a refurbishment, to be substantially completed by early 1995, the rooms are decorated in a warmer style, with dark wood furnishings and patterned fabrics, creating an art deco flavor. The best rooms are on the harbor side—the higher the better. *Albert St., tel. 09/309–8888, fax 09/379–6445. 332 rooms with bath. Facilities: bar, 3 restaurants, heated outdoor pool. AE, DC, MC, V.*

$$$ Centra. Rooms at this city landmark are equal to those in just about any of Auckland's leading hotels, but cutting down on the facilities and the glossy public areas has made the price substantially lower. Rooms have a standard, functional layout, and each has its own iron and ironing board. Accommodation begins on the 16th floor, and every room has a view. The suites on the 28th floor have great views and bigger bathrooms for just a slightly higher price. The hotel, which opened in 1991, is aimed primarily at the business traveler. Service is keen and professional. *128 Albert St., tel. 09/302–1111, fax 09/302–3111. 252 rooms with bath. Facilities: bar, restaurant, gym. AE, DC, MC, V.*

\$\$ Ascott Parnell. Accommodations and facilities in this sprawling guest house are comfortable and functional, but space and character have been sacrificed to provide rooms with en suite facilities or private bathrooms at a reasonable price. The room with the attached sunroom at the back of the house is small but pleasant. The house stands on a leafy back street, within easy walking distance of the shops and nightlife of Parnell Village. Smoking is not permitted inside, and children 2–8 are not accommodated. *36 St. Stephens Ave., Parnell, tel. 09/309–9012, fax 09/309–3729. 9 rooms with bath. Tariff includes full breakfast. AE, MC, V.*

\$\$ Devonport Villa. This guest house has just relocated to a new vil-
★ la: the former Towers Bed & Breakfast. The new location is one block away from the old one—still two minutes' walk to Cheltenham Beach, which offers safe swimming, and a bit closer to Devonport Village—and still combines tranquil, historic surroundings and fresh sea air, with the city just a boat ride away. Rooms are individually decorated and have handmade quilts, queen-size beds with Edwardian-style headboards, lace curtains, and colonial furniture. The house is a 10-minute walk from the ferry terminal, but the owner will pick up arriving guests. *46 Tainui Rd., Devonport, tel. 09/445–8397, fax 09/445–9766. 4 rooms with bath. Tariff includes full breakfast. Facilities: garden, guest lounge. AE, V.*

\$\$ Florida Motel. Located in a harborside suburb a 15-minute drive east of the city center (and close to a major bus route into the city), this motel offers exceptional value. Rooms come in three versions: studios or one- or two-bedroom units. The units have a lounge room separate from the bedroom, and the two-bedroom units are particularly good for families. All rooms have separate, fully equipped kitchens and a few extra touches of luxury, such as wall-mounted hair dryers, plunger-type coffee makers, and ironing boards with irons. The motel is immaculately maintained and extremely popular, and rooms must be booked several months in advance. *11 Speight Rd., Kohimarama, tel. 09/521–4660, fax 09/521–4662. 8 rooms with bath. AE, DC, MC, V.*

\$ Albion Hotel. If you're looking for comfortable, modern accommodations in the heart of the city and outstanding value, look no further. The rooms are modest in size and offer no views, but all are neat and well kept. The best room in the house, the Hobson Suite, is equipped with a waterbed and Jacuzzi and costs only slightly more than the standard rooms. Despite the busy corner location, the area is quiet after 6 PM. However, rooms on the lower floor can be affected by noise from the pub on the ground floor, which is especially popular on Friday nights. The Aotea Centre and the shops of Queen Street are only two blocks away. *Cnr. Hobson and Wellesley Sts., tel. 09/379–4900, fax 09/379–4901. 20 rooms with bath. Facilities: pub, brasserie. AE, DC, MC, V.*

The Arts

For a current listing of plays, opera, dance, and musical events in Auckland, a brochure called **_Auckland Alive_** is available from the Visitor Information Centre and the Aotea Centre. For current films, check the entertainment pages of the daily newspapers. Auckland's main venue for music and the performing arts is the **Aotea Centre** (at Aotea Square, near the corner of Queen and Myers streets), which hosts performances of music and drama throughout the year. For general inquiries there is an Information Desk (tel. 09/307–5050) in the Owens Foyer, level 2 of the complex. For recorded information on current events at the Aotea Centre, phone 09/309–2678. For bookings, phone **Bass New Zealand** (tel. 09/307–5000). Bass is the central booking agency for all theater, music, and dance performances, as well as for major sporting events.

Music The **Auckland Philharmonia Orchestra** performs regularly at the Aotea Centre (*see above*). The **New Zealand Symphony Orchestra** performs at the Town Hall and at the Aotea Centre.

Opera Dame Kiri Te Kanawa often performs at the Aotea Centre on return visits to her homeland, but tickets are usually sold out months in advance.

Theater **The Mercury Theatre,** the country's largest professional company, gives regular performances of the latest hits in its 700-seat auditorium. The theater has two bars and a café, open before and after all shows. *9 France St., Newton, tel. 09/303–3869. Shows Mon.–Sat.*

Nightlife

After sunset, the liveliest area of the city is Parnell, which has several restaurants, bars, and nightclubs.

Bars and Lounges **Cactus Jacks** is a mid-city bar that would like to believe it's somewhere deep in the heart of Texas. If you're looking for a convivial bar with a Tex-Mex menu and an impressive lineup of tequilas, this is the place. *Finance Plaza, 96 Albert St., tel. 09/302–0942. Open Mon.–Sat. 11 AM–1 AM.*

The Civic Tavern, at the heart of the city center, looks unremarkable from street level, but inside it, the **London Bar** has a vast selection of beers, **Murphy's Irish Bar** has jazz bands every night from Wednesday to Saturday, and **Younger's Tartan Bar** is "Auckland's only Scottish bar," with an impressive choice of Scotch whiskey. *1 Wellesley St., tel. 09/373–3684. Open Mon.–Sat. 11 AM–midnight.*

The Loaded Hog, one of the newest arrivals on Auckland's entertainment scene, is a popular, casual brewery and bistro with a choice of indoor or outdoor dining and drinking. Part of the new Hobson's Wharf development, the tavern has a vaguely nautical feel to go with its harborside location. Jazz musicians perform most evenings. *104 Quay St., tel. 09/366–6491. Open approx. 11 AM–1 AM.*

The Safari Bar, on the top floor of the Exchange Hotel, is a lively and attractive place that attracts a young, well-heeled crowd, especially on Friday and Saturday nights. On the floor below, the **Long Room** is a more subdued cocktail bar. Drinks are expensive. *99 Parnell Rd., Parnell, tel. 373–2531. Open Mon.–Sat 11 AM–midnight.*

The Shakespeare Tavern is an atmospheric and popular pub in the middle of the city. The Shakespeare makes and serves its own beers, which go by such colorful names as Willpower Stout and Falstaff's Real Ale. There are several bars inside and live rock or jazz most evenings. *Cnr. Albert and Wyndham Sts., tel. 09/373–5396. Open Mon.–Sat. 11–11.*

Nightclubs   **Number 7** is a long-standing favorite with Auckland's sophisticates, and you'll have to dress up to get through the door. On most evenings the club offers live jazz as well as disco music. *7 Windsor St., Parnell, tel. 09/379–4341. Admission: $6–$10. Open Wed.–Sat. 9 PM–3 AM.*

Rick's Blue Falcon is Auckland's version of the Hard Rock Café: a voguish interior decorated with car parts, rainbow-colored cocktails, and a steak and burger menu. Here, as elsewhere, this well-tested recipe attracts a varied clientele. Prices are moderate. The Attic Bar has live jazz or restrained rock every night. *27 Falcon St., Parnell, tel. 09/309–0854. Open daily noon–midnight.*

Studebaker Diner and Bar is a cross between a '50s-style diner and a stage set for *Phantom of the Opera*. The loud bar, disco, and café appeal to Auckland's early-20s set. Theme nights vary from rock on Tuesday to psychedelic on Sunday. *3 Lower Albert St., tel. 09/377–1950. Open Sun.–Tues. 5 PM–midnight, Wed.– Thurs. 5 PM–2 AM, Fri.–Sat. 5 PM–3 AM.*

Discos   **The New Testament,** popularly abbreviated to TNT, is still rocking and shaking on Auckland's nefarious "K Road," the nucleus of the city's sex trade. The cavernous, two-level complex is composed of the Mosaic Bar, the China Beach Bar, the Cinema Dance Club—all open to the public—and The Sanctuary—open to members only. Drinks are moderately priced. *340 Karangahape Rd., tel. 09/379–9320. Admission: $5. Open Wed.–Sun. 9 PM–5 AM.*

Northland and the Bay of Islands

Beyond Auckland, the North Island stretches a long arm into the South Pacific. This is Northland, an undulating region of farms, forests, and marvelous beaches. The main attraction here is the Bay of Islands, an island-studded seascape with a mild, subtropical climate, and one of the finest game-fishing waters in the country—witness its record catches of marlin and mako shark. Big-game fishing is expensive, but many small fishing boats will take you out for an evening of trawling for as little as $35.

It was on the Bay of Islands that the first European settlement was established, and here that New Zealand became a nation with the signing of the Treaty of Waitangi in 1840. The main town is Paihia, a strip of motels and restaurants along the waterfront. If you plan to spend more than a day in the area, the town of Russell, just a short ferry trip away, makes a more atmospheric and attractive base.

Important Addresses and Numbers

Tourist Information **Bay of Islands Visitor Information Centre.** *Maritime Reserve, Paihia, tel. 09/402–7426. Open Nov.–Mar., daily 7:30–7:30; Apr.–Oct., daily 8–5.*

Emergencies Dial 111 for **fire, police,** or **ambulance** services.

Arriving and Departing

By Car The main route from Auckland is Highway 1. Leave the city by the Harbour Bridge and follow the signs to Whangarei. Driving time for the 250-kilometer (150-mile) journey to Paihia is about four hours.

By Bus **Northliner Express** (tel. 09/307–5873), **InterCity** (tel. 09/358–4085), and **Newmans** (tel. 09/309–9738) operate several daily bus services between Auckland and Paihia.

Guided Tours

Orientation **Fullers Northland** operates one-, two-, and three-day tours from Auckland to the Bay of Islands. Recommended is its Bay Explorer tour, which includes a tour of the historic Waitangi Treaty House, a trip to Cape Reinga, a swim with dolphins, a voyage around the bay aboard a schooner, and accommodations in Russell. *Bay of Islands Travel Centre, Shop 2, Downtown Shopping Centre, Customs St., Auckland, tel. 09/358–0259. Tickets: $435 adults, $220 children 4–14.*

Russell Mini Tours offers a one-hour guided tour of the historic sights of Russell. Tours depart from the Fullers office, opposite the wharf. *Box 70, Russell, tel. 09/403–7891. Tickets: $8 adults, $4 children 5–15. Tours at 11, 1, 2, 3:30.*

Boat Tours **Fullers Northland** (*see above*) operates several cruises in the Bay of Islands, departing from both Paihia and Russell. The most popular is the half-day catamaran cruise to Cape Brett, at the eastern extremity of the bay. The Cream Trip is a six-hour cruise that stops in at many of the bay islands. *Maritime Bldg., Paihia, tel. 09/402–7421. Tickets: Cape Brett, $47 adults, $24 children 4–14; Cream Trip, $49 adults, $24 children. Cape Brett Cruise departs Paihia daily 9 AM and 1:30 PM; Cream Trip departs Paihia daily 10 AM Oct.–May; Mon., Wed., Thurs., Sat. 10 AM June–Sept.*

Exploring Northland

This tour begins at Auckland, traveling north to the Bay of Islands via Highway 1 and returning along the western side of the peninsula. The return route, Highway 12, adds almost two hours to the driving time, but the tranquil landscape makes an attractive alternative to Highway 1, which is particularly busy during the December–January holiday period.

North of Waitemata Harbour, Highway 1 quickly leaves the city and the suburbs behind and weaves into rolling green hills around the town of **Albany.** In December, the pohutukawa trees along the roadside celebrate the arrival of Christmas by erupting in a blaze of scarlet blossoms, and hence their other name—the New Zealand Christmas tree. To the Maoris, the flowers had another meaning: the beginning of the shellfish season. The spiky-leaved plants that grow in clumps by the roadside are the New Zealand flax. The fibers of this plant, the raw material for linen, were woven into clothing by the Maoris. The huge tree ferns—common throughout the forests of North Island, where they can grow as high as 10 meters (30 feet)—are known locally as "pungas."

Numbers in the margin correspond to points of interest on the Northland and the Bay of Islands map.

At the town of **Warkworth,** 69 kilometers (43 miles) from Auckland, turn right into McKinney Road, right again into Thompson Road, and then follow the signs to the **Warkworth Museum.** The main attraction here is the two giant kauri trees in the car park. The larger one, the **McKinney Kauri,** measures almost 25 feet around its base, yet this 800-year-old colossus is a mere adolescent by kauri standards. Kauri trees, once prolific in this part of the North Island, were highly prized by Maori canoe builders, because a canoe capable of carrying a hundred warriors could be made from a single trunk. Unfortunately these same characteristics—strength, size, and durability—made kauri timber ideal for ships, furniture, and housing, and the kauri forests were rapidly depleted by the early European settlers. Today the trees are protected by law, and many infant kauris are again appearing in the forests of the North Island, although their growth rate is painfully slow. The museum contains a collection of Maori artifacts and farming and domestic implements from the pioneering days of the Warkworth district. *Tudor Collins Dr., tel. 09/425–7093. Admission: $2 adults, 50¢ children 5–15. Open Dec.–Feb., daily 9:30–4; Mar.–Nov., daily 10–3:30.*

When you get to the town of **Whangarei,** cross the river and look for a sign on your left to **Clapham's Clock Museum.** Just about every conceivable method of telling time is represented in this collection of more than 1,400 clocks, from primitive water clocks to ships' chronometers to ornate masterworks from Paris and Vienna. Some of the most intriguing specimens were made by the late Mr. Clapham himself, including a World War II air force clock that automatically changed the position of aircraft over a map. Ironically, the one thing you won't find here is the correct time. If all the bells, chimes, gongs, and cuckoos went off together the noise would be deafening, so all the clocks are set to different times. *Water St., Cafler Park, Whangarei, tel. 09/438–3993. Admission: $3.50 adults, $1.20 children 5–15. Open daily 10–4.*

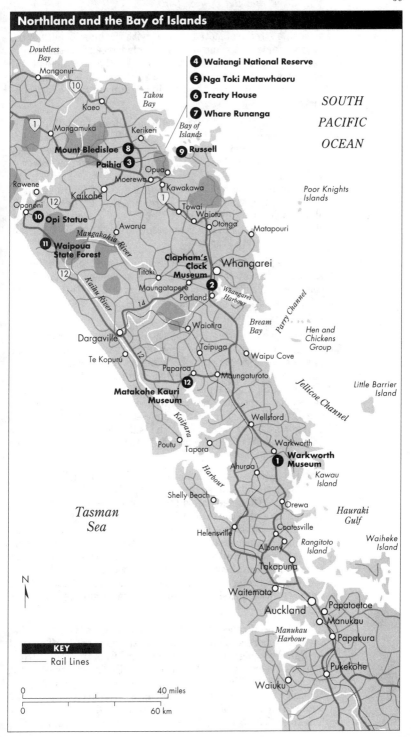

Northland and the Bay of Islands

4 Waitangi National Reserve

5 Nga Toki Matawhaoru

6 Treaty House

7 Whare Runanga

SOUTH

PACIFIC

OCEAN

Doubtless Bay

Mangonui

(10)

Kaeo

Takou Bay

Mangamuka

Kerikeri

1

Mangamuka

Bay of Islands

Mount Bledisloe **8**

9 **Russell**

Paihia **3**

Opua

Moerewa

Kawakawa

Rawene

(12)

Kaikohe

1

Opononi

Towai

10 **Opi Statue**

Awarua

Waiotu

Otonga

Matapouri

Poor Knights Islands

11
Waipoua State Forest

Mangakahia River

Clapham's Clock Museum

Whangarei

(12)

Titoki

2

Whangarei Harbour

Kaihu River

Maungatapere

Portland

14

Bream Bay

Parry Channel

Hen and Chickens Group

Waiotira

Dargaville

12

Taipuga

Waipu Cove

Jellicoe Channel

Little Barrier Island

Te Kopuru

Paparoa

12

Maungaturoto

Matakohe Kauri Museum

Wellsford

Kaipara Harbour

Poutu

Tapora

Warkworth

1 **Warkworth Museum**

Anuroa

Kawau Island

Shelly Beach

Orewa

Hauraki Gulf

Tasman Sea

Helensville

Coatesville

Waiheke Island

Albany

Rangitoto Island

Takapuna

N

Waitemata

Auckland

Papatoetoe

Manukau

Manukau Harbour

Papakura

KEY

— Rail Lines

Pukekohe

Waiuku

| 0 | 40 miles |

| 0 | 60 km |

3 **Paihia,** the main holiday base for the Bay of Islands, is an unremarkable stretch of motels at odds with the quiet beauty of the island-studded seascape and the rounded green hills that form a backdrop to the town, yet nearby Waitangi is one of the country's most important historic sites. It was near here that the Treaty of Waitangi, the founding document for modern New Zealand, was signed.

4 At the northern end of town, on the far side of the Waitangi River, a side road turns right toward the **Waitangi National Reserve.** Inside the visitor center, a 23-minute video, shown every hour on the hour, sketches the events that led to the Treaty of Waitangi. The center also houses a display of Maori artifacts and weapons, including a musket that belonged to Hone Heke Pokai, the first Maori chief to sign the treaty. After his initial display of enthusiasm for British rule, Hone Heke was quickly disillusioned, and less than five years later he attacked the British in their stronghold at Russell.

5 From the visitor center, follow the short track through the forest to **Nga Toki Matawhaoru,** a Maori war canoe. This huge kauri canoe, capable of carrying 150 warriors, is named after the vessel in which Kupe, the Polynesian navigator, is said to have discovered New Zealand.

6 Follow the shoreline track and then cross the vast lawn to the **Treaty House,** a five-minute stroll from the war canoe. There can have been few more modest beginnings on the road to nationhood than this simple white timber cottage, which has a remarkable air of dignity despite its scale. The interior is fascinating, especially at the back, where exposed walls give an insight into the difficulties that the early administrators faced—such as an acute shortage of bricks (since an insufficient number had been shipped out from New South Wales) with which to finish the walls.

The Treaty House was prefabricated in New South Wales for the British Resident, James Busby, who arrived in New Zealand in 1832. Busby had been appointed to protect British commerce and put an end to the brutalities of the whaling captains against the Maoris, but Busby lacked either the judicial authority or the force of arms necessary to impose peace. On one occasion, unable to resolve a dispute between Maori tribes, Busby was forced to shelter the wounded of one side in his house. While tattooed head hunters screamed war chants outside the windows, one of the warriors sheltered Busby's infant daughter, Sarah, in his cape.

The real significance of the Treaty House lies in the events that took place here on February 6, 1840, the day that the **Treaty of Waitangi** was signed by Maori chiefs and Captain William Hobson, representing the British crown. Under the treaty, the chiefs agreed to accept the authority of the crown; in return, the British recognized the Maoris as the legitimate landowners and granted them all the rights and privileges of British subjects. The treaty also confirmed the status of New Zealand as a British colony, forestalling French overtures in the area, and legitimized—at least according to European law—the transfer of land from Maori to European hands. In recent years the Maoris have used the treaty successfully to reclaim land that, they maintain, was misappropriated by white settlers.

The Treaty House has not always received the care its significance merits. When Lord Bledisloe bought the house and presented it to the nation in 1932, it was being used as a shelter for sheep.

On the northern boundary of Waitangi National Reserve is ❼ **Whare Runanga,** a Maori meeting house with an elaborately carved interior. Inside, an audio show offers a brief outline of traditional Maori society. *Waitangi Rd., Waitangi, tel. 09/402–7437. Admission: $5 adults, children under 15 free. Open daily 9–5.*

Three kilometers (2 miles) from the Treaty House, on the other side of the Waitangi Golf Course, there is a small parking area on the right of Waitangi Road. Stop here and take the short track, ❽ which rises above a pine forest to the summit of **Mount Bledisloe** and a splendid view across Paihia and the Bay of Islands. The handsome ceramic marker at the top showing the distances to major world cities was made by Doulton in London and presented by Lord Bledisloe in 1934 during his term as governor-general of New Zealand.

The second town in the Bay of Islands, at the tip of a peninsula ❾ opposite Paihia, is **Russell.** You can drive, but the quickest and most convenient route is by ferry. Three passenger ferries make the crossing between Paihia and Russell, with departures at least every 30 minutes in each direction from 7:30 AM to 11 PM. The one-way adult fare is $1, 50¢ for children 5–14. The car ferry is at Opua, about 5 kilometers (3 miles) south of Paihia. This ferry operates from 6:40 AM to 8:50 PM (9:50 PM Friday), with departures at approximately 20-minute intervals from either shore. The last ferry leaves from Russell at 8:50 (9:50 Friday), from Opua at 9 (10 Friday). The one-way fare is $6 for the car and driver plus $1 for each passenger.

Hard as it is to believe these days, sleepy little Russell was once dubbed the Hellhole of the Pacific. Early last century (when it was still known by its Maori name, Kororareka) it was a swashbuckling frontier town, a haven for sealers and for whalers who found one of the richest whaling grounds on earth along the east coast of New Zealand. The tales of debauchery were probably exaggerated, but the British administrators in New South Wales (as Australia was known at the time) were sufficiently concerned to dispatch a British Resident in 1832 to impose law and order. After the Treaty of Waitangi, Russell was the national capital, until in 1844 the Maori chief Hone Heke attacked the British garrison and most of the town burned to the ground. Hone Heke was finally defeated in 1846, but Russell never recovered its former prominence, and the seat of government was shifted first to Auckland, then to Wellington. Today Russell is a delightful town of timber houses and big trees that swoon low over the seafront, framing the yachts and the big-game fishing boats in the harbor. The atmosphere can best be absorbed in a stroll along the Strand, the path along the waterfront.

At the southern end of the Strand is **Pompallier House,** named after the first Catholic bishop of the South Pacific. Marist missionaries built the original structure out of rammed earth (mud mixed with dung or straw—a technique known as *pise* in their native France), since they lacked the funds to buy timber. For several years the priests and brothers operated a press here, printing Bibles in the Maori language. The original building forms the core of the elegant timber house that now stands on the site. *The Strand, Russell, tel. 09/403-7861. Admission: $5 adults, children under 15 free when accompanied by adults, $2 unaccompanied children. Open daily 9–5.*

Set back slightly from the waterfront some 50 yards to the north is the **Captain Cook Memorial Museum,** which houses a collection of Maori tools and weapons and some fine portraits. The pride of its display is a ⅕-scale replica of Captain Cook's ship, HMS *Endeavour*, which entered the bay in 1769. *York St., Russell, tel. 09/403-7701. Admission: $2 adults, 50¢ children 5–15. Open daily 10–5.*

A block farther back from the harbor is **Christ Church,** the oldest church in the country. One of the donors to its erection in 1835 was Charles Darwin, at that time a wealthy but unknown young man making his way around the globe on board HMS *Beagle*. Behind the white picket fence that borders the churchyard, the gravestones tell a fascinating and gruesome story of life in the early days of the colony. Several graves belong to sailors from HMS *Hazard* who were killed in this churchyard by Hone Heke's warriors in 1845. Another headstone marks the grave of a Nantucket sailor from the whaler *Mohawk*. As you walk around the church, look for the musket holes made when Hone Heke besieged the church. The interior is simple and charming; the embroidered cushions on the pews are examples of a folk-art tradition that is still very much alive. *Church and Robertson Sts., Russell. Open daily 8–5.*

To return to Auckland via the west coast road, turn south toward the town of Kawakawa, then right onto Highway 1, and after about 16 kilometers (10 miles), take Highway 12 left toward Kaikohe. This road winds into steep green hills before wandering down toward a broad sea inlet, Hokianga Harbour. In the town of **Opononi,** near the mouth of the harbor, a statue in front of the pub commemorates a tame dolphin, **Opi,** that came to play with swimmers in the mid-1950s, putting the town on the national map for the first and only time in its history.

South of Opononi is the **Waipoua State Forest,** the largest remnant of the kauri forests that once covered this part of the country. A short path leads from the parking area through the forest to **Tane Mahuta,** "Lord of the Forest," standing nearly 173 feet high and measuring 43 feet around its base. The largest tree in New Zealand, it's said to be 1,200 years old.

⓬ The **Matakohe Kauri Museum** is one of the most intriguing museums in the country. Its vast collection of artifacts, tools, photographs, documents, and memorabilia tells the story of the pioneers who settled this part of the country in the second half of the 19th century—a story that is interwoven with the kauri forests. Here you'll find superb examples of kauri craftsmanship and furniture, a complete kauri house, and an early example of an American-built Caterpillar bulldozer, which was used to drag logs from the forest. One of the most fascinating displays is the room of kauri gum, the transparent lumps of resin that form when the sticky sap of the kauri tree hardens. This gum, which was used to make varnish, can be polished to a warm, lustrous finish that looks remarkably like amber—right down to the insects that are sometimes trapped and preserved inside. At one time collecting this gum was an important rural industry. Many of the gum diggers, as they were known, came from Dalmatia, part of present-day Croatia. *Matakohe, tel. 09/431–7417. Admission: $5 adults, $1.50 children 5–15. Open daily 9–5.*

Twenty kilometers (12½ miles) beyond the museum, Highway 12 joins Highway 1 for the final leg of the return journey to Auckland.

What to See and Do with Children

High and dry on the banks of the Waitangi River, the *Tui* is a historic kauri sailing vessel that was built to carry sugar to a refinery in Auckland. Below decks is an exhibition of artifacts recovered from shipwrecks by the famous New Zealand salvage diver Kelly Tarlton. In addition to the brass telescopes, sextants, and diving helmets that can be tried on for size, there is an exquisite collection of jewelry that belonged to Isidore Jonah Rothschild (of the famous banking family), which was lost when the SS *Tasmania* sank in 1897. Rothschild was on a sales trip to New Zealand at the time. *Waitangi Bridge, Paihia, tel. 09/402–7018. Admission: $4 adults, $2 children under 12. Open daily 10–5.*

Sports and the Outdoors

Boating **Marine Rentals** (tel. 09/402–8105), on the waterfront at Paihia, offers catamarans, jet skis, kayaks, and aqua bikes for hire. In the same location, **Charter Pier Paihia** (tel. 09/402–7127) has 16-foot powerboats suitable for fishing and diving for up to six people, available by the hour or the day. A catamaran operated by **Straycat Day Sailing Charters** (Doves Bay Rd., Kerikeri, tel. 09/407–7342) makes one-day sailing trips in the Bay of Islands from Russell and Paihia at $50 per person.

Diving The Bay of Islands offers some of the finest scuba diving in the country, particularly around Cape Brett, where the marine life includes moray eels, stingrays, and grouper. Water temperature at the surface varies from 62°F in July to 71°F in January. From September to November, underwater visibility is often affected by a plankton bloom. **Paihia Dive Hire and Charter** (Box 210, Paihia, tel. 09/402–7551) offers complete equipment hire and regular boat trips for accredited divers.

Fishing The Bay of Islands is one of the world's premier game-fishing grounds for marlin and several species of shark. Operators in the area include **Dudley Smith** (Box 203, Russell, tel. 09/403–7200), **Nighthawk** (tel. 09/407–8999), and **NZ Billfish Charters** (Box 416, Paihia, tel. 09/402–8380). A far less expensive alternative is to fish for snapper, kingfish, and John Dory in the inshore waters of the bay. Among several boat operators in Russell and Paihia who offer a half day of fishing, including bait and rods, for about $40 per person are **Skipper Jim** (tel. 09/402–7355) and **MV Arline** (tel. 09/402–8511).

Dining

During the January summer-vacation period, dinner reservations are essential at all restaurants in the area.

$$$ **The Gables.** This trim little cottage restaurant on the waterfront at Russell is one of the more sophisticated in the Bay of Islands. First courses on the mostly seafood menu include terrine of smoked snapper and a warm salad of chicken livers. The panfried snapper fillets with balsamic vinegar and the chargrilled fillet of lamb with a ginger and honey sauce are recommended. The lunch menu is limited but less expensive. *The Strand, Russell, tel. 09/403–7618. Reservations advised. Dress: casual. AE, DC, MC, V. No lunch weekdays except during summer. Closed Mon.*

$$ **Bay of Islands Swordfish Club.** Overlooking Kororareka Bay in a pretty cream-and-white timber building, the restaurant of the Swordfish Club is dedicated to fish and fish people, from the decor to the menu to the conversation. First courses are a salad of mussels or fresh oysters; entrées include fresh scallops and asparagus with oyster sauce. Request a table at the window, and begin the evening with a drink in the friendly bar upstairs— where, in the summer holiday period, you may have to wait for a table anyway. Officially visitors must be signed in by a member of the club, but provided you look sober, neat, and capable of enthusing over marlin fishing, the barman will request a club member to countersign the visitor's book for you (after which it would be diplomatic to stand the member to a drink). *The Strand, Russell, tel. 09/403–7652. No reservations. Dress: casual. AE, MC, V. No lunch.*

$$ **Cafe Over the Bay.** This breezy, bistro-style restaurant has an unambitious menu with an Italian accent, but the fish is excellent. First courses include minestrone, seafood chowder, and sweet and sour fish. Main dishes are tortellini with a wine and cream sauce, and fish with a coconut and lime sauce. Most of the fish dishes are made with the delicate, white-fleshed orange roughy. *Waterfront, Paihia, tel. 09/402–8147. No reservations. Dress: casual but neat. DC, MC, V.*

$$ **The Quarterdeck.** The specialty of this seafront restaurant is fish al fresco—crayfish, lobster, flounder, scallops, and snapper, and chips and salads—and while the prices are rather steep for less than glamorous dining, the outdoor tables overlooking the lively harbor are a pleasant spot on a warm evening. The Quarterdeck is popular with families. *The Strand, Russell, tel. 09/403–7761. No reservations. Dress: casual. AE, DC, MC, V. BYOB. No lunch weekdays except summer.*

Lodging

$$$$ **Kimberley Lodge.** The most luxurious accommodation in the Bay
★ of Islands, this splendid white timber mansion occupies a commanding position overlooking Russell and Kororareka Bay. The house has been designed with big windows and sunny verandas to take maximum advantage of its location. Below, terraced gardens fall away down a steep hillside to the sea. The house is opulently furnished in contemporary style, and the en suite bathrooms are equipped to five-star standards. Only one bedroom at the rear of the house—Pompallier—lacks impressive views. The best room in the house is the Kimberley Suite, which costs more than the standard suites. Dinner is available by arrangement. *Pitt St., Russell, tel. 09/403–7090, fax 09/403–7239. 4 rooms with bath. Facilities: outdoor heated pool. Tariff includes breakfast. No smoking indoors. AE, DC, MC, V.*

$$ **Austria Motel.** The large, double-bed rooms at this motel are typical of motel accommodations in the area—clean and moderately comfortable. Each has a kitchenette. The motel also offers a family unit on the ground level of the two-story wing. The shops and waterfront at Paihia are a two-minute walk away. *36 Selwyn Rd., Paihia, tel. 09/402–7480. 7 rooms with bath. Facilities: spa. AE, DC, MC, V.*

$$ **Duke of Marlborough Hotel.** This historic hotel is a favorite with the yachting fraternity, for whom ready access to the harbor and the bar downstairs are the most important considerations. Rooms are clean and tidy enough, and all have en suite facilities, but they offer no memorable character despite the hotel's long and colorful history. The front rooms with harbor views are the most expensive but also the ones most likely to be affected by noise from the spirited crowd in the bar, especially on weekends. *The Waterfront, Russell, tel. 09/403–7829, fax 09/403–7760. 29 rooms with bath. Facilities: restaurant, bar. DC, MC, V.*

$$ **Waitangi Resort Hotel.** The biggest hotel north of Auckland and a favorite with coach tour groups, this complex sprawls along a peninsula within walking distance of the Treaty House. Standard rooms, which are often booked by coach parties, show signs of long and heavy use, but many "premium" rooms were renovated in 1991 and offer more stylish accommodations. *Waitangi Rd., Paihia, tel. 09/402–7411, fax 09/402–8200. 138 rooms with bath. Facilities: outdoor pool, guest laundry, 3 restaurants, 2 bars. AE, DC, MC, V.*

$ **Russell Lodge.** Surrounded by quiet gardens two streets back from the waterfront, this lodge—owned and operated by the

Salvation Army—offers neat, clean rooms in several configurations. It's an especially good value for budget travelers and families. The family units have a separate bedroom with two single beds, and either a double or a single bed in the main room. The largest room is Unit 15, a two-bedroom flat with a kitchen, which will sleep six. Backpacker-style accommodation is also available in rooms for four; towels and sheets are not provided in these rooms but may be rented. All rooms have en suite bathrooms, and five have kitchen facilities. *Chapel and Beresford Sts., Russell, tel. 09/403–7640, fax 09/403–7641. 24 rooms with bath. Facilities: outdoor pool, guest laundry. AE, MC, V.*

The Coromandel Peninsula

New Zealand has countless pockets of beauty that are not included in the standard tourist itineraries. One of the most accessible is the Coromandel Peninsula, which juts out like a hitchhiker's thumb east of Auckland. The center of the peninsula is dominated by a craggy spine of volcanic peaks that rise sharply to a height of almost 900 meters (3,000 feet). The west coast is sheltered, while on the unprotected east coast the Pacific Ocean has gnawed a succession of beaches and inlets separated by rearing headlands. From the town of Thames, the gateway to the region, Highway 25 combines with the 309 Road to circle the lower two-thirds of the peninsula—an exhilarating drive with the sea on one side and big forested peaks on the other. The journey will add a day (at the very least) to your New Zealand itinerary, but it would be hard to find a finer introduction to the country.

Important Addresses and Numbers

Tourist Information **Coromandel Visitor Information Centre.** *Kapanga Rd., Coromandel, tel. 07/866–8958. Open weekdays 10–3.*

Thames Visitor Information Centre. *405 Queen St., Thames, tel. 07/868–7284. Open weekdays 9–5, weekends 10–3.*

Emergenices Dial 111 for **fire, police,** or **ambulance** services.

Arriving and Departing

By Car From Auckland, take the Southern Motorway, following the signs to Hamilton. Just past the end of the motorway, turn left onto Highway 2 and follow the signs to Thames. Allow two hours for the 118-kilometer (73-mile) journey.

By Bus **Murphy Buses** (tel. 07/867–6829) link Whitianga, Thames, and Auckland daily. Bookings can be made through InterCity (tel. 09/358–4085).

Guided Tours

The **Coromandel Peninsula Pass** is a three-day tour that includes transport to and from Auckland, hiking through native forests, kayaking, and fishing. Meals and accommodations are not included. *Fredericks and Rings Rds., Coromandel, tel. 07/866-8468. Tickets: $110.*

Doug Johansen's full- and half-day tours are a fascinating—and often hilarious—look at a majestic part of the country that he has known and loved since birth. Glowworm caves, abandoned gold mines, flora and fauna, thermal springs, and odd bits of history and bush lore are all covered in the tour, which will provide some of the most evocative memories of your visit to New Zealand. But be warned: Doug Johansen is an incurable practical joker. *Box 76, Pauanui Beach, tel. 07/864-8859. Tickets: $75 full day, $45 half day.*

Green Beetle Tours operates from Auckland a three-day tour of the Coromandel Peninsula designed primarily for young travelers. The emphasis is on low-impact ecotourism; kayaking, hiking, swimming with dolphins, and a history tour are highlights of the trip. Meals and accommodations are not included. *Box 31-228, Auckland, tel. 09/358-5868. Tickets: $118.*

Exploring the Coromandel Peninsula

This tour begins at **Thames** and follows Highway 25 in a clockwise direction as it circles the peninsula. If you leave Auckland early in the morning, it's possible to do the trip in a single day.

Numbers in the margin correspond to points of interest on the Coromandel Peninsula map.

Leave Thames and head north along Highway 25, which snakes along the seafront at the foot of the Coromandel Ranges, with expansive views across the Firth of Thames. At the former gold-mining town of Tapu, a narrow road turns inland to follow the Tapu River upstream along a narrow gorge that becomes prettier with every turn. About 6 kilometers (4 miles) from the start of ❶ this road, a sign on the right points to **Rapaura Falls Park,** a garden of native and exotic flowering species that has been sculpted from the wilderness. Paths wind through a riot of rhododendrons, lilies, azaleas, and orchids, while giant tree ferns and rata, remu, and kauri trees lock arms to form a green canopy overhead. The combination of delicacy and rugged grandeur has moved the hardworking gardener to philosophy, or at least to nuggets of wisdom painted on signs ("Keep your values in balance and you will always find happiness"). Be sure to take the 10-minute walk from the parking lot to the waterfall. *Admission: $5 adults, $1.50 children under 15. Open Sept.–May daily 10–5.*

❷ Return to Highway 25 and continue toward **Coromandel.** In 1852 the town became the site of New Zealand's first gold strike when Charles Ring, a sawmiller, found gold-bearing quartz at Driving Creek, just north of town. The find was important for New Zealand, since the country's manpower had been severely depleted by the gold rushes in California and Australia. Ring hurried to Auckland to claim the reward that had been offered to

The Coromandel Peninsula

Cape Colville

MOEHAU RANGE

Port Charles

Hauraki Gulf

Cuvier Island

N

0   10 miles
0   15 km

Colville

Motukawao Group

Amodeo Bay

Kennedys Bay

Papaaroha

Kennedy Bay

Great Mercury Island

Whangapoua

Whangapoua Harbour

Kuaotunu

Opito Bay

Coromandel ②

Te Rerenga

Waimate Island

Coromandel Harbour

309

Whanganui Island

Te Kouma

■ **Lighthouse**

Manaia

309

Whitianga

Mercury Bay

⑤ **Cathedral Cove**

④ **Hahei**

Kaimarama

Whitianga Harbour

③ **Cook's Beach**

Mill Creek

Kereta

Coromandel Range

⑥ **Hotwater Beach**

25

Coroglen

Whenuakite

Tapu River

Waiwawa River

Tapu

① **Rapaura Falls Park**

25

Shoe Island

Waiomu

Tairua

Te Puru

Pauanui Beach

Thorntons Bay

Ngarimu Bay

COROMANDEL STATE FOREST PARK

Tairua Harbour

Whakatete Bay

Kauaeranga River

Hikuai

Puketui

Slipper Island

Tararu

■ **Park Headquarters**

Firth of Thames

Thames

Kauaeranga

25A

Kopu

Opoutere

26

Orongo

Matatoki

Tairua River

Pipiroa

Wharekawa

TO HWY. 2

Kopuarahi

Puriri

25

Whangamata

anyone finding "payable" gold. The town's population soared, but the reef gold could be mined only by heavy and expensive machinery, and within a few months Coromandel resumed its former sleepy existence as a timber town—and Charles Ring was refused the reward.

From Coromandel, drive back along Highway 25 for about 4 kilometers (2½ miles) and turn inland where a sign points to "Whitianga—309 Road." If you haven't seen kauri trees yet, stop at Waiau Falls for the kauri grove, which is a 10-minute walk beyond the waterfall and swimming hole. At the end of the 309 Road turn right toward Tairua. This road skirts Mercury Bay, where Captain James Cook observed the transit of the planet Mercury in November 1769. Cook's landfall—the first by a European—is commemorated by a plaque on the southern side **❸** of the bay at **Cook's Beach;** however, the beach itself is one of the less attractive in the area.

Turn left on the southern side of Mercury Bay where a sign **❹** points to **Hahei.** At the entrance to the town, Pa Road turns to the right off Hahei Beach Road and, after 1½ kilometers (1 mile), ends at a small parking area at the Te Pare Historic Reserve. If you're feeling fit, follow the red arrow down the hill, and after about 50 yards take the right fork, which leads through a grove of giant pohutukawa trees, then through a gate and across a grassy, open hillside. The track is steep in places and becomes increasingly overgrown as you climb, but persist until you reach the summit, and then head toward the pohutukawas off to your right at the southern end of the headland. This is the site of an old Maori *pa*, a fortified hilltop, though no trace remains of the defensive terraces and wooden spikes that once ringed the hill. Another, much larger pa was located on the hilltop overlooking this site. If you happen to be there at high tide, the blowhole at the foot of the cliffs will add its booming bass note to the crash of the waves and the sighing of the wind in the grass.

Time Out | **Calenso Orchard and Herb Garden,** on Highway 25 just south of the Hahei turnoff, is a relaxed cottage café set in a garden full of lavender. The menu lists fresh juices, vegetable soup, focaccia with ham, homemade chocolate fudge biscuits, and Devonshire teas—simple, wholesome fare that goes with the droning of the bees and the sound of the wind chimes. Prices are low. *Main Rd., Whenuakite, tel. 07/866–3275. Open daily 10–5.*

Return to Hahei Beach Road, turn right toward the sea, and then, just past the shops, turn left into Grange Road and follow **❺** the signs to **Cathedral Cove.** The road ends at a parking lot with dramatic coastal views. Cathedral Cove, a vast rock arch accessible at low tide, is a 45-minute walk each way.

❻ The popular **Hotwater Beach** lies a few kilometers to the south. To find the beach from Hahei, retrace your route toward the highway and watch for the signposts that point left. A thermal spring seeps beneath the beach, and by scooping a shallow hole in the sand you can create a pool of warm water; the deeper you dig, the hotter the water becomes. (The phenomenon occurs only at low to mid-tide.) For a swim without the spa treatment, follow Hahei Beach Road to its end at a well-protected cove, one of the finest along this coastline. The sands of this island-sheltered beach are tinted pink with crushed shells.

South of the coastal resort of Tairua, Highway 25 turns inland to skirt Tairua Harbour and then continues west across the spine of the peninsula to Thames—a short, dramatic journey between forested peaks. From Thames, the journey to Waitomo Caves or Rotorua takes about three hours.

What to See and Do with Children

Driving Creek Railway is one man's magnificent folly. Barry Brickell is a local potter who discovered that the clay on his land was perfect for his work. The problem was that the deposit lay in a remote area at the top of a steep slope; so he hacked a path through the forest and built his own miniature railroad. Visitors to his studio began asking if they could go along for the ride, and Brickell now takes passengers on a daily tour aboard his toy train. The route that the diesel-powered, narrow-gauge locomotive follows incorporates a cutting, a double-decker bridge, two tunnels, a spiral, and a switchback. The round-trip takes about 50 minutes. The "station" is located about 3 kilometers (2 miles) north of Coromandel township. *410 Kennedy's Bay Rd., Coromandel, tel. 07/866–8703. Tickets: $6 adults, $3 children 5–15. Departs Dec.–Mar., 10:30, 2, 5; Apr.–Oct., 2, 4; Nov., 2, 5.*

Sports and the Outdoors

Hiking   **Coromandel State Forest Park** has more than 30 walking trails which offer anything from a 30-minute stroll to a three-day trek. The most accessible starting point is the delightful Kauaeranga Valley Road, where the Coromandel Forest Park Headquarters provides maps and information (tel. 07/868–6381; open weekdays 8–4). To reach the Kauaeranga Valley, head south from Thames and on the outskirts of the town turn left on Banks Street, then right on Parawai Road, which becomes Kauaeranga Valley Road.

Dining

The Coromandel Peninsula is not well endowed with restaurants. In most towns the choice is between coffee shops and pubs, which usually offer cooked meals such as steaks and fish-and-chips, and sometimes salads. An outstanding exception is the dining room at the **Puka Park Lodge** (*see* Lodging, *below*), which brings an international menu and a dash of glitter to this remote part of the world. *Reservations required. Jacket required. AE, DC, MC, V. No lunch. $$$$*

American Express offers Travelers Cheques built for two.

©1994 American Express Travel Related Services Company, Inc. *Available at participating clubs.

Cheques *for Two*℠ from American Express are the Travelers Cheques that allow either of you to use them because both of you have signed them. And only one of you needs to be present to purchase them.

Cheques *for Two* are accepted anywhere regular American Express Travelers Cheques are, which is just about everywhere. So stop by your bank, AAA* or any American Express Travel Service Office and ask for Cheques *for Two*.

AMERICAN EXPRESS **Travelers Cheques**

So, you're getting away from it all.

Just make sure you can get back.

AT&T Access Numbers
Dial the number of the country you're in to reach AT&T.

AMERICAN SAMOA	633-2-USA	**INDONESIA♦**	001-801-10	***PHILIPPINES**	105-11
AUSTRALIA	**1800-881-011**	*JAPAN	0039-111	**SAIPAN†**	235-2872
CHINA, PRC♦♦	**10811**	**KOREA**	**009-11**	SINGAPORE	800-0111-111
COOK ISLANDS	09-111	KOREA◇◇	11✱	SRI LANKA	430-430
GUAM	**018-872**	MACAO	0800-111	***TAIWAN**	**0080-10288-0**
HONG KONG	**800-1111**	***MALAYSIA**	**800-0011**	THAILAND♦	0019-991-1111
INDIA♦	**000-117**	NEW ZEALAND	000-911		

Countries in bold face permit country-to-country calling in addition to calls to the U.S. **World Connect℠** prices consist of **USADirect®** rates plus an additional charge based on the country you are calling. Collect calling available to the U.S. only. *Public phones require deposit of coin or phone card. ♦Not available from public phones. ♦♦Not yet available for all areas. ◇◇From public phones only, push the red button, wait for dial tone and then dial. †May not be available from every phone. ©1994 AT&T

Here's a travel tip that will make it easy to call back to the States. Dial the access number for the country you're visiting and connect right to AT&T. It's the quick way to get English-speaking AT&T operators and can minimize hotel telephone surcharges.

If all the countries you're visiting aren't listed above, call **1 800 241-5555** for a free wallet card with all AT&T access numbers. Easy international calling from AT&T. **TrueWorld Connections.**

AT&T

Lodging

$$$$ **Puka Park Lodge.** This stylish lodge, which attracts a largely
★ European clientele, lies immersed in native bushland on
Pauanui Beach, at the seaward end of Tairua Harbour on the
east coast of the peninsula. (The turnoff from Highway 25 is
about 6 kilometers, or 4 miles, south of Tairua.) The timber chalets are smartly furnished with black cane tables and wooden
Venetian blinds; the gauze mosquito nets draped over the beds
are there for effect rather than practical reasons. Sliding glass
doors lead to a balcony perched up among the treetops. The
bathrooms are well equipped but small. The lodge offers a full
range of activities for those who want to take advantage of the
splendor of the surrounding beaches and forests. The tariff is
comparatively low for accommodations of this standard. The
food and service in the international restaurant are outstanding. *Private Bag, Pauanui Beach, tel. 07/864–8088, fax 07/864–
8112. 32 rooms with bath. Facilities: heated outdoor pool, tennis
court, bicycles, restaurant, bar. AE, DC, MC, V.*

$$ **Coromandel Colonial Cottages.** These six immaculate timber
★ cottages offer spacious and comfortable self-contained accom-
modations for about the same price as a standard motel room.
Each has two bedrooms, a lounge room with convertible beds, a
large, well-equipped kitchen, and a dining area. Arranged with
military precision in two ranks, the cottages face each other
across a tailored lawn surrounded by green hills on the northern
outskirts of Coromandel. During vacation periods, they must be
booked several months in advance. *Rings Rd., Coromandel, tel.
07/866–8857. 6 cottages. Facilities: spa, croquet lawn, minigolf,
guest laundry. AE, DC, MC, V.*

$$ **Karamana.** Mary and Bill Hoyles's historic house provides
homestay accommodations that are exceptional on the peninsu-
la. The kauri house is simply constructed yet embellished with
ornamental architraves and a delightful veranda. Guest rooms
are furnished with high-quality antiques and are scented with
potpourri. The location, at the foot of steep, forested peaks, is
majestic and serene; the view has been further enhanced by the
Hoyles's gardening skills. Dinner is available by arrangement.
*Whangapoua Rd., Coromandel, tel. and fax 07/866–7138. 3
rooms, 1 with en suite bath, 2 share 1 bath, 1 shower. Tariff includes breakfast. MC.*

4 Rotorua to Wellington

By Michael Gebicki

The first part of this chapter covers the central area of the North Island, from the Waitomo Caves to the surroundings of Lake Taupo. In this area, focused on the town of Rotorua, nature has crafted a gallery of surreal wonders that includes limestone caverns, volcanic wastelands, steaming geysers, and hissing ponds. From the shores of Lake Taupo—the country's biggest lake and the geographic bull's-eye of the North Island—Mount Ruapehu, the island's tallest peak, is plainly visible. The mountain is the site of New Zealand's largest ski area and is the dominant feature of Tongariro National Park, a haunting landscape of craters, volcanoes, and lava flows that ran with molten rock as recently as 1988.

Southeast of Lake Taupo, on the shores of Hawke's Bay, lies the town of Napier, an unexpected oasis of Art Deco architecture. Napier is also the center of an excellent wine region. Our tour of the North Island ends at its southern tip, in the charming—if windy—city of Wellington, the nation's capital.

Rotorua, the Waitomo Caves, and Lake Taupo

It's one of the most extraordinary sights in the country. Everywhere you turn the earth bubbles, boils, spits, and oozes. Drainpipes steam, flowerbeds hiss, rings tarnish, cars corrode; the rotten-egg smell of hydrogen sulfide hangs in the air, and even the local golf course has its own mud-pool hot spots where a lost ball stays lost forever.

New Zealand's most famous tourist attraction, Rotorua, sits smack on top of the most violent segment of the Taupo Volcanic Zone, which runs in a broad belt from White Island in the Bay of Plenty to Tongariro National Park, south of Lake Taupo. While the spurting geysers and sulfur springs are perfectly good reasons to visit, there's a lot more to the area than hellfire and brimstone. Drive outside the city limits and you'll find yourself in magnificent, untamed country, where spring-fed streams sprint through native forests into lakes that are home to some of the biggest rainbow trout on earth. Not only are these trout large and abundant, but they seem to be genetically programmed for suicide: Anglers still regularly pull 10-pound rainbow trout from Lake Tarawera, and there are fishing guides who guarantee that no client will come home empty-handed.

Rotorua also has a well-established Maori community tracing its ancestry back to the great Polynesian migration of the 14th century. Maori culture is stamped indelibly on the town, although the majority of visitors will have their most intimate contact with that culture at a *hangi*—a traditional feast—followed by a Maori concert.

Important Addresses and Numbers

Tourist Information **Tourism Rotorua Visitor Information Centre.** In addition to an information office, this modern complex houses a café, a film-processing service, a map shop operated by the Department of Conservation, and a lost-luggage facility. *67 Fenton St., Rotorua, tel. 07/348–5179. Open daily 8–5:30.*

Taupo Visitor Information Centre. *13 Tongariro St., Taupo, tel. 07/378–9000. Open daily 8:30–5.*

Waitomo Caves Visitor Information Centre. *Waitomo Museum of Caves, tel. 07/878–7640. Open daily 9–5:30.*

Emergencies Dial 111 for **fire, police,** and **ambulance** services.

Arriving and Departing

By Plane **Air New Zealand** (tel. 07/346–1001) and **Ansett New Zealand** (tel. 07/347–0146) have daily flights that link Rotorua with Auckland and Wellington, with further connections throughout New Zealand. **Mount Cook Airline** (tel. 0800/80–0737) schedules daily flights between Rotorua and Auckland, Wellington, Christchurch, and Queenstown. **Rotorua Airport** stands about 10 kilometers (6 miles) from the city center. Taxi fare to the city is $15.

By Car From Auckland, take Highway 1 south, following the signs to Hamilton. From Hamilton, follow Highway 3. The Waitomo Caves are located 6 kilometers (4 miles) east of the highway. Driving time for the journey is about three hours.

By Bus **InterCity** (tel. 09/358–4085) has four bus services daily between Auckland and Rotorua. InterCity also operates a daily service between Auckland and Waitomo Caves and between Waitomo Caves and Rotorua. **Newmans** (tel. 09/309–9738) operates twice daily on the Auckland–Rotorua route.

Guided Tours

Gray Line (tel. 09/377–0904) offers two-day tours of the Waitomo Caves and Rotorua from Auckland. The tour costs $359 for adults, $247 for children 5–15.

Mount Tarawera 4WD Tours offers a sensational half-day, four-wheel-drive trip to the edge of the Mount Tarawera crater. Departures are available at 8:30 AM or 1:30 PM. *Box 5157, Rotorua, tel. 07/357–4026. Cost: $52 adults, $26 children under 12, $135 family (2 adults, 2 children).*

The **Waimangu Round Trip** is probably the most complete and spectacular tour of Rotorua. The full-day tour includes an easy 5-kilometer (3-mile) hike through the Waimangu Thermal Valley to Lake Rotomahana, where a cruiser takes visitors past steaming cliffs to the narrow isthmus that divides the lake from Lake Tarawera. After crossing the lake on a second cruiser, the tour visits a village that was buried by a volcanic eruption and ends with a dip in the Polynesian Pools in Rotorua. Lunch is included. *Bookings at Rotorua Visitor Information Centre, or tel. 07/347–1199. Tickets: $125 adults, $65 children 5–14.*

Rotorua Sightseeing Shuttle is a bus service making a circuit of the city's 23 major attractions. Passengers may leave at any stop and catch any following bus. The first bus departs from Rotorua Visitor Centre at 8:15, and the service terminates at 5:10. *Bookings at Rotorua Visitor Information Centre, 67 Fenton St., tel. 07/348–5179. Tickets: $14 for half day, $20 for full day, half price for children 4–14.*

Tamaki Tours' Volcanic Wilderness Safari is a two-day trip that combines horse trekking in the Rainbow Mountain/Mount Tarawera area, rafting on the Rangitaki River, and an introduction to traditional Maori legends and lifestyle. The company is a Maori-owned and -operated venture. *Box 1492, Rotorua, tel. 07/346–2823. Cost: $320.*

Tarawera Helicopters (tel. 07/348–1223) offers a choice of scenic flights, from a short flight over the city and Whakarewarewa Thermal Reserve ($50 per person) to a longer flight over crater lakes and the Waimangu Valley, with a landing on top of Mount Tarawera ($325 per person).

Tour Magic (tel. 07/345–6080) has a choice of half- and full-day minibus tours of Rotorua's prime attractions, with pickup and drop-off at your accommodation. These tours are recommended for their personal, attentive style. Half-day tours cost $38–$54 per person.

The **MV *Wairaka*** (tel. 07/374–8338) is a vintage riverboat that cruises from Taupo to Huka Falls daily at 10 and 2. The two-hour cruise costs $18 for adults, $8 for children under 12. A barbecue cruise departs at 12:30 and costs $35 for adults, $15 for children.

Exploring the Waitomo Caves

This itinerary begins at Auckland and travels south through Hamilton to the Waitomo Caves, east to Rotorua, and finally south again to Lake Taupo. It's possible to complete the journey in three days, but for those who want to experience the vast range of activities in the area, four days is a practical minimum.

Numbers in the margin correspond to points of interest on the Central North Island map.

❶ The **Waitomo Caves** are an ancient seabed that was lifted and then spectacularly eroded into a surreal landscape of limestone formations and caves, many of them still unexplored. Only two caves are open to the public for guided tours: the Aranui and the Waitomo, or Glowworm Cave. The **Waitomo Cave** takes its name from the Maori words *wai* and *tomo*, water and cave, since the Waitomo River vanishes into the hillside here. Visitors are taken through by boat, and the highlight is the **Glowworm Grotto**. The glowworm is the larva of *Arachnocampa luminosa*, a member of the gnat family, which looks like a small daddy longlegs

later when it emerges from its cocoon. The larva, measuring between one and two inches, lives on the roof of caves and snares its prey by dangling filaments of tiny, sticky beads; insects attracted to the light it emits through a chemical oxidation process get trapped in the deadly necklace. In one of nature's crueler ironies, it is often the adult *Arachnocampa luminosa* that is caught and eaten by the infant of the species. A single glowworm produces far less light than any firefly, but when massed in great numbers, the effect is electrifying. **Aranui Cave,** 2 kilometers (1¼ miles) beyond the Glowworm Cave, is a very different experience. Eons of dripping water have sculpted a delicate garden in pink and white limestone. The cave is named after a local Maori, Te Rutuku Aranui, who discovered the cave in 1910 when his dog disappeared inside in pursuit of a wild pig. Each cave tour lasts 45 minutes. The Glowworm Cave is high on the list of every coach tour, so try to avoid visiting between 11 and 2, when many tour groups arrive from Auckland. *Te Anga Rd., tel. 07/ 878–8227. Admission to Aranui Cave: $13.50 adults, $6.75 children under 12. Admission to both caves: $21 adults, $10.50 children under 12. Glowworm Cave tours: every hr on the hr 9–4, with late tours at 4:30 and 5:30 Nov.–Easter. Aranui Cave tours: 10, 11, 1, 2, 3.*

In the center of the caves village, the **Museum of Caves** provides an entertaining and informative look at the formation of the caves and the life cycle of the glowworm, with a number of interactive displays designed especially for children. *Waitomo Caves Village, tel. 07/878–7640. Admission: $3 adults, children under 15 free. Open daily 9–5:30.*

The **Waitomo Walkway** is a 5-kilometer (3-mile), 2½-hour walk that begins across the road from the Museum of Caves and follows the Waitomo River. The track, which passes through forests and impressive limestone outcrops, provides many visitors with their fondest memories of Waitomo. It is relatively easy and highly recommended, but there is no transport from the end of the walk back to Waitomo Caves Village. If you prefer an alternative to the complete walk, take Te Anga Road from the village, turn left onto Tumutumu Road, park at Ruakuri Reserve, and walk the short final section of the track through this delightful reserve.

From Waitomo Caves Village, return to Highway 3 and turn right to the town of Te Kuiti, where Highway 30 turns east to Rotorua. Driving time for the 150-kilometer (95-mile) journey is 2½ hours.

Exploring Rotorua and Lake Taupo

This driving tour begins at the Visitor Information Centre on Fenton Street and takes a day. (If you take the 11 AM cruise on Lake Tarawera, which is highly recommended, it will mean rearranging the tour to reach Tarawera Landing in time for the boat's departure.) From Rotorua, allow 25 minutes for the drive to Tarawera Landing. Limited picnic supplies are available from the café at the Buried Village, about 1½ kilometers (1 mile) before the landing.

From the front door of the Visitor Centre, turn right and follow
❷ Fenton Street for 3 kilometers (2 miles) to **Whakarewarewa**— a mouthful of a name that the locals reduce to "Whaka." (In Maori names, "wh" is pronounced as "f," and "Whaka" is therefore spoken as "Faka.") This is easily the most accessible and popular of Rotorua's thermal areas, and also the most varied, since it gives an insight into Maori culture. Visitors are free to wander at their own pace, but you'll gain far more from the experience if you take one of the guided tours, which leave at frequent intervals from the Arts and Crafts Institute, near the ticket office. The trails that wind through the complex pass sinister, steaming pools, spitting mud ponds, and smooth silica terraces that appear to be coated in melted candle wax. The highlight is **Pohutu** ("the big splash"), a geyser that sometimes shoots to a height of over 80 feet; however, its eruptions are erratic. At the top end of the complex is a reconstructed Maori village with houses, gates, and a *marai*, a meeting house. At the lower end is a modern Maori village, but its people still cook in the traditional manner by placing meat and vegetables in flax baskets and dunking them in the steaming pools at the back of the village. At the village entrance is a graveyard in which the graves are all above ground, since it's impossible to dig down into the earth. A one-hour Maori concert takes place daily at 12:15 in the Arts and Crafts Institute. *Hemo Rd., Rotorua, tel. 07/348–9047. Admission: $10 adults, $4 children 5–14, $26 family. Concert: $10 adults, $4 children, $26 family. Open daily Nov.–Easter 8–6; Easter–Oct. 8–5.*

Return to the city along Fenton Street and turn right into Amohau Street, which is easy to identify by the McDonalds on the left corner. After almost 3 kilometers (2 miles), turn right
❸ where a sign points to Tarawera and the **Blue and Green Lakes.** This road loops through forests and skirts the edge of the two lakes. The color contrast varies with the time of year and the weather conditions.

❹ Just past the lakes is **Te Wairoa,** the buried village. At the end of the 19th century this village was the starting point for expeditions to the pink and white terraces of Rotomahana, on the slopes of Mount Tarawera. These silica terraces were formed by the mineral-rich water from a geyser. As the water cascaded down the mountainside, it formed a series of baths, which became progressively cooler as they neared the lake. In the latter half of the last century these fabulous terraces were the country's major tourist attraction, but they were completely destroyed when Mount Tarawera erupted in 1886. The explosion, which was heard as far away as Auckland, killed 153 people and buried the village of Te Wairoa under a sea of mud and hot ash. The village has been excavated, and today a path makes a circuit of this fascinating and deceptively tranquil spot, complete with grazing deer. Of special interest is the *whare* (hut) of the *tohunga* (priest) Tuhoto Ariki, who predicted the destruction of the village. Eleven days before the eruption, two separate tourist parties saw a Maori war canoe emerge from the mists of Lake Tarawera and disappear again—a vision the tohunga interpreted as a sign of impending disaster. Four days after the eruption, the hundred-year-old tohunga was dug out of his buried whare still alive, only to die in the hospital a few days later. The path, after circling the village, dives down the hill alongside Te Wairoa Falls, then passes through a cave, crosses a bridge, and ascends the moist, fern-covered slope on the far side. The walk is a delight, although the lower section of the track is steep and slippery in places. *Tarawera Rd., tel. 07/362–8287. Admission: $8 adults, $2 children 6–15, $18 family. Open daily 9–4:30, summer 8:30–5:30.*

Four kilometers (2½ miles) beyond the village is Spencer Road, where a sign points to "Launch Cruises." This road leads to a parking lot on the shores of Lake Tarawera, where a restored lake cruiser, the **MV *Reremoana,*** makes regular scenic runs. Especially recommended is the two-hour cruise, which departs at 11 AM and stops for 30 minutes at the foot of Mount Tarawera, where passengers can picnic, swim, or walk across the isthmus to Lake Rotomahana. Forty-five-minute cruises depart from the landing at one-hour intervals from 1:30 to 4:30. *Tarawera Launch Cruises, tel. 07/362–8595. Tickets: $15 adults, $7.50 children under 15, $35 family.*

Return to Rotorua by the same route and turn right into Hinemaru Street, then right again through the gates of the **Government Gardens.** The Maoris call this area *Whangapiro,* "evil-smelling place"—a far more appropriate name for these bizarre gardens, where sulfur pits bubble and fume behind the manicured rose beds. The focus of interest here is the extraordinary neo-Tudor **Bath House.** Built as a spa at the turn of the century, this building is now Rotorua's Art and History Museum. One room on the ground floor is devoted to the eruption of Mount Tarawera, with a number of artifacts that were unearthed from the debris and a remarkable collection of photographs that show the terraces of Rotomahana before the eruption. *Arawa St., tel. 07/348–4199. Admission free. Open weekdays 10–4:30, weekends 1–4:30.*

Leave the gardens by the main gate, turn left into Hinemaru Street, and take the first left, Hinemoa Street. This road ends at the **Polynesian Pools.** A trip to Rotorua would hardly be complete without a dip in these soothing, naturally heated mineral baths. A wide choice of baths is available, from large communal pools to family pools to small, private baths for two. Massage and saunas are also available. *Hinemoa St., tel. 07/348–1328. Admission to family pool: $6.50 adults, $2 children 5–14; adult pool: $6.50; private pool (per half hr): $7.50 adults, $2 children 5–14. Open 6:30 AM–10 PM.*

Leave Rotorua by Fenton Street, which becomes Highway 5, and follow the signs to Taupo. After 30 kilometers (19 miles), turn left where a sign points to **Waiotapu.** This is a complete thermal wonderland—a freakish, fantastic landscape of deep, sulfur-crusted pits, jade-color ponds, silica terraces, and a steaming lake edged with red algae and bubbling with tiny beads of carbon dioxide. The most spectacular feature is the **Lady Knox Geyser,** which erupts precisely at 10:15 daily—but not through some miracle of Mother Nature's. Five pounds of soap powder poured into the vent of the geyser causes the water to boil, and the vent is then blocked with rags until the pressure builds sufficiently for the geyser to explode. The phenomenon was discovered early this century. Wardens from a nearby prison farm would bring convicts to a pool here to wash their clothes. They found that when the water became soapy the pool would boil fiercely, and one of the wardens built a rock cairn to serve as a nozzle, concentrating the force of the boiling water and making the geyser rise even higher. *State Hwy. 5, tel. 07/ 366–6333. Admission: $8 adults, $3 children 5–15, $20 family. Open daily 8:30–5.*

Continue toward Taupo along Highway 5. At Mihi Bridge, just past Golden Springs, turn right along a road signposted "Orakei Korako." If by now you think you've seen enough bubbling mud pools and fuming craters to last a lifetime, this captivating thermal valley will change your mind. On the shores of Lake ❾ Ohakuri, a jet boat waits to take passengers across to **Orakei Korako,** where geyser-fed streams hiss and steam as they flow into the waters of the lake. One of the most impressive features of this area is the multicolored silica terrace, believed to be the largest in the world since the destruction of the terraces of Rotomahana. At the bottom of Aladdin's Cave, the vent of an ancient volcano, is a jade-green pool that was once used exclusively by Maori women as a beauty parlor, which is where the name Orakei Korako—"a place of adorning"—originated. *Tel. 07/ 378–3131. Admission: $10 adults, $4.50 children 5–15, $25 family. Open daily 8:30–4:30, winter 8:30–4.*

Return to Highway 5 and proceed toward Taupo. Just past the ❿ junction with Highway 1 you can see the **Wairakai Geothermal Project** in the distance, wreathed in swirling clouds of steam. The steam, tapped through underground shafts, drives generators that provide about 5% of New Zealand's electrical power. There are no guided tours of the plant, but the Geothermal Information Centre close to the highway has an informative display of the process by which steam is converted into electricity. *State Hwy. 1, tel. 07/374–8216. Admission free. Open daily 9– noon, 1–4.*

Beyond the power station, at the top of the next hill, a road turns ⓫ left off the highway toward **Huka Falls,** where the Waikato River thunders through a narrow chasm and over a 35-foot rock ledge before it pours into Lake Taupo. The view from the footbridge is superb.

⓬ The town of **Taupo** is the services base for Lake Taupo, the largest lake in New Zealand. You can take your pick here from a wide range of water sports—sailing, cruising, waterskiing, swimming, but most of all, fishing: Taupo is the rainbow-trout capital of the universe. The average Taupo trout weighs in at around 4 pounds, and there is no closed season. For nonanglers, several sailing boats, modern catamarans, and vintage riverboats offer sightseeing cruises. From Taupo, the driving time back to Rotorua is about 90 minutes.

⓭ At the southern end of Lake Taupo is **Tongariro National Park,** the country's first, established on land donated by a Maori chief. The park is dominated by the peaks of three active volcanoes, one of which, Mount Ruapehu, is, at 2,752 meters (9,175 feet), the tallest mountain on the North Island. Ruapehu last erupted in 1988, spewing a shower of volcanic rocks. Tongariro's spectacular combination of dense rimu forests, crater lakes, barren lava fields, and bird life makes it the most impressive and popular of the North Island's national parks. It has many walking trails, from the 40-minute Ridge Track to the Mount Tongariro Traverse, which crosses the mountain from one side to the other and is one of the finest one-day walks in the country. The longest walk in the park is the six-day Round the Mountain track. The Whakapapa ski area, on the north side of Mount Ruapehu, is New Zealand's largest. On the southern side of the mountain is a second ski area, Turoa, which generally offers a longer ski season than Whakapapa's June to October.

Highway 1 skirts the eastern side of the park, but the easiest access is from Highway 47, on the western side. For more information, contact the Department of Conservation Field Centre at Whakapapa Village off Highway 47 (mailing address: Whakapapa Visitor Centre, Private Bag, Mount Ruapehu, tel. 07/892–3729). Accommodations in the village range from the **THC Tongariro Hotel** (Mount Ruapehu, tel. 07/892–3809; $$$$) to the cabins and campsites in the motor camp. The park has nine huts for hikers.

What to See and Do with Children

Agrodome. Most of this sprawling complex is dedicated to the four-footed woolly New Zealander. Shows daily at 9:15, 11, and 2:30 demonstrate the different breeds of sheep, shearing techniques, and sheepdogs at work. Children can participate by feeding lambs and milking a cow. In another part of the complex, **Trainworld,** scale-model trains rumble through a miniature slice of English countryside. The complex is part of a 320-acre farm, a 10-minute drive northwest of Rotorua. *Riverdale Park, Western Rd., Ngongotaha, tel. 07/357–4350. Admission to Agrodome: $9 adults, $4.50 children 5–15; Trainworld: $5 adults, $3 children. Open daily 9–4:30.*

Leisure World. This giant complex includes waterslides, three-wheeler dirt bikes, slot cars, a minigolf course, and video games. *Marguerita St., Rotorua, tel. 07/348–9674. Admission free. Rides cost $3–$6 per person. Open weekdays 10–5, weekends 10–6.*

Rainbow Springs. Situated some 5 kilometers (3 miles) from Rotorua, this leafy park is home to many species of New Zealand wildlife, including deer, kiwis and other native birds, wild pigs, and most of all, trout. The trout that congregate for feeding sessions at the Rainbow and Fairy Springs are the King Kongs of the trout world. On the other side of State Highway 5 is the second part of the complex, Rainbow Farm, which demonstrates New Zealand farming life. A show similar to the one at the Agrodome takes place daily at 10:30, 11:45, 1, and 2:30. *Fairy Springs Rd., tel. 07/347–9301. Admission (Rainbow Springs or Rainbow Farm): $9.70 adults, $3 children 5–15. Open daily 8–5.*

Off the Beaten Track

At the northern end of Rotorua, on the shores of the lake, stands **St. Faith's,** the Anglican church for the Maori village of Ohinemutu. Before the present Tudor-style church was built in 1910, one of the ministers was Seymour Spencer Mills, of Hartford, Connecticut, who preached to the Arawa people for 50 years. He is commemorated in a small window above the organ chancel, preaching to a group of Maoris as he holds his habitual umbrella. The interior of the church, which is richly decorated with carvings inset with mother-of-pearl, deserves attention at any time, but it's at its best during Sunday services, when the rich, melodic voices of the Maori choir rise in hymns. The service at 8 AM is in the Maori language; the 10 AM service is in both Maori and English. *Memorial Dr., Rotorua.*

Sports and the Outdoors

Fishing   The lakes of the Rotorua/Taupo region are one of the few places where tales of the big one can be believed. If you want to keep the trout of a lifetime from becoming just another fish story, it pays to have a boat with some expert advice on board. Expect to pay about $55 per hour for a fishing guide and a 20-foot cruiser that will take up to six passengers. The minimum charter period is two hours, and fishing gear and bait are included in the price. A one-day fishing license costs $11 per person and is available on board the boat. In Rotorua, fishing operators include **Clark Gregor** (tel. 07/347–1730), **Bryan Colman** (tel. 07/348–7766), and **Ray Dodunski** (tel. 07/349–2555). Highly recommended is *Clear Water Pride* (tel. 07/362–8590), a luxury 38-foot launch that operates fishing trips on Lake Tarawera. The cost for up to seven passengers is $80 per hour, including all gear and light refreshments. For 8 to 15, the cost is $120 per hour and a hostess is provided. In Taupo, contact **Richard Staines** (tel. 07/378–2736) or **Punch Wilson** (tel. 07/378–5596). At the other end of the scale, a luxury cruiser on Lake Taupo costs about $150 per hour; for more information, contact **Chris Jolly Boats** (Box 1020, Taupo, tel. 07/378–0623).

Rafting   The center of the North Island has a number of rivers with grade-3 to grade-5 rapids that make excellent white-water rafting. For scenic beauty, the Rangitaki River is recommended. For experienced rafters who want a challenge, the Wairoa and the Mohaka rivers have exhilarating grade-5 rapids. The climax of a rafting trip on the Kaituna River is the drop over a 21-foot waterfall, probably the highest to be rafted by a commercial operator anywhere. In Taupo, contact **Rapid Descents** (tel. 07/377–0419); in Rotorua, **Rafting Kaituna** (tel. 07/348–0223). Transport, wet suits, and meals are provided. The price of a one-day trip is about $65 per person.

Black-Water Rafting This is an unusual way to see the caves, and a lot of fun. Participants must first prove themselves with a giant leap into the Huhunoa Stream; the next three hours are spent dressed in wet suits and equipped with cavers' helmets and inflated inner tubes, floating through underground caverns. While the combination of darkness and freezing water might sound like a refined form of torture, the trip is an exhilarating one that will live vividly in your memory long after the goose bumps have disappeared. The cost is $50 per person. Departure times vary, depending on daily demand. *Information and bookings: Black Water Rafting, Box 13, Waitomo Caves, tel. 07/878–7640.*

Dining

Rotorua offers a unique New Zealand dining experience: the *hangi,* or Maori feast. Traditionally, meat and vegetables placed in flax baskets were gently steamed in an earth oven lined with heated stones and wet leaves. Several of the larger hotels in Rotorua offer a hangi, and although the food is still cooked by steam, it's unlikely that it will be buried in the traditional earth oven. Lamb, pork, and seafood are usually available at the buffet-style meals, together with pumpkin and *kumara* (sweet potato), a staple of the Maori diet. Almost without exception, hangis in Rotorua are followed by a Maori concert, a performance of traditional songs and dances. The hangis at the **Sheraton** (tel. 07/348–7139) and the **Lake Plaza** (tel. 07/348–1174) enjoy long-standing reputations as two of the best in town. Expect to pay about $40 per person. **Tamaki Tours'** (tel. 07/346–2823) hangi is the only one that takes place at a Maori *marae,* or meeting house, on the shores of Lake Rotoiti.

$$$ **Poppy's Villa Restaurant.** This florid restaurant with its pink walls and scalloped, flower-patterned blinds is Rotorua's big-occasion restaurant, yet prices are relatively moderate. First courses on the modern, European-style menu include mussels poached in a spicy tomato and Parmesan sauce as well as sweetbreads in wine and tarragon sauce served with a walnut brioche. Baby rack of lamb with honey, mustard, and a rosemary glaze served in a red-berry sauce is a long-standing favorite main course. *4 Marguerita St., Rotorua, tel. 07/347–1700. Reservations advised. Dress: casual but neat. AE, DC, MC, V. No lunch.*

$$$ **You and Me.** Despite the restaurant's furry pink-and-black decor, the food at least pays lip service to modern trends with a fashionable eastern accent. The menu offers smoked salmon marinated in lime juice and served with avocado; fillet of lamb marinated in lemongrass and olive oil; and cervena venison with zucchini flowers stuffed with scallops and roasted garlic. Gour-

met opinions regard this as the only restaurant in Rotorua that has achieved a notable culinary style. *31 Pukuatua St., Rotorua, tel. 07/347–6178. Reservations advised. Dress: casual but neat. AE, DC, MC, V. BYOB. No lunch. Closed Sun. and Mon.*

$$ Incas Cafe. This casual café caters to most tastes, with beef bourguignon, vegetable moussaka, spare ribs, steamed mussels, and coconut lamb curry, but despite the name, nothing south-of-the-border appears on the menu. The restaurant's 1 AM closing time draws the night owls. *Pukaki and Fenton Sts., Rotorua, tel. 07/348–3831. Reservations not required. Dress: casual. AE, DC, MC, V. No lunch.*

$$ Zanelli's Italian Cafe. Rotorua's favorite Italian restaurant offers a predictable range of dishes—spaghetti bolognese, lasagna, cannelloni, and fettuccine with various sauces—but the food is well flavored and the service is efficient. The decor—walls lined with split cane, a stone-tile floor, Formica tables—and the up-tempo Italian music create a slightly hectic atmosphere. *23 Amohia St., Rotorua, tel. 07/348–4908. Reservations not required. Dress: casual. DC, MC, V. No lunch. Closed Sun.*

$ International Cafe. Situated beneath the veranda of the Princes Gate Hotel, this outdoor café is the perfect place for warmweather eating. The menu lists soups, focaccia, salads, bruschetta, grilled chicken, eggplant lasagna, and burgers. *1 Arawa St., Rotorua, tel. 07/348–1179. No reservations. Dress: casual. AE, DC, MC, V. No dinner.*

$ Orchid Gardens Cafe. If you are staying close to the city and want an alternative to hotel breakfasts, this is just the place. The café is located at the end of the Government Gardens, and diners are treated to a breakfast surrounded by palm trees and the sound of bird calls and trickling water. The breakfast menu lists fruit juices, cereals, toast, eggs, and bacon. Later in the day the menu expands to include soup, quiche, shrimp cocktail, and steaks. The café opens at 8 on weekdays, 7 on weekends. *Government Gardens, Hinemaru St., Rotorua, tel. 07/347–6182. No reservations. Dress: casual. MC, V. No dinner.*

Lodging

The accommodations scene in Rotorua is highly competitive. For most of the year there are many more hotel beds than visitors, and a number of hotels and motels offer significant discounts on their standard rates. The Tourism Rotorua Visitor Centre on Fenton Street acts as a clearinghouse for discount accommodations, and you can often save up to half the published rate of a particular hotel by booking through the center on arrival in Rotorua. The exception is school holidays, when accommodations should be booked in advance.

$$$$ Huka Lodge. Buried in parklike grounds at the edge of the
★ frisky Waikato River, this superb lodge is the standard by which New Zealand's other sporting lodges are judged. It is run in the European style, however, and the atmosphere of aristocratic privilege may be a little overwhelming for some tastes. The large, lavish guest rooms, decorated in muted grays and whites,

are arranged in blocks of two or three. All have sliding glass doors that open to a view across lawns to the river. In the interest of tranquillity, guest rooms are not equipped with telephones, televisions, or radios. The five-course formal dinners are gourmet affairs served at a communal dining table. The wine list is a showcase of the very best New Zealand has to offer. Breakfasts include such luxuries as fresh croissants, brioches, and pastries. *Huka Falls Rd., Taupo (mailing address: Box 95, Taupo), tel. 07/378–5791, fax 07/378–0427. 17 rooms with bath. Facilities: tennis court, fishing, spa, bar, restaurant. Tariff includes breakfast and dinner. AE, DC, MC, V.*

$$$$ **Muriaroha Lodge.** Although it lacks trout streams and lake views, when it comes to style, facilities, food, and comfort, this handsome lodge on the outskirts of Rotorua evokes the finest traditions of the luxury sporting lodge—at a much reduced rate. Guest rooms are paired in bungalows, which are separate from the main building; to ensure privacy, the adjoining room is not assigned when one of the pair is occupied. The guest rooms, gardens, lounge, and dining room all have an English country house flavor. For the duration of their stay, guests are extended complimentary membership at the Arikikapaka Golf Course just across the road. *411 Old Taupo Rd., Rotorua, tel. 07/346–1220, fax 07/346–1338. 8 rooms with bath. Facilities: outdoor pool, bar, restaurant. AE, DC, MC, V.*

$$$$ **Sheraton Rotorua.** Close to the Whakarewarewa thermal area on the outskirts of town, this hotel offers the chain's usual high standard of comforts and amenities. Request a room on one of the top two floors overlooking the golf course. The hotel's nightly hangi is one of the best in town. *Fenton and Sala Sts., Rotorua, tel. 07/348–7139, fax 07/348–8378. 130 rooms with bath. Facilities: outdoor pool, spa, sauna, gym, tennis court, 2 restaurants, bar. AE, DC, MC, V.*

$$$$ **Solitaire Lodge.** It would be difficult to imagine a finer backdrop than the lakes, forests, and volcanoes that surround this plush retreat. Set high on a peninsula that juts out into Lake Tarawera, the lodge has been designed as a sophisticated hideaway where a few guests at a time can enjoy the scenery in a relaxed, informal atmosphere. All the suites are luxuriously equipped, though the bathrooms in the junior suites are modest in size. The best room is the Tarawera Suite, which has panoramic views. The surrounding lakes and forests hold many possibilities for hiking, boating, and fishing. Lake Tarawera is well-known for its king-size rainbow trout, and the lodge has boats and fishing gear. Smoking is not permitted indoors. *Ronald Rd., Lake Tarawera, Rotorua, tel. 07/362–8208, fax 07/362–8445. 10 rooms with bath. Facilities: spa, bar, restaurant, sailing boats, motorboat, fishing. Tariff includes all meals. AE, DC, MC, V.*

$$ ★ **Cascades Motor Lodge.** Set on the shores of Lake Taupo, these attractive brick and timber rooms are large, comfortable, and furnished and decorated in a smart contemporary style. The two-story "luxury" apartments, which sleep up to seven, have a lounge room, bedroom, kitchen, and dining room on the ground floor in an open-plan design, glass doors leading to a large patio,

and a second bedroom and bathroom on the upper floor. Studio rooms have only one bedroom. All rooms are equipped with a spa bath. Room 1 is closest to the lake and the small beach. *Lake Terr., Taupo, tel. 07/378–3774, fax 07/378–0372. 22 rooms with bath. Facilities: heated outdoor pool. AE, DC, MC, V.*

$$ **Cedar Lodge Motel.** These spacious modern units, about a half-mile from the city center, are good value, especially for families. All the double-story units have a kitchen and lounge room on the lower floor and a bedroom on the mezzanine floor above. All have at least one queen-size and one single bed, and some have a queen-size bed and three singles. Every unit has its own spa pool in the private courtyard at the back. The gray-flecked carpet, smoked-glass tables, and recessed lighting have a clean, contemporary flavor. Request a room at the back, away from Fenton Street. *296 Fenton St., Rotorua, tel. 07/349–0300, fax 07/349–1115. 15 rooms with shower. Facilities: guest laundry. AE, DC, MC, V.*

$$ **Princes Gate Hotel.** This ornate timber hotel occupies a prime position across the road from the Government Gardens. It was built in 1897 on the Coromandel Peninsula and brought here in 1917, and efforts have been made to re-create a turn-of-the-century flavor inside. The rooms are large and comfortable, although the old-fashioned carpets and furnishings look slightly dowdy. The motel rooms, located in a separate wing, have been renovated to make suites with kitchens; these make a better choice for families. *1 Arawa St., Rotorua, tel. 07/348–1179, fax 07/348–6215. 28 hotel rooms, 12 motel units. Facilities: spa pool, mineral baths, tennis court, 2 restaurants, bar. AE, DC, MC, V.*

$ **Eaton Hall.** This well-kept, friendly guest house has an outstanding location one street from the heart of Rotorua. Guest rooms are homey and comfortable and maintained to a standard well above that in most guest houses. Room 4, a twin-bedded room with its own shower, is available at no extra charge. *39 Hinemaru St., Rotorua, tel. 07/347–0366, fax 07/348–6287. 8 rooms share 2 baths. Facilities: spa. Tariff includes breakfast. AE, DC, MC, V.*

Napier and Hawke's Bay

New Zealand is a country that prides itself on natural wonders, but Napier is an exception: This city of 50,000, situated about two-thirds of the way down the east coast of the North Island, is best known for its architecture. After an earthquake devastated Napier in 1931, the citizens rebuilt it in the Art Deco style fashionable at the time. Today the city is an Art Deco treasure.

The mild climate and beaches of Hawke Bay make this a popular vacation area for New Zealanders. (*Hawke* Bay is the body of water; *Hawke's* Bay is the region.) Another attraction is wine: The region produces some of New Zealand's best.

Important Addresses and Numbers

Tourist Information   **Napier Visitor Information Centre.** *Marine Parade, Napier, tel. 06/835–4949. Open weekdays 8:30–5, weekends 9–5.*

Emergencies   Dial 111 for **fire, police,** and **ambulance** services.

Arriving and Departing

By Plane   **Air New Zealand** (tel. 06/835–3288) has several flights daily between Napier and Auckland, Wellington, and Christchurch.

By Car   The main route between Napier and the north is Highway 5. Driving time from Taupo is 2½ hours. Highway 2 is the main southern route. Driving time to Wellington is five hours.

By Bus   **Newmans** (tel. 09/309–9738) and **InterCity** (tel. 09/358–4085) both operate daily bus services between Napier and Auckland, Rotorua, and Wellington.

Guided Tours

Bay Tours features a four-hour tour of the various wineries in the area. It offers a chance to sample some of the boutique wines unavailable to independent travelers. *Napier Visitor Information Centre, tel. 06/843–6953. Tickets: $34 adults, first child and children under 10 free, other children $17. Sun.–Fri. 10:30, Sat. 1:15.*

The Art Deco Trust offers an excellent and informative guided walking tour of Napier. The 1-mile walk takes two hours. *Hawke's Bay Museum, 9 Herschell St., tel. 06/835–0022. Cost: $5 adults, children under 13 free. Tours Sun., Wed. 2 PM.*

Exploring Napier and Hawke's Bay

Numbers in the margin correspond to points of interest on the Central North Island map.

⑭   This tour begins with a short walk around the center of **Napier,** focusing on the city's Art Deco buildings. Art Deco, the style born at the 1925 International Exposition of Modern Decorative and Industrial Arts in Paris, can be recognized by its stylized decorative motifs, such as chevrons, zigzags, sunbursts, and deer or dancers silhouetted in mid-leap. In some cases, Napier's Art Deco heritage has been spoiled by the addition of garish advertising or unsympathetic alterations to shopfronts. The classic Art Deco features that remain are often found above ground-floor level, and the first part of this tour might well result in a stiff neck. The walk is followed by a brief wine-tasting tour. The visit to the gannet colony at the end of the tour is possible only between October and March.

Numbers in the margin correspond to points of interest on the Napier map.

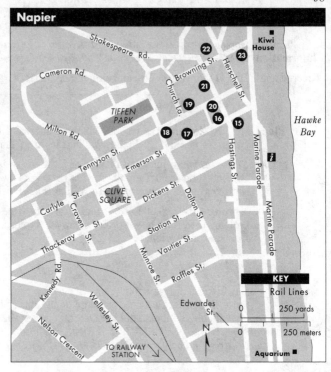

Begin at the **Napier Visitor Information Centre** in Marine Parade. Walk north along Marine Parade with the sea on your right and turn left at the clocktower of the A & B Building. The ⓯ first notable building is the **ASB Bank,** on the left. The Maori theme on the lintels above the main entrance is echoed in the ceiling inside the building.

Continue along Emerson Street and cross into the pedestrian ⓰ mall. The **Criterion Hotel** on the right is typical of the Spanish Mission style, whose popularity in the reconstructed Napier was due largely to its success in Santa Barbara, California, which had been devastated by its own earthquake just a few years before. Buildings along both sides of this mall number among Napier's finest examples of Art Deco, including ⓱ **Hannahs,** the **Bowman's Building, McGruers,** and the **Hawke's Bay Chambers.** Detour left into Dalton Street and look across the road to the balcony of the pink **Countrywide Bank Building,** one of Napier's Art Deco masterpieces.

Return to the intersection of Emerson Street and continue along Dalton Street to the next corner. Cross to the left side of the ⓲ street to view the decorative frieze on **Hildebrand's,** the building on the corner of Tennyson Street. Hildebrand was a German who migrated to New Zealand—thus the German flag at one end, the New Zealand at the other, and the wavy lines in the middle to symbolize the sea passage between the two countries.

Turn right into Tennyson Street; just past the next corner on the

(19) left is the **Daily Telegraph Building,** an Art Deco classic. On the

(20) right at the corner of Hastings Street is the **Market Reserve Building,** the first to rise from the rubble following the earth-

(21) quake. Turn left into Hastings Street. The facade of **Hartson's Bar,** on the left, has altered little since its previous incarnation as Hartson's Music Shop, which survived the quake.

Turn right into Browning Street; on the opposite corner is the

(22) **Ministry of Works** building with its decorative lighthouse pillar at the front, still considered Art Deco despite its slightly forbidding appearance.

(23) On the next corner, on the right, is the **Hawke's Bay Art Gallery and Museum.** Using newspaper reports, photographs, and audiovisuals, the museum re-creates the suffering caused by the earthquake. The museum also houses a unique display of artifacts of the Ngati Kahungunu people of the east coast. *65 Marine Pde., tel. 06/835–9668. Admission: adults $3, children under 14 free. Open daily 10–4:30.*

Numbers in the margin correspond to points of interest on the Central North Island map.

Leave Napier by Kennedy Road, which runs southwest from the city center toward Taradale. Just past Anderson Park, turn right into Avenue Road. At the end of this road on the other side

(24) of Church Road is the entrance to the **Mission Vineyard,** the oldest in the country. The vineyard at Taradale was established by Catholic Marist brothers in the late 1850s, after an earlier vineyard farther to the north at Poverty Bay was abandoned. Legend has it that in 1852 one of the brothers made a barrel of sacramental wine and shipped it to Napier; the seamen broached the cargo, drank the wine, and filled the empty cask with seawater. The pinot noir and semillon/sauvignon blanc blend both deserve attention. *Church Rd., Taradale, tel. 06/844–2259. Open Mon.–Sat. 8–5, Sun. 1–4.*

Drive back to Church Road, turn right, and about ½ kilometer

(25) (¼ mile) farther is the **McDonald Winery.** This long-established vineyard benefited from an injection of capital and expertise when it became part of the Montana wine-making group in 1989. The Church Road Chardonnay and Cabernet Sauvignon have excited oenophiles. The winery operates free tours on weekdays at 11 and 2, weekends at 11, 1, 2, and 3. *200 Church Rd., Taradale, tel. 06/844–2053. Open summer Mon.–Thurs. 9–5, Fri.–Sat. 10–6, Sun. 11–5; Mar.–Nov., Mon.–Sat. 9–5, Sun. 11–4.*

Farther along Church Road, turn left at the intersection of Puketapu Road; follow it as it changes its name to Meeanee Road, and after about 6 kilometers (4 miles) turn right into

(26) Brookfields Road and follow the signs to **Brookfields Winery.** This is one of the most attractive wineries in the area, befitting its status as a premier producer. The Reserve Chardonnay and the pinot gris are usually outstanding, but the showpiece is the cabernet-merlot blend, characterized by intense fruit and assertive oak. *Brookfields Rd., Meeanee, tel. 06/834–4615. Open daily 9–5.*

Return toward Napier along Brookfields Road, and at the intersection with State Highway 2 turn right and then left, following the signs to Te Awange and Clifton. The road follows the southern curve of Hawke Bay and ends at **Cape Kidnapper.** Named by Captain James Cook after local Maoris tried to kidnap the servant of Cook's Tahitian interpreter, the cape is the site of a large **gannet colony.** The gannet is a big white sea bird with black-tipped flight feathers, a golden crown, and wings that can reach a span of up to 6 feet. When the birds find a shoal of fish, they fold their wings and plunge straight into the sea at tremendous speed. Their migratory pattern ranges from western Australia to the Chatham Islands, about 800 kilometers (500 miles) east of Christchurch, but they generally nest only on remote islands. The gannet colony at Cape Kidnappers is believed to be the only mainland sanctuary in existence. Between October and March, about 15,000 gannets build their nests here, hatch their young, and prepare them for their long migratory flight. It is possible to walk to the sanctuary along the beach from Clifton, which is about 24 kilometers (15 miles) south of Napier, but the journey cannot be made at high tide. The 8-kilometer (5-mile) walk must begin no earlier than three hours after high tide; the return journey must begin no later than four hours before the next high tide. Tidal information is available at Clifton. A rest hut with refreshments is available near the colony. A far easier alternative is to ride aboard one of the **Garret Beach Adventures** (tel. 06/875–0898) tractor-trailers that are pulled along the beach starting from Charlton Road, Te Awanga, 21 kilometers (13 miles) south of Napier. The fare is $14 for adults, $11 for children 12–17, $9 for children under 12; the tractors depart two hours before low tide. The trip takes 4–4½ hours. If tides prevent the trip along the beach, the only other access is across private farmland. However, **Gannet Safaris** (tel. 06/875–0511) operates a four-wheel-drive bus to Cape Kidnappers from Summerlee Station, just past Te Awanga. A minimum of four is required for this tour, and the fare is $35 adults, $17 children 4–15. **Kidnappers Sea Escape** (tel. 06/875–0556) offers boat rides to view the gannet colony from the sea. The boats depart from Te Awanga; the fare is $45 per person.

Northeast of Napier is **Urewera National Park,** a vast, remote region of forests and lakes straddling the Huiarau Range. The park's outstanding feature is the glorious **Lake Waikaremoana** ("Sea of Rippling Waters"), a forest-girded lake with good swimming, boating, fishing, and walks. The lake is circled by a 50-kilometer (31-mile) walking track; the three- to four-day walk is popular and in the summer months the lakeside tramping huts are often heavily used. There are many other short walks nearby. The one-hour walk to Lake Waikareiti Track is especially recommended. For information, contact the Department of Conservation Field Centre at Aniwaniwa, on the eastern arm of Lake Waikaremoana (mailing address: Aniwaniwa, Private Bag, Wairoa, tel. 06/837–3803). The motor camp on the lakeshore has cabins, chalets, and motel units. In the summer months a launch operates sightseeing and fishing trips from the motor camp.

What to See and Do with Children

Kiwi House. New Zealand's national symbol is the star attraction at this nocturnal wildlife house. After the half-hour educational and environmental show at 1, visitors may handle the kiwis. *Marine Pde., Napier, tel. 06/835–7553. Admission: $3 adults, $1.50 children 5–15, $7.50 family. Open daily 11–3.*

Napier Aquarium. Sharks, rays, tropical fish, saltwater crocodiles, turtles, and piranha are displayed in this drum-shape building on the waterfront. *Marine Pde., Napier, tel. 06/835–7579. Admission: $6.50 adults, $3.25 children 5–15, $17 family. Open daily 9–5.*

Dining

$$$ **Bayswater on the Beach.** This bayside restaurant has a long-
★ standing reputation as Napier's finest. Fillet of salmon with a scallop mousse, boned quails stuffed with a puree of zucchini and sweet peppers, and a warm salad of mussels filled with mozzarella are listed on a summer dinner menu that scores high marks for originality. The voguish, white interior has a faintly art deco flavor and big doors that open to a sparkling sea view. The moderately priced wine list offers some of the best that Hawke's Bay produces. In warm weather, request a table on the deck outside; otherwise, a table at the window. The restaurant can be hard to spot at night, but look for the chicken take-away, about 2 kilometers (1 mile) from the town center. *Hardinge Rd., Napier, tel. 06/835–8517. Reservations advised. Dress: casual. AE, DC, MC, V.*

$$$ **Bucks Great Wall Restaurant.** Housed in a landmark building on
★ Napier's Marine Parade, this opulent and sophisticated restaurant is a real treat for anyone who enjoys Cantonese cooking. The menu lists almost 100 dishes, from Peking duck to crayfish to sautéed prawns with crispy rice, and while it rarely ventures into unfamiliar territory, the food is delicious and beautifully presented. The earthen-pot dishes are particularly good. In addition to the à la carte menu, there are three fixed-price selections, from $30 to $40 per person. The gregarious owner imports her chefs and even installed a laundry on the premises when the local service sent back tablecloths that were not quite whiter than white. *Marine Pde. and Emerson St., Napier, tel. 06/835–0088. Reservations not required. Dress: casual. AE, DC, MC, V. No lunch weekends.*

$$ **Brookfields Winery Restaurant.** A simple, satisfying menu and an outdoor setting amid the vines make this prestige boutique winery a good choice for sunny-weather lunches. Salads, sandwiches on rye and sourdough bread, pasta, and homemade cakes are offered, as is wine by the glass. *Brookfields Rd., Meeanee,* *tel. 06/834–4615. No reservations. Dress: casual. AE, DC, MC, V. No dinner. No lunch Mon.–Thurs. except during Jan.*

$$ **Pierre sur le quai.** This spare, smart, modern bistro is the back-
★ drop for Pierre Vuilleumier's robust French provincial cooking.
Braised lamb shanks with a tomato and white wine sauce, baked
eel in red wine with rice, and a seafood casserole with spring
vegetables in a champagne sauce are examples from a menu that
allows the flavors to speak for themselves and also offers outstanding value. Combined, the ambience, service, price, and
uncluttered cooking should serve as an example to the rest of
New Zealand. This waterfront restaurant may take some finding, but make the effort. *62 West Quay, Ahuriri, tel. 06/834–
0189. Reservations advised. Dress: casual. MC.*

$$ **Vidal's Barrel Room Restaurant.** Set in a vineyard on the south-
ern outskirts of Hastings, this restaurant has a relaxed country
atmosphere that's perfect for family dining. The menu relies
heavily on steaks, but there is usually a choice of grilled salmon,
spare ribs, and pasta dishes, plus a changing blackboard menu.
Old wine barrels, chunky furniture, and stained-glass windows
give the restaurant an earthy appeal. In the winter there are
open fires; in summer, a courtyard for open-air dining. If time
allows, visit the wine shop and take a vineyard tour. *913 St.
Aubyn St., East Hastings, tel. 06/876–8105. Reservations ad-
vised weekends. Dress: casual but neat. DC, MC, V. Closed
Sun.*

Lodging

$$$ **Ormlie Lodge.** This ornate, sprawling timber house offers a
taste of gracious country living at a reasonable price. Guest
rooms, located on the upper level of the double-story house, are
large, comfortable, and furnished with antiques. Room 4 has a
Jacuzzi and French doors onto the balcony. To one side of the
lodge is a group of four comfortable, modern timber chalets, an
especially good value for a family. The hosts are warm and welcoming people who will happily point out golf courses or prime
fishing spots in the area. The lodge is located in pastoral winegrowing country, about a 15-minute drive south of Napier.
*Omarunui Rd., Waiohiki, Taradale, tel. 06/844–5774, fax 06/
844–5499. 4 lodge rooms, 4 chalets. Facilities: restaurant, bar.
AE, DC, MC, V.*

$$ **Edgewater Motor Lodge.** These motel rooms are about average
in size, facilities, and character, but they offer a central location
and sea views. Rooms on the upper level have balconies, and
there are several room styles to suit couples or families. *359 Ma-
rine Pde., Napier, tel. 06/835–1140, fax 06/835–6600. 20 rooms
with bath. Facilities: spa pool, outdoor pool, guest laundry.
AE, DC, MC, V.*

$$ **Mon Logis Hôtel Privé.** The French owner of this seafront house
★ has modeled his accommodation on the *logis* of his homeland—a
refined version of traditional bed-and-breakfast accommodations. Rooms are large and prettily decorated in a Continental
style with eiderdowns and feather pillows. Although they lack
the sea view, the two rooms at the back of the house are quieter:

Buttes Chaumont has an en suite bathroom, while Paris's bathroom is located off the hall. But what most sets this place apart from the standard B&B is the food. In the morning guests have complimentary coffee and a basket of freshly baked French breads delivered to their rooms. Children are not accommodated. A four-course dinner at $45 per person, including wine, is available by arrangement. *415 Marine Pde., Napier, tel. 06/ 835–2125, fax 06/435–4196. 4 rooms with bath. Tariff includes breakfast. AE, DC, MC, V.*

Wellington

Most visitors find themselves in the capital more by necessity than by choice. Perched at the southern tip of the North Island, Wellington is the jumping-off point for the ferry south, and many travelers, in their rush to the South Island, pass through without a second glance. Yet those who delay their departure for even a single day will discover a sociable city of real charm, small enough to be easily explored on foot, yet large enough to cater to cultured tastes.

The city was named after the Duke of Wellington, the conqueror of Napoléon in his final defeat at Waterloo, and originally settled by English pioneers who purchased land from the New Zealand Company. Shortly after the Treaty of Waitangi was concluded in 1840, Auckland was chosen as the site for the new national capital, but the prosperous and influential gold miners of the South Island waged a campaign for a more central capital, and in 1865 the seat of government was shifted to Wellington.

This city of 354,000 sits in a glorious location on the western shores of Port Nicholson, squeezed against the sea by peaks that rear up to almost 900 meters (3,000 feet). Behind it, suburbs of quaint timber houses spill down precipitous slopes. "Windy Wellington" is a nickname that springs readily to the lips of every New Zealander. Frequently the streets are roped to help pedestrians avoid being bowled over. The cause of this bitter wind is the air currents funneled through the narrow neck of Cook Strait, the 18-kilometer (11-mile) channel between the two islands.

Important Addresses and Numbers

Tourist Information **Wellington Visitor Information Centre.** *Civic Administration Bldg., Victoria and Wakefield Sts., tel. 04/801–4000. Open weekdays 8:30–6, weekends 9–5.*

Embassies and High Commissions **Australian High Commission.** *72–78 Hobson St., Thorndon, tel. 04/473–6411. Open weekdays 8:45–12:15.*
British High Commission. *44 Hill St., tel. 04/472–6049. Open weekdays 9:30–noon and 2–3:30.*
Canadian High Commission. *61 Molesworth St., Thorndon, tel. 04/473–9577. Open weekdays 8:30–4:30.*
United States Embassy. *29 Fitzherbert Terr., Thorndon, tel. 04/ 472–2068. Open weekdays 10–noon and 2–4.*

Emergencies Dial 111 for **fire, police,** or **ambulance** services.

Hospital **Wellington Hospital.** *Riddiford St., Newtown, tel. 04/385–5999.*

Late-Night Pharmacy **The After-Hours Pharmacy.** *17 Adelaide Rd., Newtown, tel. 04/385–8810. Open weekdays 5 AM–11 PM, Sat. 9 AM–11 PM, Sun. 10–10.*

Travel Agencies **American Express Travel Service.** *203 Lambton Quay, tel. 04/473–1221.*
Thomas Cook. *108 Lambton Quay, tel. 04/473–5167.*

Arriving and Departing

By Plane **Wellington International Airport** lies about 8 kilometers (5 miles) from the city. **Super Shuttle** (tel. 04/387–8787) operates a 10-seater bus between the airport and any address in the city ($8 for one person, $10 for two). The bus meets all incoming flights; tickets are available from the driver.

By Car The main access to the city is via the Wellington Urban Motorway, an extension of National Highway 1, which links the city center with all towns and cities to the north.

By Train The **Wellington Railway Station** (tel. 04/498–3000) is on Bunny Street, less than 1 kilometer (½ mile) from the city center.

By Bus **InterCity** buses (tel. 04/495–2443) arrive and depart from Wellington Railway Station. The terminal for **Newmans** buses (tel. 04/499–3261) is the InterIslander Ferry Terminal, 3 kilometers (2 miles) from the city center.

By Ferry The **InterIsland Line** (tel. 04/498–3999) operates vehicle and passenger ferries between Wellington and Picton, at the northern tip of the South Island. The one-way adult fare is $38 during school holidays, $30 at other times. Children ages 4–14 pay half price. The fare for a medium-size sedan is $114 during school holidays, $92 at other times. The crossing takes about three hours and can be very rough. There are at least two departures in each direction every day, and bookings should be made in advance, particularly during holiday periods. The ferry terminal is about 3 kilometers (2 miles) from the city. A free bus leaves Platform 9 at the Wellington Railway Station for the ferry terminal 35 minutes before sailings.

Getting Around

By Bus Wellington's public bus network is known as **Ridewell.** For trips around the inner city, the fare is $1 for adults and 50¢ for children 4–14. **Daytripper** tickets ($5), allowing unlimited travel for one adult and two children, are available from bus drivers after 9 AM. For maps and timetables, contact the information center (142–146 Wakefield St., tel. 04/801–7000).

By Bicycle If the sun is shining and the wind is still, a bicycle is an ideal way to explore the city and its surrounding bays. **Penny Farthing Cy-**

cles (89 Courtenay Pl., tel. 04/385–2772) hires out mountain bikes for $25 per day or $140 per week, including helmet.

Guided Tours

Harbour Capital Bus Tours' Coastline Tour takes in attractions in the city center as well as along the Miramar Peninsula to the east. The 2¾-hour tour departs from the Visitor Information Centre at the corner of Victoria and Wakefield streets. *Tel. 04/ 499–1282. Tickets: $21 adults, $10 children under 15.*

Wally Hammond, a tour operator with a great anecdotal knowledge and a fund of stories about the city, offers a 2½-hour minibus tour of the city and Marine Drive. Tours depart from Travel World, Mercer and Victoria streets, at 10 and 2. Passengers can be picked up at their city hotels at no extra cost. *Tel. 04/472– 0869. Tickets: $20 per person.*

The **Trust Bank Ferry,** a commuter service between the city and Days Bay, on the eastern side of Port Nicholson, is one of the best-value tours in the city. Weekdays the catamaran departs from Queens Wharf at 7:10, 8:20, noon, 2, 4:15, and 5:30; weekends, at 10:30, noon, 2, and 4:15. The trip takes about 25 minutes. *Queens Wharf, City, tel. 04/499–1273. Round-trip tickets: $12 adults, $6 children 3–15.*

Exploring Wellington

This walking tour of the city includes city views, formal gardens, literary history, some fine examples of 19th-century architecture, and the seat of government. Allow about three hours.

Numbers in the margin correspond to points of interest on the Wellington map.

❶ Begin at the **Kelburn Cable Car** terminus in Cable Car Lane off Lambton Quay, opposite Grey Street. The Swiss-built funicular railway makes a short but sharp climb to Kelburn Terminal, which offers views across parks and city buildings to Port Nicholson. Sit on the left side during the six-minute journey for the best scenery. *Cost: $1.50 adults, 70¢ children 4–15. Departures about every 10 min, weekdays 7 AM–10 PM, Sat. 9:20–6, Sun. 10:30–6.*

Leave the Kelburn Terminal and take the Northern Walkway, following the arrow that points to St. Mary Street. This path **❷** skirts the edge of the **Botanic Garden,** with city views on one side and the domes of the Dominion Observatory on the other. As you round the hilltop, you'll see an immense green hill with transmission towers on top; this is Tinakori Hill, known to the Maoris as Ahumairangi—"sloping down from the sky."

Continue along the path, which becomes quite steep as it **❸** plunges down toward the **Lady Norwood Rose Garden** and the **Begonia House.** There are more than 100 types of roses in the

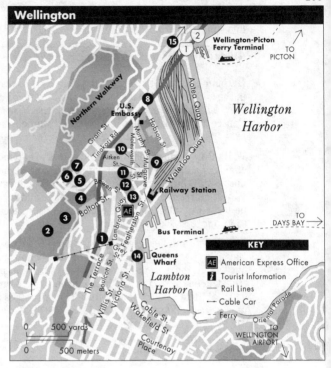

garden, which erupts in a blaze of color between November and
the end of April.

Turn your back on the roses and walk to the right around the
enclosed Anderson Park, following the sign to Bolton Street
Memorial Park. At the end of this short road, make a detour to
the monument on the right. The **John Seddon Memorial** is dedicated to the colorful and popular liberal politician who was
prime minister from 1893 to 1906. Under Seddon's leadership,
New Zealand became the first country to pay its citizens an old-
age pension, and the first to give women the vote.

Close to the memorial a track zigzags down the hill beneath a
stand of pohutukawa trees. At the bottom, cross Bowen Street,
walk downhill, take the path to your left, and climb narrow
Ascot Street. The tiny, doll-like cottages along this street were
built in the 1870s, and this remains the finest example of a 19th-
century streetscape in Wellington. At the top of the rise, stop
for a breather on the bench that has been thoughtfully provided
in the shady courtyard.

Turn right into **Tinakori Road.** The lack of suitable local stone
combined with the collapse of most of Wellington's brick buildings in the earthquake of 1848 ensured that timber was used almost exclusively for building here in the second half of the 19th
century. Most of the carpenters of the period had learned their

skills as cabinetmakers and shipwrights in Europe, and the sturdy houses in this street are a tribute to their craftsmanship.

6 Another fact of early life in Wellington is illustrated by **No. 306,** the pasta shop. Pressed for level ground, the citizens of early Wellington tended to build tall, narrow houses. This example— one room wide and five stories high—took things to extremes. Just below the house, make a short detour to see the three superbly restored timber houses side by side in Upton Terrace. Behind a green fence a few steps farther down Tinakori Road is
7 **Premier House,** the official residence of the prime minister until 1935, when the new Labour government, caught up in the reforming zeal of socialism, turned it into a dental clinic.

Continue down a relatively drab part of Tinakori Road to No. 25,
8 just beyond the Hobson Street bridge. This is the **Katherine Mansfield House,** where the writer was born (as Kathleen Beauchamp) and lived the first five years of her life. Mansfield left to pursue her career in Europe when she was only 20, but many of her short stories are set in Wellington. A year before her death in 1923, she wrote, "New Zealand is in my very bones. What wouldn't I give to have a look at it!" The house, which has been restored as a typical Victorian family home, contains furnishings, photographs, videos, and tapes that elucidate Mansfield's life and times. *25 Tinakori Rd., Thorndon, tel. 04/ 473-7268. Admission: $4 adults, $1 children 4-15. Open Tues.- Sun. 10-4.*

Walk back along Tinakori Road to the Hobson Street overpass, and on the far side of the motorway turn right to walk through the elms of Katherine Mansfield Memorial Park. Turn left around the rather stern compound of the U.S. Embassy, and walk down Murphy Street, which becomes Mulgrave Street, to
9 **Old St. Paul's Cathedral.** Consecrated in 1866, the church is a splendid example of the English neo-Gothic style executed in wood. Even the trusses that support the roof transcend their mundane function with their splendid craftsmanship. The hexagonal oak pulpit was a gift from the widow of Prime Minister Richard Seddon, in memory of her husband. *Mulgrave St., Thorndon, tel. 04/473-6722. Open Mon.-Sat. 10-4:30, Sun. 1- 4:30.*

Walk down Mulgrave Street and turn right at Archives House into Aitken Street. The modern building on the right is the
10 **National Library,** which houses the largest collection of books in the nation as well as the remarkable Alexander Turnbull Library. This latter collection, named after the noted bibliophile who founded it, contains a particularly impressive Pacific history section, which includes accounts of every important European voyage of discovery since Magellan. The art collection includes many sketches of New Zealand made by early visitors; these are displayed in changing exhibitions. *Molesworth and Aitken Sts., tel. 04/474-3000. Open weekdays 9-5, Sat. 9-1.*

Cross Molesworth Street and walk through the gate to the
11 **Parliament Buildings** on the far side. The green Gothic struc-

ture on the right is the General Assembly Library, a soaring, graceful building compared with the ponderous gray bulk of the Parliament House next door. The layout of the House of Representatives, where legislation is presented, debated, and either passed or rejected by majority vote, is a copy of the British Houses of Parliament at Westminster, right down to the Speaker's mace and the despatch boxes. Tours of the building explain the parliamentary process in detail. *Molesworth St., tel. 04/471–9999. Admission free. Tours depart weekdays at varying times.*

⑫ It would be difficult to imagine a more complete contrast in architectural styles than the **Executive Office** building to the left of the Parliament House, known for obvious reasons as "the Beehive"—though the people of Wellington will often add that it produces nothing sweet. This building houses the offices of parliamentarians and their staffs.

⑬ Walk down the hill from the Beehive to the **Cenotaph,** the memorial to New Zealanders killed in battle. New Zealand has a proud and distinguished war record. "Few Americans appreciate the tremendous sacrifices made by New Zealanders in the last two world wars," James A. Michener wrote in *Return to Paradise.* "Among the allies, she had the highest percentage of men in arms—much higher than the United States—the greatest percentage overseas, and the largest percentage killed."

The wide street that curves away to the back of the bronze lions is **Lambton Quay.** As its name suggests, this was once Wellington's waterfront. All the land between your feet and the present-day shoreline has been reclaimed. From this point, the shops of the city center are within easy walking distance along Lambton Quay.

Other Places of Interest

⑭ **Maritime Museum.** Housed in the handsome Harbour Board Building, this museum has paintings, figureheads, various nautical apparatuses, and some fine scale models of ships, including the *Wahine,* which sank in Cook Strait in 1968 with the loss of 51 lives. However, most of the displays belong to the old-fashioned, glass-cabinet school of museum design. *Queens Wharf, tel. 04/472–8904. Admission: $2 adults, 50¢ children under 12. Open weekdays 9:30–4, weekends 1–4:30.*

⑮ **Southward Museum.** The largest collection of vintage and veteran cars in the Southern Hemisphere, this amazing collection of more than 250 vehicles includes Bugattis, a Hispano-Suiza, one of only 17 Davis three-wheelers ever made, a De Lorean, a gullwing 1955 Mercedes 300SL, gangster Micky Cohen's armorplated 1950 Cadillac, and another Cadillac once owned by Marlene Dietriech. The motorcycle collection, which has a number of early Harley-Davidsons and Indians, a Brough Superior, and a Vincent V-twin, is almost as impressive. The museum is located just off Highway 1, about a 45-minute drive north of Wellington. *Otaihanga Rd., Paraparaumu, tel. 04/297–1221. Admission: $4 adults, $1 children 5–14. Open daily 9–4:30.*

Dining

Courtenay Place is Wellington's restaurant row. Turkish, Indian, French, and Italian restaurants jostle for attention, along with several bar/brasseries that make this a favorite nightspot for the city's sophisticates.

$$$$ Le Petit Lyon. The anonymous brick wall at the front hides what
★ many regard as the finest epicurean restaurant in the country. Inside, classical French cuisine is presented with all the trimmings: silver, crystal, plush surroundings, and solicitous service. The menu degustation, at $125 per person including wines, is recommended for those who want to totally indulge themselves. *8 Courtenay Pl., tel. 04/364–9402. Reservations required. Jacket and tie required. AE, DC, MC, V. No lunch Sat. Closed Sun.*

$$$ Brasserie Flipp. Highly fashionable with Wellington's sophisti-
★ cates, the innovative international menu makes this restaurant a good choice for lunch or dinner. Main courses include smoked pork kassler sausage with red cabbage, char-grilled baby octopus salad, and grilled lamb steak with a green pea puree. The decor is smart and stylish: polished timber floors, dazzling white napery, and subdued lighting. The wine list has a good selection of New Zealand wines, and a token bottle from just about everywhere else. *RSA Bldg., 103 Ghuznee St., Wellington, tel. 04/385–9493. No reservations. Dress: casual. AE, DC, MC, V.*

$$$ Tinakori Bistro. Set in a miniature Thorndon shopfront, this popular bistro has a modern, French-influenced menu and a long-standing reputation for reliability. Main courses include char-grilled scotch fillet with sour cream and horseradish dressing, and grilled venison medallions with a blackberry and port sauce. *328 Tinakori Rd., Thorndon, tel. 04/499–0567. Reservations advised. Dress: casual but neat. AE, MC, V. BYOB. No lunch weekends. Closed Sun.*

$$ Bellissimo Trattoria Italiana. This is simply great Italian food—
★ served with far more style and panache than the name "trattoria" might suggest. First courses include fish carpaccio with olive oil and calamari in a chili sauce. Among the mains might be panfried veal stuffed with vegetables or venison stew. All the pasta is made on the premises by the Neapolitan owner/chef. *Dukes Arcade, Manners St., tel. 04/499–1154. Reservations not required. Dress: casual. AE, DC, MC, V. No lunch weekends.*

$$ Chevy's. With a name like that and a flashing neon cowboy out front, the burgers, nachos, chicken wings, BLTs, and barbecue spareribs come as little surprise. The salads are crisp, the fries are crunchy, the service is prompt, the quasi-American decor is bright and attractive, and the restaurant stays open until at least 10:30. *97 Dixon St., Wellington, tel. 04/384–2724. No reservations. Dress: casual. AE, DC, MC, V. BYOB.*

$$ Dockside. Part of the redeveloped warehouse complex on the waterfront, this new, informal restaurant has a nautical theme, a reasonably priced menu, and a choice of casual dining in either the bar or the upstairs restaurant. *Moules marinières* (pasta with mussels in a tomato and chili sauce), *salad niçoise,* smoked chicken salad, and a salad of warm vegetables and cervena venison appear on a menu that is particularly strong on seafood. *Shed 3, Queens Wharf, Jervois Quay, tel. 04/499–9900. Reservations not required. Dress: casual. AE, DC, MC, V.*

$ ★ **Dixon Street Gourmet Deli.** This city-center delicatessen stocks one of the best ranges of gourmet treats in the country. There are home-baked breads and bagels, an international choice of meats, cheeses, pickles, and preserves, plus local smoked fish and oysters—everything you need for a superior picnic. *45–47 Dixon St., tel. 04/384–2436. No credit cards. Closed weekends.*

$ **Gourmet Lane.** These half-dozen cafés in the basement of the Bank of New Zealand Building offer a choice of light meals, from spring rolls to fish and chips to pies, pastries, and salads. Try to avoid the 12:30 crush, when the place is crowded with office workers. *1 Willis St. No credit cards. Lunch only. Closed weekends.*

$ **The Lido.** This popular, bustling corner café across from the tourist information center is a particularly good choice if you're looking for budget-priced breakfast or lunch. *Victoria and Wakefield Sts., tel. 04/499–6666. No reservations. Dress: casual but neat. No credit cards.*

Lodging

Lodging in Wellington is peculiarly polarized, with elegant and expensive hotels on one end, homestays on the other, and nothing in between.

$$$$ ★ **Parkroyal Wellington.** If you are looking for the luxury, facilities, gloss, and glamour that only a big international hotel can deliver, this is the best in town—and possibly the best in the country. Opened in 1990, the bronze tower building has an art deco flavor in its public areas. Guest rooms are decorated in sea greens and blues with blond wood furnishings, and each has its own iron and ironing board. The bureau rooms, which have a desk and a queen-size bed instead of two doubles, are tailored especially for traveling executives. Request a room with ocean views. Service by the young staff is excellent throughout the hotel. The Parkroyal is located in the city center, within walking distance of shops, restaurants, and the central business district. The Panama Street Brasserie is a favorite breakfast spot for the city's power brokers. *Featherston and Grey Sts., Wellington, tel. 04/72–2722, fax 04/472–4724. 232 rooms with bath. Facilities: spa pool, sauna, gym, heated indoor pool, guest laundry, 2 bars, 2 restaurants. AE, DC, MC, V.*

$ **Halswell Lodge.** Rooms at this hotel on the edge of the city center are compact and functional, but each has en suite facilities and a reasonable standard of comfort. The surroundings offer a wide choice of restaurants. Rooms at the front are affected by street noise during the daytime. *21 Kent Terr., Wellington, tel. 04/385–0196, fax 04/385–0503. 19 rooms with bath. AE, DC, MC, V.*

$ **Homestay.** Located just a five-minute drive from the city center, this timber house offers comfort, style, and good value for those looking for homestay accommodations. The ground-level guest room is rather small and does not have an en suite bathroom, but the apartment on the floor below has a separate kitchen, bathroom, lounge, and room for four. Throughout, the owners (one is an Austrian, one a New Zealander) have decorated their house simply but stylishly with bunches of dried wildflowers, rustic wooden furniture, Oriental rugs, and polished timber floors. The house has marvelous views across timber houses and gardens that spill down to the harbor in the distance. *33 Mortimer Terr., tel. 04/385-3667. 1 room, 1 apartment with bath. Tariff includes breakfast. No credit cards.*

$ **Tinakori Lodge.** Situated in a historic suburb overlooking the city, this lodge offers atmospheric bed-and-breakfast accommodations in tranquil surroundings at a reasonable price. The rooms, which can sleep up to three, are simply furnished but comfortable. The city center is a 10-minute walk away, and there are several restaurants in the vicinity. The owners are extremely friendly and helpful. Children are accommodated by arrangement. *182 Tinakori Rd., Thorndon, tel. 04/473-3478, fax 04/472-5554. 10 rooms share 3 baths. Tariff includes breakfast. AE, DC, MC, V.*

The Arts and Nightlife

The Arts Wellington is the home of the **New Zealand Ballet Company** and the **New Zealand Symphony Orchestra.** The main venue for the performing arts is the **Michael Fowler Centre** (Wakefield Street, tel. 04/472-3088).

The **Downstage Theatre** holds frequent performances of stage classics. *Hannah Playhouse, Courtenay Pl. and Cambridge Terr., tel. 04/384-9639.*

Nightlife At the heart of the city, the **St. George Hotel** has several bars, live jazz music most nights of the week, and Legends of the George, a late-night restaurant. *Willis and Boulcott Sts., tel. 04/473-9139. Open 11 AM–midnight.*

The most vigorous sign of life after dark in Wellington is found in its bars. On the ground floor of the Parkroyal Hotel at the corner of Grey and Featherstone streets, the **Arizona Bar** (tel. 04/495-7867) is packed on Friday and Saturday nights, as is the nearby **Malthouse** at 47 Willis St. (tel. 04/499-4355). However, the main action is on Courtenay Place, where the bar scene operates at fever pitch on Friday and Saturday nights.

5 The South Island

By Michael Gebicki

The South Island is separated from the North Island by Cook Strait, an expanse of just 17 kilometers (11 miles); yet the difference is far greater than the distance suggests. Whether you first glimpse the South Island from the deck of the ferry as it noses into Marlborough Sounds or through the window of a plane bound for Christchurch, the immediate impression is that the landscape has turned feral: The green, mellow beauty of the North Island has given way to jagged snowcapped mountains and rivers that charge down from them and sprawl across vast shingle beds. The locals will tell you that you haven't seen rain until you've been drenched by a rainstorm on the west coast—one of the wettest places on earth.

The headline attractions are Queenstown, the adventure-sport capital of the country; Mount Cook and its glaciers; and the sounds of Fiordland National Park. Beyond the well-defined tourist routes, the island's beech forests, lakes, trout streams, mountain trails, and beaches form a paradise for hikers, anglers, and just about anyone who enjoys a dose of fresh air. Sperm whales, dolphins, penguins, seals, and royal albatrosses can be seen in the wild along the coastline. And Stewart Island, off the southern tip of South Island, is remote enough to satisfy even the most determined escapist.

Marlborough, Nelson, and the West Coast

These three regions, which form the northern and western coasts of the South Island, offer an immense variety of scenery, from the siren seascapes of Marlborough Sounds to the mellow river valleys of the north coast to the icy world of the glaciers and the Southern Alps, where 12,000-foot peaks rise within 32 kilometers (20 miles) of the shore.

After the well-ordered serenity of the North Island, the wild grandeur of the west coast will come as a surprise. This is Mother Nature with her hair down, flaying the coastline with huge seas and drenching rains and littering its beaches with bleached driftwood sculptures. It is a country that creates a special breed, and the rough-hewn and powerfully independent people—known to the rest of the country as "coasters"—occupy a special place in New Zealand folklore.

For visitors who ferry across from Wellington, Marlborough Sounds will provide the first taste of the South Island. Together with the city of Nelson and Abel Tasman National Park to the west, this is a sporting paradise, with a mild climate that allows a year-round array of adventure activities.

Important Addresses and Numbers

Tourist Information **Nelson Visitor Information Centre.** *Trafalgar and Halifax Sts., tel. 03/548–2304. Open daily 9–5.*

Franz Josef Glacier Visitor Information Centre. *State Hwy. 6, Franz Josef, tel. 03/752–0796. Open daily 8–4:30.*

Greymouth Visitor Information Centre. *Regent Theatre Bldg., McKay and Herbert Sts., tel. 03/768–5101. Open weekdays 9–5.*

Emergencies Dial 111 for **fire, police,** or **ambulance** services.

Arriving and Departing

By Plane **Air New Zealand** (tel. 03/546–9300) and **Ansett New Zealand** (tel. 04/471–1044) link Nelson with Christchurch, Queenstown, Dunedin, the west coast town of Hokitika, and all major cities on the North Island. **Nelson Airport** lies 10 kilometers (6 miles) west of the city. **Super Shuttle** (tel. 03/547–5782) operates buses that meet all incoming flights and charge $6 to the city for one passenger, $5 each for two. The taxi fare to the city center is about $12.

By Car From Nelson, Highway 6 runs southwest to the west coast, down the coast to the glaciers, then south to Queenstown and Invercargill. Highway 1 follows the east coast to Christchurch and Dunedin. Allow at least seven hours for the 458-kilometer (284-mile) journey from Nelson to Franz Josef.

By Bus From Nelson, **InterCity** buses travel the length of both the west and east coasts daily. For bookings from Nelson, tel. 03/548–1539; Greymouth, tel. 03/768–1435; Franz Josef, tel. 03/752–0780.

By Ferry The berth for the **InterIsland Ferries** from Wellington is at Picton, 145 kilometers (90 miles) east of Nelson. At the ferry terminal, buses are readily available for travel either east to Blenheim and Christchurch or west to Nelson.

By Train The west coast in general is poorly served by the rail network, but one glowing exception is the **TranzAlpine Express,** which ranks as one of the world's great rail journeys. This passenger train crosses the Southern Alps between Christchurch and Greymouth, winding through beech forests and mountains that are covered by snow for most of the year. The bridges and tunnels along this line, including the 8-kilometer (5-mile) Otira Tunnel, represent a prodigious feat of engineering. The train is modern and comfortable, with panoramic windows as well as dining and bar service. Smoking is not permitted on board. The train departs Christchurch daily at 9:15 AM and arrives in Greymouth at 1:25 PM; the return train departs Greymouth at 2:35 PM and arrives at Christchurch at 6:40 PM. The one-way fare is $66 adults, $33 children 4–14. For bookings, tel. 800/802–802.

Guided Tours

Abel Tasman National Park Enterprises operate launches that follow the majestic shoreline of the park. A popular option is to leave the boat at Bark Bay on the outward voyage, take a two-hour walk through the forests, and reboard the boat at Torrent Bay. The 6½-hour cruise departs daily from Kaiteriteri, a one-hour drive northwest of Nelson, at 9 AM. A bus connection from Nelson leaves the Visitor Information Centre at 7:35 AM. A cruise/flight option is also available. Passengers should buy a take-out lunch at Motueka—supplies on board are basic. *Old Cedarman House, Main Rd., Riwaka, tel. 03/528–7801. Cost: cruise (from Kaiteriteri), $42 adults, $14 children 4–14; cruise/flight (from Nelson): $112 adults, $97 children 4–14; bus (Nelson–Kaiteriteri round-trip), $17.*

The *Glenmore,* a small launch that makes a daylong trip ferrying mail and supplies around the reaches of Pelorus Sound, offers one of the best ways to discover this waterway and meet the people who live there. The boat departs from Havelock Tuesday to Thursday at 9:30 and returns about 5:30. *Glenmore Cruises, 73 Main Rd., Havelock, tel. 03/574–2276. Tickets: $45 adults, $22.50 children 4–14.*

The **Helicopter Line** operates several scenic flights over the glaciers from the heliport at Franz Josef. The shortest is the 20-minute flight over the Franz Josef Glacier ($40 per person); the longest is the Mountain Scenic Spectacular, a one-hour flight that includes a landing on the head of the glacier and a circuit of Mount Cook and Mount Tasman ($130 per person). *Box 45, Franz Josef, tel. 02/883–1767.*

The **Scenic Mail Run** is a five-hour tour aboard the bus that delivers the mail and supplies to isolated farming communities around Cape Farewell, at the northern tip of the South Island. The tour includes lunch on a 2,500-acre grazing property. The eight-seater bus departs from the Collingwood post office. *Collingwood Bus Services, P.O. Collingwood, tel. 03/524–8188. Tickets: $25 adults, $15 children under 12. Tour departs 9:30 weekdays.*

Exploring Marlborough, Nelson, and the West Coast

This driving tour begins at Picton, where the InterIslander Ferries berth, and travels west to Nelson and Motueka, then south on Highway 6 along the coast. The detour through Motueka adds almost two hours; anyone who intends to make the seven-hour drive from Nelson to the glaciers in a single day should ignore this section of the tour and leave Nelson by Highway 6 instead.

Numbers in the margin correspond to points of interest on the Marlborough, Nelson, and the West Coast map.

❶ Picton is the base for cruising holidays in the **Marlborough Sounds,** the labyrinth of waterways that was formed when the sea invaded a series of river valleys at the northern tip of the South Island. Backed by forested hills that at times rise almost vertically from the water, the Sounds are a wild, majestic place edged with tiny beaches and rocky coves and studded with islands where such native wildlife as gannets and the primitive tuatara have remained undisturbed by introduced species. These waterways are the country's second-favorite cruising waters,

Marlborough, Nelson, and the West Coast

Cook Strait

★ Wellington

D'Urville Island

Marlborough Sounds ❶

Pelorus Sound

Queen Charlotte Drive

❷ Picton

Blenheim

Cape Farewell

Golden Bay ❽

Tasman Bay

Abel Tasman National Park Totaranui ❼ Marahau **Nelson** ❸

Collingwood (60)

Takaka Kaiteriteri

Tasman Mts. Riwaka Tasman

Motueka Valley ❾ ❻ Mapua ❹ **Isel Park**

Nature Smoke ❺

N.W. NELSON FOREST PARK (61) **Broadgreen**

MOUNT RICHMOND FOREST PARK

Hillersden

Cape Campbell

Wharanui

Karamea

(67)

Molesworth

NELSON LAKES NATIONAL PARK

Clarence

SOUTH PACIFIC OCEAN

Waimarie

(6) Murchison

Kaikoura

Karamea Bight

Lyell ❿ **Buller River**

(70)

Hanmer Springs

Cheviot

Westport (69)

PAPAROA NATIONAL PARK

Maruia Springs

(7)

LAKE SUMMER FOREST PARK

(7)

(1)

Motunau

Pancake Rocks ⓫

(6)

(7)

Amberley

Pegasus Bay

Jade Boulder Gallery ⓬

Lake Brunner

ARTHURS PASS NATIONAL PARK

Greymouth

Shantytown ⓭

Oxford

Belfast

Christchurch

Hokitika

TranzAlpine Express

Cass

(73)

Lake Coleridge

Darfield

Burnham

Banks Peninsula

(75)

Tasman Sea

(6)

Rakaia

Dorie

Canterbury Bight

Methven

Harihari

Hakatere

Ashburton

N↗

Fox and Franz Josef Glaciers ⓮

MOUNT COOK NATIONAL PARK

(79)

Rangitata

WESTLAND NATIONAL PARK

Geraldine

Lake Matheson ⓯

Lake Tekapo

Winchester

Point

Fairlie (8)

Timaru

(80) *Lake Pukaki*

Pareora

KEY

— Rail Lines

0 ———— 40 miles

0 ———— 60 km

after the Bay of Islands, but in terms of isolation and rugged grandeur they are in a class of their own. Much of the area is a national park; it has changed little since the 1770s, when Captain James Cook called in on five separate occasions to repair his ships and stock up with fresh provisions. There are rudimentary roads on the long fingers of land jutting into the Sounds, but the most convenient access is by water. One of the best ways to discover the area is hitching a ride at Havelock aboard the launch *Glenmore,* which delivers mail and supplies to outlying settlements scattered around Pelorus Sound (*see* Guided Tours, *above*).

From the InterIslander ferry terminal, turn right and follow the signs to **Queen Charlotte Drive.** This road rises spectacularly along the edge of the sound, then cuts across the base of the peninsula that separates Queen Charlotte Sound from Pelorus Sound. Beyond Havelock the road winds through forested river valleys before it rounds the eastern side of Tasman Bay and reaches Nelson.

Set on the broad curve of its bay with views of the Tasman Mountains on the far side, it would be hard to find a city and a climate better suited for year-round adventure than **Nelson.** To the east are the sheltered waters of Marlborough Sounds; to the west, the sandy crescents of the Abel Tasman National Park; and to the south, mellow river valleys and the peaks and glacial lakes of the Nelson Lakes National Park, a pristine wonderland for hikers, mountaineers, and cross-country skiers. Beyond those geographic splendors, Nelson has a mild climate with more hours of sunlight than any other city in the country. New Zealanders are well aware of these attractions, and in December and January the city is swamped with vacationers. Apart from this brief burst of activity, you can expect to have the roads and beaches almost to yourself.

Nelson is dominated by **Christ Church Cathedral,** which sits on a hilltop surrounded by gardens. Work on the cathedral began in 1925 and dragged on for the next 40 years. During construction the design was altered to withstand earthquakes, and despite its promising location, it looks like a church designed by a committee.

Leave Nelson by **Rutherford Street,** named in honor of the eminent nuclear physicist Ernest Rutherford, who was born nearby and educated at school here. On the outskirts of the city, take the right fork off this road, Waimea Road, and continue as it becomes Main Road. Turn left into Marsden Road, where a sign points to **Isel Park.** The **Nelson Provincial Museum** in the grounds of the park has a small but outstanding collection of Maori carvings. The museum also has a number of artifacts relating to the "Maungatapu murders," a grisly goldfields killing committed near Nelson in 1866. *Isel Park, Stoke, tel. 03/547–9740. Admission: $2 adults, $1 children 5–15, $5 family. Open Tues.–Fri. 10–4, weekends 2–5.*

Isel House, near the museum, was built for Thomas Marsden, one of the region's prosperous pioneers. The Marsden family's impressive collection of porcelain and furniture is displayed inside. It was Marsden who laid out the magnificent gardens surrounding the house, which include a towering California redwood and a 42-meter (140-foot) Monterey pine. *Isel Park, tel. 03/547–9740. Admission to house: $2.50 adults, $1 children 5–15. House open weekends 2–4. Closed June–Aug.*

Return to Main Road, turn right at the next set of traffic lights into Songer Street, turn right into Nayland Road, and stop at ⑤ the park on the left. In the middle is **Broadgreen,** a fine example of a Victorian "cob" house. Cob houses, made from straw and horsehair bonded together with mud and clay, are commonly found in the southern English county of Devon, where many of Nelson's pioneers originated. The house is furnished as it might have been in the 1850s, with patchwork quilts and kauri furniture. *276 Nayland Rd., Stoke, tel. 03/546–0283. Admission: $2 adults, 50¢ children 5–15. Open Nov.–Apr., Tues.–Fri. 10:30–4:30, weekends 1:30–4:30; May–Oct., Wed. and weekends 2–4:30.*

Return to Main Road and turn right onto Highway 6. Unless time is short, turn right again onto Highway 60, following the "coastal route" signs to Motueka. Turn right where a sign points to Mapua and continue to Mapua Port. This road ends at a tiny dock with a couple of ramshackle warehouses; in the blue ⑥ corrugated iron building on the wharf is **Nature Smoke.** The business is operated by Dennis Crawford, who buys his fish right off the fishing boats, fillets it, marinates it according to a secret recipe, and smokes it. The result is delicious, and Crawford will happily offer samples. If you're headed south, you won't find a better lunch along the way than a slab of smoked snapper or albacore tuna with a loaf of crusty bread from the bakery in Motueka and apples from one of the roadside orchard stalls. *Mapua Wharf, tel. 03/540–2280. Open daily 9–5:30, extended hrs in summer.*

West of Mapua, Highway 60 loops around quiet little sea coves that, for all but the warmest months of the year, mirror the snow-frosted peaks on the far shore. The tall vines along the roadside are hops, used in the making of beer.

Beyond the town of Motueka, Highway 60 passes close to the fine swimming beach at Kaiteriteri, then turns inland to skirt ⑦ the **Abel Tasman National Park,** the smallest of New Zealand's national parks. Its coastline is a succession of idyllic beaches backed by a rugged hinterland of beech forests, granite gorges, and waterfalls. The park has a number of walking trails, both from Totaranui at its northern end and Marahau in the south. The most popular is the two- to three-day **Coastal Track,** open year-round. Launches of the Abel Tasman National Park Enterprises (tel. 03/528–7801) will drop off and pick up hikers from several points along the track. A popular way to explore the coastline is by sea kayak (*see* Sports and the Outdoors, *below*). The park information center is at the Department of Conservation Field Centre (1 Commercial St., Takaka, tel. 03/525–9136). The main accommodations base for the national park is Motueka.

8 Highway 60 returns to the sea near the town of Takaka. The sweep of sand to the north is known, deservedly, as **Golden Bay,** but it once had a very different name. The Dutch navigator Abel Tasman anchored here briefly just a few days before Christmas 1642; his visit ended tragically when four of his crew were killed by Maoris. Bitterly disappointed, Tasman named the place Moordenaers, or Murderers' Bay, and sailed away without ever setting foot on New Zealand soil. For those who have time to explore, Golden Bay is a delight—a sunny 40-kilometer (25-mile) crescent of rocks and sand with a supremely relaxed crew of locals who firmly believe they live in paradise.

Time Out Next door to the Motueka Museum, **Annabelles Café** serves snacks and light, inexpensive meals: scones, muffins, salads, sandwiches, and great espresso. The café offers a choice of indoor or outdoor tables. *140 High St., Motueka, tel. 03/528–8696. Open daily 11–3.*

9 At the entrance to Motueka, at the Rothmans Clock Tower, turn south onto Highway 61, following the sign to Murchison. The road snakes through **Motueka Valley** alongside the Motueka River, which is edged with poplars and yellow gorse, with the green valley walls pressing close alongside. If this river could talk, it would probably scream "Trout!" There are many deer farms in the area, easily identified by their high fences.

10 Fifty-seven kilometers (35 miles) beyond Motueka, Highway 61 joins Highway 6 for the journey south. Beyond Murchison, the road parallels the broad **Buller River** as it carves a deep gorge from the jagged mountain peaks. Nineteen kilometers (12 miles) south of Murchison, the **Newtown Hotel,** no longer licensed, teeters on the brink of the gorge, surrounded by a fantastic junkyard of obsolete farm machinery. The Buller once carried a fabulous cargo of gold, but you have to use your imagination to reconstruct the days when places such as Lyell, 34 kilometers (21 miles) beyond Murchison, were bustling mining towns. **Hawk's Crag,** where the highway passes beneath a rock overhang with the river wheeling alongside, is the scenic climax of the trip along the Buller. Before the town of Westport, turn left to continue along Highway 6.

11 After a journey through coastal scrub, Highway 6 meets the sea; shortly thereafter it arrives at a tiny collection of shops called **Punakaiki.** From the visitor center, an easy 10-minute walk leads to a fantastic maze of limestone rocks stacked high above the sea. These are commonly known as the **Pancake Rocks,** and they are the outstanding feature of the surrounding **Paparoa National Park.** At high tide, the blowhole spouts a thundering geyser of spray. Mount Cook is sometimes visible to the south. *Paparoa National Park, tel. 03/731–1895.*

The town of Greymouth is aptly named—a dull, dispirited strip of motels and timber mills. Yet the **Jade Boulder Gallery** is a great place to pick up a distinctive souvenir. The gallery exhibits the work of Ian Boustridge, one of the country's most accomplished sculptors of greenstone, the jade that was highly prized by the Maoris. Earrings start at about $35, and sculptures can cost anything up to $1,000. *1 Guiness St., Greymouth, tel. 03/768-0700. Open daily 8-5.*

On the southern outskirts of Greymouth, **Shantytown** is a lively reenactment of a gold-mining town of the 1880s. Except for the church and the town hall, most of the buildings are replicas, but the gold diggings are authentic and fascinating. Displays include a water jet for blasting the gold-bearing quartz from the hillside, water sluices, and a stamper battery or crusher powered by a 30-foot water wheel. Visitors can pan for gold, and since the creek is salted with gold dust, there is a good chance of striking "color." *Rutherglen, Greymouth, tel. 03/762-6634. Admission: $7 adults, $4 children 5-15. Open daily 8:30-5.*

South of Greymouth the highway threads through farming country as it heads toward the Southern Alps and the glaciers of **Westland National Park.** The glaciers are formed by the massive rainfall of the west coast—up to 300 inches per annum—which descends as snow on the névé, or head, of the glacier. The snow is compressed into ice, which flows downhill under its own weight. There are more than 60 glaciers in the park; the most famous and accessible are **Fox** and **Franz Josef,** the only glaciers on earth that grind through a rain forest. They lie about 24 kilometers (15 miles) apart. You can park a 15-minute walk away from the terminal face of Fox Glacier, and a 30-minute walk from the Franz Josef terminal. Both parking lots are terrorized by keas—mountain parrots—which specialize in destroying the rubber molding around car windows. (Keas are harmless to humans, and a coating of insect repellent around the window frames should safeguard your vehicle.)

Trails from the parking lots wind across the valley floor to the glacier faces, where a tormented vocabulary of squeaks, creaks, groans, and gurgles can be heard as the glacier creeps down the mountainside at an average rate of 5 feet per day. Care must be taken here, since rocks and chunks of ice frequently drop from the melting face. These being New Zealand glaciers, there is much to do besides admire them. You can fly over them and land on their névé, walk on them, even make a bloodcurdling and very cold white-water rafting trip down the Waiho River where it emerges from the base of Franz Josef (*see* Guided Tours, *above*, and Sports and the Outdoors, *below*). Flights should be made early in the morning, when the visibility is better. Fox Glacier is slightly larger and longer than Franz Josef, but you'll miss nothing important if you see only one. Both glaciers have separate townships, and if you are spending the night, Franz Josef is marginally preferable.

At the town of Fox Glacier, turn toward the sea where a sign points to Gillespies Beach, then turn right toward **Lake**

Matheson for one of the country's most famous views. A walking trail winds along the lakeshore, and the snowcapped peaks of Mount Cook and Mount Tasman are reflected in the water. Allow at least an hour for the complete walk to the "View of Views." The best time is early morning, before the mirrorlike reflections are fractured by the wind.

Beyond the glaciers Highway 6 continues along the south coast to Haast, where it turns inland to Wanaka and Queenstown. The driving time between Fox Glacier and Wanaka is six hours. The best accommodation along this road is the Lake Moeraki Wilderness Lodge, just north of Haast (*see* Lodging, *below*).

Sports and the Outdoors

Boating and Rafting   **Abel Tasman Kayaks** has one- and two-person kayaks for hire at Marahau, at the southern end of Abel Tasman National Park, which gives paddlers ready access to beaches and campsites often inaccessible to hikers. The company does not rent to solo kayakers, and a minimum two-day rental is required. The cost is $90 for two days. Guided kayak tours cost $80 for one day, $260 for three days. *Marahau, RD 2 Motueka, tel. 03/527–8022.*

The **Marlborough Sounds Adventure Company** offers one- and four-day guided kayak tours of the Sounds, as well as kayak rentals for experienced paddlers. The cost is $60 for a one-day guided tour, $450 for a four-day guided tour. A kayak rental costs $35 per day. *1 Russell St., Picton, tel. 03/573–6078.*

Nelson Raft Company has various trips along the Motueka and Buller Rivers, from $28 for two hours to $95 for a full day. Transport to and from Nelson is included. *Lodder La., RD 3, Motueka, tel. 03/546–6212.*

Cycling   **Cycle Treks** offers several escorted cycle tours, from a two-day trip through mountains and lakes ($185) to a seven-day tour of Marlborough Sounds ($1,379). Cyclists are supplied with 21-speed mountain bikes, group size is limited to 10, a backup van is provided, and trips begin and end at either Nelson or Picton. *Box 733, Nelson, tel. 03/547–9122.*

Hiking   **Abel Tasman Enterprises** operates two-, three-, and four-day guided treks along the southern half of the Abel Tasman Track. Travelers spend all nights in comfortable lodges; during the days they explore the coastline and forests of the national park. One day of the four-day trip is spent sea kayaking. Walkers carry only a light day pack, and all meals are provided. The guided walks, which have an "easy" grading, depart each Tuesday and Friday. *Old Cedarman House, Main Rd., Riwaka, tel. 03/528–7801. Cost: $250–$680 adults, $175–$500 children 8–14.*

Alpine Guides offers guided walks on Fox Glacier, the only way to safely experience the ethereal beauty of the ice caves, pinnacles, and crevasses on top of the glaciers. The three-hour walks travel about 2 kilometers (1 mile) up the glacier. The climb is quite strenuous and extremely slippery, despite the metal-pointed staves and spiked boots supplied to hikers. *Box 38, Fox*

Glacier, tel. 03/751–0825. Cost: $32. Tours depart daily at 9:30 and 2.

Dining

Apart from Nelson, gourmet highlights are rare in this area.

$$ Chez Eelco Coffee House. The menu, with its array of steaks, burgers, seafood, and salads, may not try too hard, but it's impossible to ignore this cheerful sidewalk café at the foot of the cathedral on Nelson's main street. In warm weather, the outside tables are recommended; otherwise, try elsewhere. *296 Trafalgar St., Nelson, tel. 03/548–7595. No reservations. Dress: casual. No credit cards. BYOB.*

$$ La Bonne Vie. This attractive seafood restaurant is a favorite
★ with the locals for its lively atmosphere, brisk service, and a menu that pairs the excellent local seafood with delicate sauces. Main courses include salmon fillet with lime and coriander, and a baked flounder stuffed with cottage cheese and almonds. Outdoor seating is available in summer. Vegetarians and steak-eaters are also provided for. *75 Bridge St., Nelson, tel. 03/548–0270. Reservations advised. Dress: casual. AE, DC, MC, V. No lunch.*

$$ Pomeroy's. This smart, popular bistro brings a modern European selection and a touch of class to Nelson's dining scene. The menu offers croissants, focaccia, bagels, and more substantial fare such as lamb stuffed with sun-dried tomatoes and served with a spinach salad. *276 Trafalgar St., Nelson, tel. 03/548–7524. Reservations not required. Dress: casual. AE, DC, MC, V. BYOB. No dinner Mon.–Wed. Closed Sun.*

Lodging

$$$$ Lake Brunner Sporting Lodge. Set on the southern shore of Lake
★ Brunner a 40-minute drive southeast of Greymouth, this sprawling lodge offers excellent fishing, a variety of activities, and a high level of comfort at a price that is relatively low by the standards of New Zealand's elite lodges. Guest rooms are large and well equipped, with the emphasis on comfort rather than opulence. The best rooms are at the front of the house, overlooking the lake. The lodge is known for its "clear water stalking," since the brown trout can be easily seen in the clear waters of the surrounding rivers. Hunting, hiking, boating, mountain biking, and bird-watching are also available. Children are welcome, a rare concession at sporting lodges. *Mitchells, R. D. 1, Kumara, Westland, tel. and fax 03/738–0163. 9 rooms with bath. Facilities: fishing, mountain bikes, nature tours, hunting. Tariff includes all meals. AE, DC, MC, V. Closed July–Sept.*

$$$$ Motueka River Lodge. A recent addition to New Zealand's list of exclusive fishing retreats, this lodge offers tranquillity, marvelous scenery, and a superb standard of comfort. Owned and operated by a former Auckland adman, the lodge is set on a hillside with views across a deer farm to the valley of the Motueka River. Inside, the rustic flavor of the house is accented with folk art collected around the world. Guest rooms are luxuriously equipped but do not have telephones or TVs. The lodge offers a range of activities—tramping, river rafting, golf, tennis—but its specialty is fishing, especially dry-fly fishing for brown trout in the wild river country, which can be reached only by helicopter. The activities are restricted outside the October–April fishing season. *Hwy. 61, Ngatimoti, Motueka, tel. and fax 03/526–8668. 4 rooms with bath. Facilities: fishing, tennis court. Tariff includes all meals. AE, DC, MC, V.*

$$$ **California Guest House.** Set at the end of a garden brimming
★ with flowers, this country charmer is recommended for anyone looking for a bed-and-breakfast with character. Guest rooms are moderately large and comfortable and furnished with antiques. The best rooms are the slightly more expensive Victorian Rose and Everett. Breakfasts include muffins, filter coffee, ham-and-sour-cream omelets, fresh fruit, and pancakes with strawberries and cream. Children are not accommodated. Smoking is not permitted indoors. *29 Collingwood St., Nelson, tel. 03/548–4173. 4 rooms with bath. Tariff includes breakfast. MC, V.*

$$$ **Cambria House.** Built for a sea captain, this 1860 house has been
★ sympathetically modernized to offer B&B accommodations with personality and a dash of luxury. The furnishings mix antiques and floral-print fabrics, and the rooms are very comfortable. Each has an en suite bathroom. The house is located in a quiet street within easy walking distance of the center of Nelson. Children are not accommodated. *7 Cambria St., Nelson, tel. 03/548–4681, fax 03/546–6649. 5 rooms with bath. Tariff includes breakfast. MC, V.*

$$$ **Doone Cottage.** This serene, homey farmstay is set in a pretty part of the Motueka River Valley, within easy reach of five trout streams and a 40-minute drive from Nelson. The hosts are a relaxed, hospitable couple who have lived in this valley for many years. Guest accommodations are comfortable and crowded with family memorabilia. Dinners are likely to feature organically grown vegetables, local meat, and fish fresh from the rivers. Children are not accommodated. *R. D. 1, Motueka, tel. 03/526–8740. 2 rooms with bath. Tariff includes breakfast and dinner. V.*

$$$ **Lake Moeraki Wilderness Lodge.** While these simple motel
★ suites lack the luxurious frills of many other lodges, the natural splendor of the surroundings is the equal of any—and the price is a bargain. The lodge is located on Lake Moeraki, just north of the west coast town of Haast. There are penguins and seals along the beaches, a feisty river on the doorstep, canoes and kayaks for paddling the lake, and forest trails that echo with the sound of rushing streams and birdcalls. The lodge is owned and operated by Dr. Gerry McSweeney and his family. Dr. McSweeney, a leading voice in New Zealand's conservation movement, took over the lodge with the intention of demonstrating that tourism was an economic alternative to logging in the forests of South Westland. His knowledge and feeling for the area contribute much to any visit. *Private Bag, Hokitika, tel. and fax 03/750–0881. 20 rooms with bath. Facilities: nature tours, canoes, fishing, restaurant, bar. AE, DC, MC, V.*

$$ **Ashley Motor Inn.** This motor inn has modern, comfortable rooms, though Greymouth and its surroundings, compared with other parts of the west coast, have little to justify an overnight stop. *70 Tasman St., Greymouth, tel. 03/768–5135. 60 rooms with bath. Facilities: indoor pool, spa, guest laundry, restaurant, bar. AE, DC, MC, V.*

$$ **Westland Motor Inn.** The largest motel in the glacier region, this complex at the center of Franz Josef village offers rooms a cut above the average in size and furnishings. Larger suites with upgraded facilities are also available, and the motor lodge has a choice of dining facilities. *State Hwy. 6, Franz Josef, tel. 02/883–1729. 100 rooms with bath. Facilities: 2 spa pools, guest laundry, restaurant, bar. AE, DC, MC, V.*

Christchurch and Canterbury

The Canterbury region includes both the Canterbury Plains, the flattest land in the country, and the Southern Alps, the steepest. Its capital is New Zealand's third-largest city, Christchurch, which has a population approaching 300,000. Christchurch is the only South Island city with an international airport, and many travelers begin or end their New Zealand journeys here.

Christchurch is something of a paradox—a city under the grand delusion that it is somewhere in southern England. The drive from the airport into town takes you through pristine suburbs of houses lapped by seas of flowers and past playing fields where children flail at one another's legs with hockey sticks. The heart of this pancake-flat city is dominated by church spires; its streets are named Durham, Gloucester, and Hereford; and instead of the usual boulder-leaping New Zealand torrent there bubbles, between banks lined with willows and oaks, the serene River Avon, suitable only for punting. The city is compact and easy to explore, and most of its major sights can be seen on a half-day walking tour.

The big attraction in this region is Mount Cook National Park—a wonderland of snow and ice—but if you have an extra day, the sperm whales that spout off the coast at Kaikoura provide a memorable trip. For a rewarding half-day excursion through delectable country scenery and seascapes, journey out to Akaroa, a pretty little town on a big blue bay.

Important Addresses and Numbers

Tourist Information **Christchurch Visitor Information Centre.** *Worcester St. and Oxford Terr., Christchurch, tel. 03/379–9629. Open weekdays 8:30–5, weekends 8:30–4.*

Mount Cook Visitor Information Centre. *Mount Cook Village, tel. 03/435–1818. Open daily 8–5.*

Emergencies Dial 111 for **fire, police,** or **ambulance** services.

Arriving and Departing

By Plane **Ansett New Zealand** (tel. 03/371–1146) and **Air New Zealand** (tel. 03/379–5200) link Christchurch with cities on both the North and South islands. **Mount Cook Airline** (tel. 03/379–0690) flies from Christchurch to Queenstown and Mount Cook. **Christchurch Airport** is located 10 kilometers (6 miles) northwest of the city. **Avon City Shuttle** buses (tel. 03/379–9999) meet all incoming flights and charge $7 per passenger to city hotels. **CANRIDE** buses operate between the airport and Cathedral Square from 6 AM to 11 PM daily. The fare is $2.40 for adults, $1.20 for children 4–14. A **taxi** to the city costs about $15.

By Car Highway 1 links Christchurch with Kaikoura and Blenheim in the north and Dunedin in the south. Driving time for the 330-kilometer (205-mile) journey between Christchurch and Mount Cook Village is five hours; between Christchurch and Dunedin, 5½ hours.

By Bus **Mount Cook Landline** (tel. 03/343–8085) and **InterCity** (tel. 03/377–0951) operate daily bus services between Christchurch and Dunedin, Mount Cook, Nelson, and Queenstown.

Getting Around

The city of Christchurch is flat and compact, and the best way to explore it is on two legs. It's unlikely that visitors will have occasion to use the public bus system, which is just as well since the once efficient, city-owned system has recently been divided among several different companies and is now a mess. Timetables and maps are unobtainable. The only reliable way to find out whether a bus is going your way is to ask the drivers at the terminal in Cathedral Square. Another option is bicycle. **Trailblazers** hires out mountain bikes for $25 per day. *96 Worcester St., tel. 03/366–6033. Open weekdays 9–5:30, weekends 10–4.*

Guided Tours

Guided walking tours of the city depart daily at 10 and 2 from the red-and-black booth in Cathedral Square. The cost of the two-hour tour is $8 per person.

Punting on the Avon is perfectly suited to the languid motion of Christchurch. Punts with expert boatmen may be hired from the Worcester Street bridge, near the corner of Oxford Terrace, from 10 to 6 in summer and 10 to 4 the rest of the year. The price of a 20-minute trip is $8 per adult, $4 for children under 12.

The **Gray Line** (tel. 03/343–3874) operates a half-day Morning Sights tour ($25) and a full-day tour of Akaroa ($52), both daily at 9 AM. All tours leave from the Christchurch Visitor Information Centre. Children 5–14 pay half fare.

Exploring Christchurch

This is a gentle stroll from the Visitor Centre through the heart of the city. Aim to finish at 1 PM, in time to catch the Wizard in Cathedral Square.

Numbers in the margin correspond to points of interest on the Christchurch map.

❶ From the front door of the Visitor Centre, cross Worcester Street to the statue of **Captain Robert Falcon Scott** (1868–1912), "Scott of the Antarctic," who visited Christchurch during his two Antarctic expeditions. The statue was sculpted by his widow, Kathleen Lady Kennett, and inscribed with his last words, written as he and his party lay dying in a blizzard on their return journey from the South Pole.

❷ Follow the curve of the River Avon past the arched **Bridge of Remembrance.** The bridge was built in memory of the soldiers who crossed the river here from King Edward Barracks, just down Cashel Street, on their way to the battlefields of Europe during the First World War.

❸ A little farther along the riverbank is the white timber **St. Michael and All Saints Anglican Church.** Christchurch was founded in 1850 by the Canterbury Association, a group of leading British churchmen, politicians, and peers who envisioned a settlement that would serve as a model of industry and ideals, governed by the principles of the Anglican faith. The first settlers the Association sent out were known as the "Canterbury Pilgrims," and their churches were a focal point for the whole community. Built in 1872, St Michael's is an outstanding example. One of the bells in the wooden belfry came from England aboard one of the four ships that carried the Canterbury Pilgrims. *Oxford Terr. and Durham St. Open daily noon–2 PM.*

❹ Follow the Avon upstream, cross to the far bank at the next bridge, and turn immediately left along the avenue of chestnuts and silver birches to the **Antigua Boatshed.** Built for the Christchurch Boating Club, this is the only boat shed that remains of the half dozen that once stood along the Avon. Canoes may be hired for short river trips. *Rolleston Ave., tel. 03/366–5885. Single canoes $5 per hr, double $10 per hr. Open daily 9:30–4:30.*

❺ Walk along Rolleston Avenue and turn left at the first gate into the **Botanic Gardens,** a green jewel of woodland and rose gardens that might easily have been transplanted from the home counties of England. *Rolleston Ave., tel. 03/366–1701. Open daily dawn–dusk.*

❻ At the northern end of the gardens is the **Canterbury Museum.** Of special interest here are the reconstruction of an early Christchurch streetscape and the display of Maori artifacts. The Hall of Antarctic Discovery charts the links between the city and the U.S. bases on the frozen continent from the days of Captain Scott; Christchurch is still used as a forward supply de-

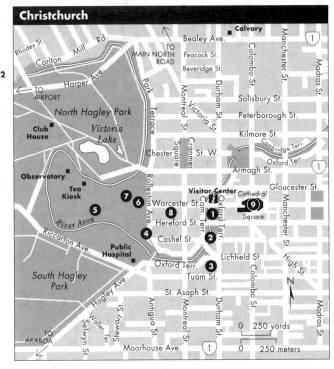

pot for U.S. Antarctic bases. *Rolleston Ave., tel. 03/366–8379. Admission by donation. Open daily 9:30–4:30.*

7 Behind the museum is the **Robert McDougal Art Gallery,** built in the 1930s by a prominent businessman. The gallery has works by 19th-century New Zealand artists and an international collection of painting and sculpture, including two Rodins. *Rolleston Ave., tel. 03/365–0915. Admission free. Open daily 10–4:30.*

From the museum, cross Rolleston Avenue into Worcester
8 Street and turn right into the **Arts Centre.** These Gothic stone buildings once housed Canterbury University, whose most illustrious pupil was Ernest Rutherford (1871–1937). Just past the information desk inside is "Rutherford's Den," the modest stone chamber where the eminent physicist conducted experiments in what was at the time a new field, radioactivity. It was Rutherford who first succeeded in splitting the atom, a crucial step in the harnessing of atomic power. In 1908 Rutherford's work earned him the Nobel prize—not for physics but for chemistry. *Worcester St., tel. 03/366–0989. Open weekdays 8:30–5, weekends 10–4.*

Time out Housed in a mock-Tudor building, **Dux de Lux** is a popular cafeteria-style restaurant that bills itself as "gourmet vegetarian." The blackboard menu offers quiches, crepes, sandwiches, pies, fresh vegetable juices, and a range of crisp salads and breads.

The courtyard is a great spot on a sunny day, especially with a beer from the brewery next door. *41 Hereford St., near Montreal St., tel. 03/366–6919. No credit cards. $*

Continue along Worcester Street and cross the river to **Cathedral Square.** The square is the city's focal point, functioning as a bus terminal and a venue for an arts and crafts market, food stalls, and street musicians, as well as a hangout for the city's unemployed youth. **Christchurch Cathedral,** the city's dominating landmark, was begun in 1864, 14 years after the arrival of the Canterbury Pilgrims, but not consecrated until 1904. Carvings inside commemorate the work of the Anglican missionaries, including Tamihana Te Rauparaha, the son of a fierce and, for the settlers, troublesome Maori chief. Free guided tours begin daily at 11 and 2. For a view across the city to the Southern Alps, climb the 133 steps to the top of the bell tower. The cathedral is known for its boys choir, which can be heard singing evensong at 4:30 Friday, except during school holidays. *Cathedral Sq. Open daily 8:30 AM–9 PM. Admission to tower: $2 adults, $1 children 5–15.*

If it's close to 1 PM when you emerge from the cathedral, look for the bearded gentleman with long hair, who is easy to spot because of the crowd that instantly forms around him. This is **the Wizard,** who offers funny and irreverent dissertations on just about any controversial subject—especially religion, politics, sex, and women's issues. Originally a freelance soapbox orator, the Wizard (whose real name is Ian Channel) became so popular that he is now employed by the city council—one of his frequent targets. *1 PM, Cathedral Sq. No performances May–Oct.*

Shopping

Inside the Christchurch Arts Centre is the **Galleria,** a dozen shops and studios for artisans and craftworkers. The quality of the work, however, is not representative of the finest of New Zealand's craftsmanship. Most of the shops are open 10 to 4; some are closed weekends. Most do not take credit cards. *Worcester St., tel. 03/379–7573.*

Bivouac sells a complete range of outdoor gear and maps. *76 Cashel St., tel. 03/366–3197. Open weekdays 9–5:30, Sat. 10–1.*

Dining

$$$$ **Sign of the Takahe.** Set in a splendid baronial castle that overlooks the city and the Southern Alps from the heights of the Cashmere Hills, this mock gothic restaurant is well known for its game and lobster, the house specialty. The buffet lunch is a less expensive option, but it lacks the stiff white napery, silver service, and candlelit tables that make the dinners magic. The restaurant is a 20-minute drive from the city center. Dinners are heavily booked by Japanese tour groups, and other diners may face long delays. *Dyers Pass and Hackthorne Rds., Cashmere*

Hills, tel. 03/332-4052. Reservations required. Jacket and tie required at dinner. AE, DC, MC, V.

$$ Bardellis. The name says it all—a bar, a deli, and an Italian accent. Stylish and medium loud, this bar/brasserie is where Christchurch's chic crowd comes for marinated octopus salads and Coronas straight from the bottle. The international menu, which changes frequently, is heavy on seafood, salads, pizza, and pasta. Typical dishes are fresh pasta with mussels in a tomato and chili sauce, and grilled chicken focaccia. Steaks and the standard New Zealand rack of lamb also make an appearance. This is a good choice for casual outdoor eating on a warm summer evening. *98 Cashel Mall, tel. 03/353-0001. Reservations advised for dinner. Dress: casual. AE, DC, MC, V.*

$$ Espresso 124. This smart, modern restaurant is a good bet for
★ mid-morning coffee or midnight snacks. Simplicity is the key on a menu that features char-grilled steaks, lamb, and seafood, and salads dressed with olive oil and balsamic vinegar. The restaurant has a high-energy atmosphere generated by the fashionable crowd that frequents it. The river and the heart of the city are both conveniently close. Next door to the restaurant is a lunch deli, which offers inexpensive sandwiches, focaccia, pasta, and savory pies, and a choice of indoor or outdoor dining. *124 Oxford Terr., tel. 03/365-0547. Reservations advised for dinner. Dress: casual but neat. AE, DC, MC, V.*

$$ Lone Star Cafe. Quarterback-size servings of steaks, chicken, ribs, burgers, and french fries are the specialty at this big, pleasant restaurant within a five-minute walk of the city center. *26 Manchester St., tel. 03/365-7086. No reservations. Dress: casual but neat. AE, DC, MC, V. BYOB. No lunch.*

Lodging

$$$$ Parkroyal Christchurch. This plush hotel, in a prime location
★ overlooking Victoria Square and the river, brings a touch of glamour to the city's accommodation scene. The rooms are large, luxurious, and styled in a powder-blue-and-cream color scheme. Be sure to request one overlooking Victoria Square. The hotel is especially well equipped with restaurants and bars. The Canterbury Tales dining room and the Japanese restaurant, Yamagen, are among the city's finest. *Kilmore and Durham Sts., tel. 03/365-7799, fax 03/365-0082. 297 rooms with bath. Facilities: gym, sauna, bicycles, 4 restaurants, 3 bars. AE, DC, MC, V.*

$$ Pacific Park. Rooms at this attractive peach-and-white complex on the northern fringe of the city are marginally better than at the average motel; all were refurbished during 1991–1992. Two-bedroom executive suites are available. Special rates apply on weekends and during winter. The motel is about 2 kilometers (1¼ miles) from the city center. *263 Bealey Ave., tel. 03/379-8660, fax 03/366-9973. 66 rooms with bath. Facilities: restaurant, bar. AE, DC, MC, V.*

$$ Riverview Lodge. This grand Edwardian manor overlooking the
★ Avon is the pick of the bed-and-breakfast accommodation in Christchurch. Completely restored in 1991, it offers superbly

comfortable, historic accommodations and a cooked breakfast at about the same price as a motel room. The best room is the Turret Room, which has access to the front balcony. Children are accommodated by arrangement. The city center is a 15-minute walk along the river. *361 Cambridge Terr., tel. and fax 03/365–2860. 3 rooms with bath. Facilities: canoe, bicycles, golf clubs. Tariff includes breakfast. MC, V.*

$$ **Turret House.** This century-old lodge has comfortable, well-maintained rooms and a friendly atmosphere that makes it a standout among Christchurch's bed-and-breakfast accommodations. All the rooms are different, and prices vary accordingly. The largest, the Apartment, has a lounge room, a separate bedroom, and a kitchen, and could easily sleep four. For a couple, the medium-size rooms offer a good combination of space and value. Despite its location close to a major intersection, noise is not a problem. *435 Durham St., tel. 03/365–3900. 8 rooms with bath. Tariff includes breakfast. AE, DC, MC, V.*

Excursion to Akaroa

Allow at least a half day for this trip to the scenic Banks Peninsula.

Getting There The main route to Akaroa is Highway 75, which leaves the southwest corner of Christchurch as Lincoln Road. The 82-kilometer (50-mile) drive takes about 90 minutes. **Akaroa Tours** (tel. 03/379–9629) operates a shuttle service between the Christchurch Visitor Information Centre and Akaroa; buses depart Christchurch weekdays at 10:30 and 4, Saturday at noon, and Sunday at noon and 6:45; buses depart Akaroa weekdays at 8:20 and 2:20, weekends at 10:30 ($30 adults, $16 children 5–15 round-trip).

Exploring *Numbers in the margin correspond to points of interest on the Canterbury map.*

Dominated by tall volcanic peaks, the **Banks Peninsula**—the knobbly landform that juts into the Pacific Ocean south of Christchurch—has a wonderful coastline indented with small bays where sheep graze almost to the water's edge. Its main ❶ source of fame is the town of **Akaroa,** which was chosen as the site for a French colony in 1838. The first French settlers arrived in 1840 only to find that the British had already established sovereignty over New Zealand by the Treaty of Waitangi. Less than 10 years later, the French abandoned their attempt at colonization, but the settlers remained and gradually intermarried with the local English community. Apart from the street names and a few surnames, there is little sign of a French connection any more, but the village has a splendid setting, and on a sunny day it makes a marvelous trip from Christchurch.

The best way to get the feel of the town is to stroll along the waterfront from the lighthouse to Jubilee Park. The focus of historic interest is the **Akaroa Museum,** which has a display of Maori greenstone and embroidery and dolls dating from the days of the French settlement. The museum includes Langlois-

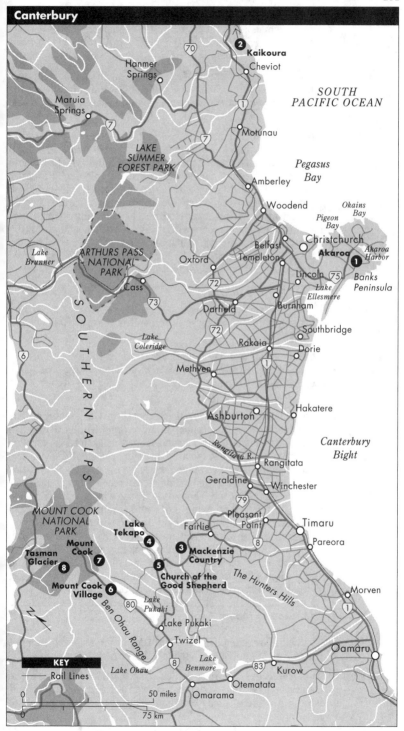

Eteveneaux House, the two-room cottage of an early French settler, which bears the imprint of his homeland in its architecture. *Rue Lavaud and Rue Balguerie, tel. 03/304–7614. Admission: $2.50 adults, 50¢ children 5–15. Open daily 10:30–4:30.*

The picture-book **Church of St. Patrick,** near the museum, was built in 1864 to replace two previous Catholic churches—the first destroyed by fire, the second by tempest. *Rue Pompallier. Open daily 8–5.*

Lodging **Glencarrig.** Buried in greenery on a hillside a three-minute walk
$$ from Akaroa, this charming lodge offers a high standard of B&B
★ accommodations at a reasonable price. Built in 1851, the house is filled with antiques and kilims, which complement its rustic character. The best of the three rooms is the Aylmer, which opens onto the veranda; however, Catherine's Room has an en suite bathroom at no extra charge. The rambling country garden, bordered by a stream with its own waterwheel, is a real delight. This is a nonsmoking house. *7 Percy St., Akaroa, tel. 03/ 304–7008. 1 room with bath, 2 rooms share 1 bath. Facilities: outdoor pool. Tariff includes breakfast. No credit cards.*

Excursion to Kaikoura

This excursion from Christchurch up the coast to Kaikoura requires a full day.

Getting The 190-kilometer (120-mile) drive up Highway 1 takes 3½
There hours. InterCity (tel. 03/72–8297) and Mount Cook Landline (tel. 03/79–0690) operate daily buses between Christchurch and Kaikoura.

Exploring The town of **Kaikoura** lies to the north of Christchurch. The
2 name means "to eat crayfish" in Maori, and while the crayfish sold from roadside stalls are an excellent reason to go, an even better one is the sperm whales that can be seen off the coast in greater numbers than anywhere else on earth. The sperm whale, the largest toothed mammal, can reach a length of 60 feet and a weight of 70 tons. The reason for the whales' concentration in this area is the abundance of squid, their main food, in the deep trench just off the continental shelf, barely a kilometer off Kaikoura. Sperm whales are most likely to be seen between October and August. **Whale Watch Kaikoura Ltd.** (tel. 0800/65–5121) operates three-hour whale-spotting trips at varying times, depending on weather ($85 adults, $50 children 5–15). Even in calm weather, the sea often has a sizable swell.

Excursion to Mount Cook

The 330-kilometer (205-mile) drive from Christchurch straight through to Mount Cook Village takes five hours.

Exploring The **Canterbury Plains,** which ring Christchurch, are the country's finest sheep pastures, as well as its largest area of flat land. But while this may be sheep heaven, the drive south along the plain is mundane by New Zealand standards—until you leave Highway 1 and head toward the Southern Alps.

At Rangitata, on the south bank of the wide Rangitata River, Highway 79 turns inland from Highway 1 and travels toward the distant mountains through the town of Geraldine to Fairlie, where Highway 8 takes up the journey. When the highway crosses Burkes Pass, the woodland is suddenly replaced by the high-country tussock grassland, which is dotted with lupines in the summer months. This is known as the **Mackenzie Country** after James ("Jock") Mackenzie, one of the most intriguing and enigmatic figures in New Zealand history. Mackenzie was a Scot who may or may not have stolen the thousand sheep that were found with him in these secluded upland pastures in 1855. Arrested, tried, and convicted, he made several escapes from jail before he was granted a free pardon nine months after his trial—and disappeared from the pages of history. Regardless of his innocence or guilt, there can be no doubt that Mackenzie was a master bushman and herdsman.

Cradled by snowy mountain peaks, the long, narrow expanse of **Lake Tekapo** is one of the most photographed sights in New Zealand. Its extraordinary milky-turquoise color comes from rockflour—rock ground by glacial action and held in a soupy suspension. On the eastern side of the lakeside power station is the tiny **Church of the Good Shepherd,** which strikes a dignified note of piety in these majestic surroundings. A nearby memorial commemorates the sheepdogs of the area. Before fences were erected around their runs, shepherds would tether dogs at strategic points to stop their sheep from straying.

At Lake Pukaki, Highway 80 turns north between the lake and the Ben Ohau Range, a scenic spectacular that reaches its climax when the road ends at **Mount Cook Village.** The village consists of a visitor center, a grocery store, and a couple of hotels, one of which, the Hermitage, is probably the most famous in the country (*see* Lodging, *below*). Surrounding the village is Mount Cook National Park. The park includes 22 peaks topping the 3,000-meter (10,000-foot) mark, the tallest of which is **Mount Cook—** at approximately 3,684 meters (12,283 feet), the highest peak between Papua New Guinea and the Andes. The mountain was dramatically first scaled in 1894 by three New Zealanders, Fyfe, Graham, and Clarke, just after it was announced that an English climber and an Italian mountain guide were about to attempt the summit. In a frantic surge of national pride, the New Zealand trio resolved to beat them to it, which they did on Christmas Day. Mount Cook is still considered a difficult ascent. In the summer of 1991 a chunk of it broke away, but fortunately there were no climbers in the path of the massive avalanches. High Peak, the summit of the mountain, is now about 20 meters (66 feet) lower, but a much more difficult ascent. Provided the sun is shining, the views are spectacular and the walks are inspiring. If the cloud ceiling is low, however, you may wonder why you came—and the mountain weather is notoriously changeable. Since a lengthy detour is required to reach Mount

Cook Village, it is advisable to contact the Visitor Information Centre (tel. 03/435–1818) to check weather conditions.

Radiating from the visitor center is a network of trails offering walks of varying difficulty, from the 10-minute Bowen Track to the 5½-hour climb to the 1,445-meter (4,818-foot) summit of Mount Sebastapol. Particularly recommended is the walk along the Hooker Valley, a two- to four-hour round-trip. There are frequent ranger-guided walks from the visitor center, with informative talks on flora, fauna, and geology along the way.

The other main activity at Mount Cook is **flightseeing.** From the airfield at Mount Cook Village, helicopters and fixed-wing aircraft make spectacular scenic flights across the Southern Alps. One of the most exciting is the one-hour trip aboard the ski-planes that touch down on the **Tasman Glacier** after a dazzling scenic flight. The 10-minute stop on the glacier doesn't allow time for much more than a snapshot, but the sensation is tremendous. The moving tongue of ice beneath your feet—one of the largest glaciers outside the Himalayas—is 29 kilometers (18 miles) long and up to 600 meters (2,000 feet) thick in places. The intensity of light on the glacier can be dazzling, and sunglasses are a must. Generally, the best time for flights is early morning. During winter the planes drop skiers on the glacier at 3,000 meters (10,000 feet), and they ski down through 13 kilometers (8 miles) of powder snow and fantastic ice formations. With guides, this run is suitable even for intermediate skiers. Skiplane flights cost about $184 for adults, $138 for children under 12; helicopter flights range from $120 to $270. Ski-plane flights are operated by **Mount Cook Line** (tel. 03/435–1848), helicopters by the **Helicopter Line** (tel. 03/435–1801). **Alpine Guides Ltd.** (Box 20, Mount Cook, tel. 03/435–1834) can assist with guides for all treks and ski trips in the national park.

Dining **Panorama Room.** It's the view rather than the food that dazzles
$$$ at the dining room of the Hermitage (*see* Lodging, *below*). The service is efficient and the food well presented, but the meals are vastly more expensive than in the neighboring Alpine Restaurant. Choices from the menu include fillet of sole stuffed with spinach, crayfish thermidor, and hare with a juniper berry and wild mushroom sauce. *Mount Cook Village, tel. 03/435–1809. Reservations required. Jacket required. AE, DC, MC, V. No lunch. Closed Apr.–Sept.*

Lodging **The Hermitage.** Famed for its stupendous mountain views, this
$$$$ rambling hotel is the luxury option at Mount Cook Village. The guest rooms are gradually being remodeled and decorated with green plaid–upholstered wood furniture and brass accents to enhance the rustic-lodge atmosphere. Request one of these renovated rooms. *Mount Cook Village, tel. 03/435–1809, fax 03/ 435–1879. 104 rooms with bath. Facilities: sauna, 3 restaurants, bar. AE, DC, MC, V.*

$$$ **Kimbell Colonial Cottages.** These neat, self-contained cottages are located in the Mackenzie Country north of Fairlie, about midway between Christchurch and Mount Cook. Prettiest of the three is Laurel, a simple timber cottage in the midst of flower beds and sheep pastures. Furnishings in each are simple and appropriately rustic. The surroundings offer trout fishing and deer hunting, and the Kimbell pub is a great source of local color. *RD 17, Fairlie, South Canterbury, tel. 03/658–8170, fax 03/685–8179. 3 cottages with bath. Tariff includes breakfast. AE, MC, V.*

$$$ **Mount Cook Travelodge.** The views here are similar to those at the Hermitage, but the drop in the quality of rooms and facilities is far greater than the drop in price. *Mount Cook Village, tel. 03/627–1809, fax 03/435–1879. 55 rooms with bath. Facilities: restaurant. Tariff includes breakfast. AE, DC, MC, V. Closed early May–Oct. (actual dates vary).*

$$ **Mount Cook Chalets.** These metal-roof A-frames with cooking facilities are the budget option at Mount Cook Village, although in terms of comfort and facilities they are vastly overpriced. Each has two small bedrooms plus a fold-down couch and can sleep up to six. *Mount Cook Village, tel. 03/627–1809, fax 03/435–1879. 18 chalets. AE, DC, MC, V.*

Southland, Otago, and Stewart Island

These areas make up the lower third of the South Island. Most of Southland (to the west) is taken up by two giant national parks, Fiordland and Mount Aspiring. Fiordland, the name generally given to the southwest coast, is a majestic wilderness of rocks, ice, and beech forests, where glaciers have carved deep notches into the coast. The scenic climax of this area—and perhaps of the whole country—is Milford Sound. The cruise on the Sound is a must, but anyone who wants to experience Fiordland in all its raw grandeur should hike along one of the many trails in the area, among them the famous four-day Milford Track, "the finest walk in the world." The accommodation base and adventure center for the region is Queenstown.

To the southeast is the flatter area known as Otago. Its capital, Dunedin, is one of the unexpected treasures of New Zealand: a harbor city of steep streets and prim Victorian architecture, with a royal albatross colony on its doorstep. Invercargill, at the southern tip of this region, is essentially a farm service community that few travelers will find any reason to visit unless they are traveling on to Stewart Island, the southernmost of New Zealand's three main islands.

Queenstown to Milford Sound

Tourist Information **Queenstown Visitor Information Centre.** *Clocktower Centre, Shotover and Camp Sts., tel. 03/442–8238. Open daily 7–7.*

Emergencies Dial 111 for **fire, police,** and **ambulance** services.

Arriving and Departing

By Plane: Queenstown is linked with Auckland, Christchurch, Rotorua, and Wellington by both **Ansett New Zealand** (tel. 03/442–6161) and **Mount Cook Airlines** (tel. 03/442–7650), which also flies several times daily to Mount Cook. **Queenstown Airport** is 9 kilometers (6 miles) east of town. The **Johnston's Shuttle Express** (tel. 03/442–3639) meets all incoming flights and charges $5 per person to hotels in town. The taxi fare is about $13.

By Car: Highway 6 enters Queenstown from the west coast; driving time for the 350-kilometer (220-mile) journey from Franz Josef is eight hours. From Queenstown, Highway 6 continues south to Invercargill—a 190-kilometer (120-mile) distance that takes about three hours to drive. The fastest route from Queenstown to Dunedin is via Highway 6 to Cromwell, south on Highway 8 to Milton, then north along Highway 1, a distance of 280 kilometers (175 miles) that can be covered in five hours.

By Bus: From Queenstown, both **Mount Cook Landline** (tel. 03/442–7650) and **InterCity** (tel. 03/442–8238) operate daily bus service to Christchurch, Mount Cook, and Dunedin. **InterCity** buses operate daily to Nelson via the west coast glaciers.

Guided Tours

Fiordland Travel has a wide choice of fly/drive tour options to Milford and Doubtful sounds from Queenstown. The cost of a one-day bus tour and cruise on Milford Sound is $132, $66 for children 4–14. *Steamer Wharf, Queenstown, tel. 03/442–7500.*

Milford Sound Adventure Tours offers a bus/cruise trip to Milford Sound from Te Anau ($85) that includes a cycling option. From the Homer Tunnel, passengers can leave the bus and coast 13 kilometers (8 miles) down to the Sound on mountain bikes. *Box 134, Te Anau, tel. 03/249–7227. Tour departs Te Anau 7:30 AM.*

The **T.S.S.** *Earnslaw* is a vintage lake steamer that has been restored to brassy, wood-paneled splendor and put to work cruising Lake Wakatipu from Queenstown. A lunch cruise, an afternoon cruise across the lake to a sheep station, and a dinner cruise are available from July to May. *Steamer Wharf, Queenstown, tel. 03/442–7500.*

The **Double Decker** (tel. 03/442–6067) is an original London bus that makes a 2½-hour circuit from Queenstown to Arrowtown and the bungee-jumping platform on the Karawau River. Tours ($25 adults, $10 children 5–15) depart Queenstown daily at 10 and 2 from the Mall and the Earnslaw wharf.

Exploring

Set on the edge of a glacial lake beneath the saw-toothed peaks of the Remarkables, **Queenstown** is the most popular tourist destination on the South Island. Once prized by the Maoris as a source of greenstone, the town boomed when gold was discovered in the Shotover, which quickly became famous as "the richest river in the world." Queenstown could easily have become a ghost town when the gold gave out—except for its location. With ready access to mountains, lakes, rivers, ski fields, and the glacier-carved coastline of Fiordland National Park, Queenstown has become the adventure capital of New Zealand. Its shop windows are crammed with skis, Gore-tex jackets, Asolo walking boots, and Marin mountain bikes. Along Shotover Street, the travel agents offer white-water rafting, jet boating, caving, trekking, heliskiing, parachuting, and bungee jumping.

Numbers in the margin correspond to points of interest on the Southland, Otago, and Stewart Island map.

Despite its marvelous location, Queenstown is basically a comfortable, cosmopolitan base camp. The best views of the town ❶ are from the **Queenstown Gardens,** on the peninsula that encloses Queenstown Bay, and from the heights of Bob's Peak, 435 ❷ meters above the lake. The **Skyline Gondola** whisks passengers to the top for a panoramic view of the town and the Remarkables on the far side of the lake. The summit terminal has a cafeteria, a carvery restaurant, and *Kiwi Magic,* a 25-minute aerial film tour of the country with stunning effects. *Brecon St., Queenstown, tel. 03/442–7540. Gondola: $20 adults, $3 children 4–15, $20 family. Open daily 10–10. Kiwi Magic screens every hr on the hr, 11–9. Admission: $6 adults, $3 children under 15.*

❸ Another gold-mining town, **Arrowtown,** lies 20 kilometers (13 miles) to the northeast. It had long been suspected that there was gold along the Arrow River, and when Edward Fox, an American, was seen selling large quantities of the precious metal in nearby Clyde, the hunt was on. Others attempted to follow the wily Fox back to his diggings, but he kept giving his pursuers the slip, on one occasion even abandoning his tent and provisions in the middle of the night. Eventually a large party of prospectors stumbled on Fox and his team of 40 miners. The secret was out, miners rushed to stake their claims, and Arrowtown was born.

After the gold rush ended, the place was just another sleepy rural town until tourism created a new boom. Lodged at the foot of the steep Crown Range, this atmospheric little village of weathered-timber shop fronts and white stone churches shaded by ancient sycamores was simply too gorgeous to escape the attention of the tour buses. These days it has become a tourist trap, but a highly photogenic one, especially when autumn gilds the hillsides.

In a less visited part of the town is the former **Chinese settlement.** Chinese miners were common on the goldfields in the late 1860s, but local prejudice forced them to live in their own separate enclave. A number of their huts and Ah Lum's Store, one of the few Chinese goldfield buildings to survive intact, have been preserved. *Bush Creek, at the western end of town. Open daily 9–5.*

❹ On Highway 6 not far from Arrowtown is the **Kawarau Suspension Bridge,** where the bungee jumpers make their leaps—a spectacle well worth the short detour. As a promotional stunt, the AJ Hackett company (*see* Sports and the Outdoors, *below*) once offered a free jump to anyone who would jump nude, but there were so many takers that the scheme had to be abandoned.

Southland, Otago, and Stewart Island

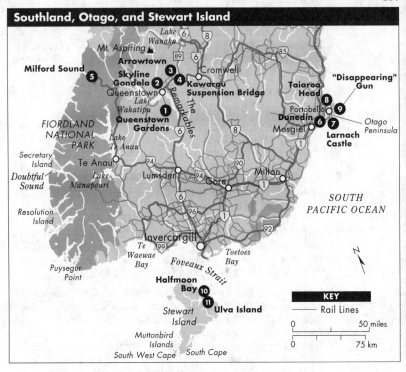

From Queenstown, the road to Milford Sound passes through the town of Te Anau, then winds through deep, stony valleys where waterfalls cascade into mossy beech forests as it enters **Fiordland National Park.** Allow at least 2½ hours for the 119-kilometer (74-mile) journey from Te Anau to Milford Sound. Fiordland, the largest national park in New Zealand, takes its name from the deep sea inlets, or sounds, on its western flank. This is the most rugged part of the country. Parts of the park are so remote that they have never been explored, and visitor activities are mostly confined to a few of the sounds and the walking trails. The nearest services base is the town of Te Anau, which offers a choice of motel, hotel, or motor camp accommodation. For information, contact the Fiordland National Park Visitor Centre (Box 29, Te Anau, tel. 03/249–7921).

⑤ For most visitors, Fiordland's greatest attraction is **Milford Sound**—the sort of overpowering place where photographers run out of film. Hemmed in by walls of rock that rise, almost sheer, from the sea up to 4,000 feet, the 16-kilometer-long (10 mile) inlet was carved by a succession of glaciers as they gouged a track to the sea. Its dominant feature is the 5,560-foot pinnacle of Mitre Peak, which is capped with snow for all but the warmest months of the year. Opposite the peak, Bowen Falls tumbles 520 feet before exploding into the sea. Milford Sound is also spectacularly wet: The average annual rainfall is around 20 feet. An inch an hour for 12 hours straight isn't uncommon, and two days without rain is reckoned to be a drought. In addition to a rain-coat you'll need insect repellent—the sound is renowned for its sandflies. From the road end, a number of cruise boats depart frequently, from about 11 AM to 3 PM, for trips around the sound; expect to pay about $40 for adults, $15 for children. During the summer holiday period it's essential to book ahead. *Fiordland Travel, Steamer Wharf, Queenstown, tel. 03/442–7500.*

Sports and the Outdoors

Bungee Jumping **AJ Hackett Bungy,** the pioneer in the sport, offers two jumps in the area. Kawarau Bridge is the original jump site, 23 kilometers (14 miles) from Queenstown on State Highway 6. Daredevils who graduate from the 143-foot plunge might like to test themselves on the 230-foot Skippers Canyon Bridge. The price is $89 for the Kawarau jump, $145 for Skippers Canyon. *Box 488, Queenstown, tel. 03/442–1177. Open winter, daily 8:30–5; summer, daily 9–7.*

Horse Trekking **Moonlight Stables** offers a choice of full- or half-day rides along the scenic Moonlight Trail, which follows the Shotover Gorge. No previous riding experience is necessary. Transport from Queenstown is provided. *Box 784, Queenstown, tel. 03/442–8892. $45 per person for ½-day trip.*

Jet Boat Rides The **Dart River Jet Boat Safari** is a 2½-hour journey 32 kilometers (20 miles) upstream into the ranges of the Mount Aspiring National Park. This rugged area is one of the most spectacular parts of the South Island, and the trip is highly recommended. Buses depart Queenstown daily at 8, 11, and 2 for the 45-minute ride to the boats. *Box 76, Queenstown, tel. 03/442–9992. Tickets: $99 adults, $55 children 5–16.*

The **Shotover Jet** is the most famous jet boat ride in the country (and one of the most exciting): a high-speed, heart-stopping adventure on which the boat pirouettes within inches of canyon walls. If you want to stay relatively dry, sit beside the driver. The boats are based at the Shotover Bridge, a 10-minute drive from Queenstown, and depart frequently between 8 AM and 7 PM from December to April, 9:30–4:30 the rest of the year. *Shotover River Canyon, Queenstown, tel. 03/442–8570. Tickets: $65 adults, $24 children under 15.*

Rafting **Kawarau Raft Expeditions** offers various half-, full-, and two-day white-water rafting trips in the Queenstown area. For intrepid rafters, the grade-4 to -5 rapids of the Shotover River provide an unforgettable journey, which ends with the rafts shooting through the 560-foot Oxenbridge Tunnel. *35 Shotover St., Queenstown, tel. 03/442–9792. Cost: $94 to $239 per person.*

Dining
$$ **Avanti.** This restaurant at the heart of Queenstown serves better-than-average Italian dishes at a far lower price than most in this resort area. Pastas and pizzas are prominent on the extensive menu, but so are more substantial meals such as venison goulash and several veal dishes. Servings are designed for appetites honed on the mountain slopes. *The Mall, Queenstown, tel. 03/442–8503. No reservations. Dress: casual. AE, DC, MC, V. BYOB.*

$$ **The Continental.** At the lake end of Queenstown Mall, this clublike bar/bistro is a notch up the smartness stakes from most of the town's restaurants. Among the main courses, you might choose the lamb cutlets with a sauce of thyme and mustard or the salmon with a cream, pepper, and dill sauce. The service is professional and friendly. *5 The Mall, Queenstown, tel. 03/442–8372. No reservations. Dress: casual. AE.*

$$ **The Cow.** The pizzas and pastas at this tiny, stone-wall restaurant are some of the best-value meals in town, but the place is immensely popular, so be prepared to wait for a table. A roaring fire provides a cozy atmosphere on chilly evenings, but patrons aren't encouraged to linger over dinner, and you may be asked to share your table. *Cow La., Queenstown, tel. 03/442–8588. No reservations. Dress: casual. MC, V. BYOB. No lunch.*

$ **Gourmet Express.** The food may not reach gourmet standards, but the service is certainly express. A popular breakfast spot, this casual diner at the front of a shopping arcade serves pancakes with maple syrup, eggs any way you want, and heart-starting coffee. A variety of inexpensive grills and burgers is available for lunch and dinner. *Bay Centre, Shotover St., Queenstown, tel. 03/442–9619. No reservations. Dress: casual. AE, DC, MC, V. BYOB.*

$ **Stonewall Cafe.** There is nothing remarkable about the sandwiches, salads, soups, and pasta at this center-of-town café, but the outdoor tables are a good choice for lunch on a sunny day. *The Mall, Queenstown, tel. 03/442–6429. No reservations. Dress: casual. AE, MC, V. Closed weekends.*

Lodging
$$$$
★   **Millbrook Resort.** A 20-minute drive from Queenstown, this glamorous new resort offers luxurious, self-contained accommodation with special appeal for golfers. The resort is an elevated cluster of big, comfortable, two-story villas surrounded by an 18-hole golf course that was designed by New Zealand professional Bob Charles. The villas are decorated in country style: pine tables, textured walls, shuttered windows, and a cream-and-cornflower-blue color scheme. Each has a fully equipped kitchen, laundry facilities, a large lounge/dining room, ski closet, and two bedrooms, each with an en suite bathroom, and the price is a bargain. *Malaghans Rd., Arrowtown, tel. 03/442–1563, fax 03/442–1145. 20 villas with bath. Facilities: golf course, tennis court, bar. AE, DC, MC, V.*

$$$$
★   **Nugget Point.** Poised high above the Shotover River, this modern, stylish retreat offers the finest accommodation in the Queenstown area. Rooms are cozy and luxuriously large, and each has a balcony, a kitchenette, and a bedroom separate from the lounge area. The lodge is a 10-minute drive from Queenstown on the road to Coronet Peak, one of the top ski areas in the country. *Arthurs Point Rd., Queenstown, tel. 03/442–7630, fax 03/442–7308. 35 rooms with bath. Facilities: heated pool, sauna, spa, squash, tennis, bar. AE, DC, MC, V.*

$$$$ **Queenstown Parkroyal.** This modern resort complex sits in a prime position close to town. Guest rooms are large and luxuriously equipped, and about half overlook the steamer wharf. Re-

quest one on the top floor. *Beach St., Queenstown, tel. 03/442–7800, fax 03/442–8895. 139 rooms with bath. Facilities: heated pool, sauna, restaurant, bar. AE, DC, MC, V.*

$$$ **Hulbert House.** Set in tranquil gardens overlooking Queenstown and the lake, this century-old timber home offers a high standard of bed-and-breakfast lodging. Rooms are large and comfortably furnished with antiques. Request one with lake and mountain views. The city center is a five-minute walk away down a very steep hill. *68 Ballarat St., Queenstown, tel. 03/442–8767. 5 rooms with bath. Tariff includes breakfast. MC.*

$$ **Trelawn Place.** Perched on the brink of the Shotover Gorge 3 kilometers (1½ miles) from Queenstown, this stone and timber colonial-style house offers homey comforts and million-dollar views. The most popular of the three spacious guest rooms is the blue room, on the ground floor. For guests who want more privacy and the option of making their own meals, the two-bedroom cottage, which costs $20 more, is recommended. *Box 117, Queenstown, tel. 03/442–9160. 3 rooms with bath, 1 cottage with bath. Facilities: spa. Tariff includes breakfast. No credit cards.*

Dunedin and Otago

Tourist Information
Dunedin Visitor Information Centre. *48 The Octagon, tel. 03/474–3300. Open weekdays 8:30–5, weekends 9–5.*

Emergencies
Dial 111 for **fire, police,** and **ambulance** services.

Arriving and Departing
By Plane: Dunedin is linked with all other New Zealand cities by **Ansett New Zealand** (tel. 03/477–4146) and **Air New Zealand** (tel. 03/477–5769). **Dunedin Airport** lies 20 kilometers (13 miles) south of the city. **Johnston's Shuttle Express** (tel. 03/476–2519), a shuttle service between the airport and the city, meets all incoming flights and charges $10 per person. Taxi fare to the city is about $30.

By Car: Driving time along the 280 kilometers (175 miles) between Queenstown and Dunedin (via Highway 6 and Highway 1) is five hours. The main route between Dunedin and Invercargill is Highway 1—a 3½-hour drive. A slower, scenic alternative is Highway 92 along the coast, which adds another 90 minutes to the journey.

By Bus: Dunedin is served by **Mount Cook Landline** (tel. 03/474–0674) and **InterCity** buses (tel. 03/477–8860).

Guided Tours
Twilight Tours offer various minibus tours of Dunedin and its surroundings, including an afternoon tour that focuses on the albatrosses, penguins, and seals of the Otago Peninsula. The penguin sanctuary is a privately operated venture, and this tour is the only way to see the rare yellow-eyed and little blue penguins. The tour price does not include admission to the albatross colony. *Box 963, Dunedin, tel. 03/474–3300. Cost: $48 adults, $40 children under 15. Tours depart daily at 1:45 from Dunedin Visitor Information Centre.*

Exploring
Numbers in the margin correspond to points of interest on the Southland, Otago, and Stewart Island map.

Clinging to the walls of the natural amphitheater at the western end of Otago Harbour, the South Island's second-largest city, **Dunedin,** combines wildlife, inspiring seascapes, and a handsome Victorian townscape. Dunedin also has a large number of university students, who give the city a vitality far greater than its population of 120,000 might suggest.

Dunedin is the Gaelic name for Edinburgh, and the city's Scottish roots are obvious. It was founded in 1848 by settlers of the Free Church of Scotland, a breakaway group from the Presbyterian Church; today it has the only kilt shop in the country and the only whiskey distillery. A giant statue of Robert Burns presides over the heart of the city. The most compelling attraction for visitors is probably the royal albatross colony at Taiaroa Head, the only place on earth where these majestic seabirds can be seen with relative ease. The city is noted for its rhododendrons, which are at their best in October.

This walking tour begins at the Visitor Information Centre in the **Octagon,** the city's navel. Dunedin prospered mightily during the gold rush of the 1860s. For a while it was the largest city in the country, and the riches of the Otago goldfields are reflected in the bricks and mortar of Dunedin, most notably in the Italianate Municipal Chambers building.

Turn away from the figure of Burns, who sits in front of the cathedral "with his back to the kirk and his face to the pub," and walk down the hill along Stuart Street. On the corner of Dunbar Street you'll come to the late-Victorian **Law Courts.** Above the Stuart Street entrance stands the figure of Justice, scales in hand but without her customary blindfold (though the low helmet she wears probably has the same effect).

On the far side of Anzac Avenue is the **Dunedin Railway Station,** a cathedral to the power of steam. The massive bluestone structure in the Flemish Renaissance style is lavishly decorated with heraldic beasts, coats of arms, nymphs, scrolls, a mosaic floor, and even stained-glass windows portraying steaming locomotives. This extravagant building earned its architect, George Troup, the nickname "Gingerbread George" from the people of Dunedin, and a knighthood from the king. The station has far outlived the steam engine, and for all its magnificence it receives few trains these days. *Open daily 7–6.*

Walk away from the front of the station into High Street; on the corner of Cumberland Street stands the **Early Settlers Museum.** The museum preserves an impressive collection of artifacts, from the years when this was a whaling station to the days of the early Scottish settlers to the prosperous gold-rush era of the late 19th century. *220 Cumberland St., tel. 03/477–5052. Admission: $4 adults, children under 15 free. Open weekdays 10–5, weekends 1–5.*

Overlooking the museum is the spire of the **First Presbyterian Church,** perhaps the finest example of a Norman Gothic building the country. Turn into Burlington Street and walk to the left of the church, turn left into Moray Place, and cross the Octagon into George Street. Turn left into Pitt Street and left again at Royal Terrace to **Olveston.** This 35-room Jacobean-style mansion was built in 1904–1906 for David Theomin, a wealthy businessman and patron of the arts, who amassed a handsome collection of antiques and contemporary furnishings. The house and its furnishings are undoubtedly a treasure from an elegant age, but apart from some paintings collected by Theomin's daughter there is very little in it to suggest that it's in New Zealand. Even the oak staircase and balustrade were prefabricated in England. The one-hour guided tour is recommended. *42 Royal Terr., tel. 03/477–3320. Admission: $9 adults, $3 children 5–15. Open daily 9–5. Tours daily 9:30, 10:45, 12, 1:30, 2:45, 4.*

The Otago Peninsula The main areas of interest on the claw-shaped peninsula that extends northeast from Dunedin are the albatross colony and Larnach Castle. On the return journey to Dunedin, the Highcliff Road, which turns inland at the village of Portobello, is a scenic alternative to the coastal Portobello Road.

❼ Set high on a hilltop with commanding views from its battlements, **Larnach Castle** is the grand baronial fantasy of William Larnach, an Australian-born businessman and politician. The castle was a vast extravagance even in the free-spending atmosphere of the gold rush. Larnach imported an English craftsman to carve the ceilings, which took 12 years to complete, and the solid marble bath, the marble fireplaces, tiles, glass, and even much of the wood came from Europe. The mosaic in the foyer depicts Larnach's family crest and the modest name he gave to his stately pile: The Camp. Larnach rose to a prominent position in the New Zealand government of the late 1800s, but in 1898, beset by a series of financial disasters and possible marital problems, he committed suicide in Parliament House. (According to one romantic version, Larnach's third wife, whom he married at an advanced age, ran off with his eldest son; devastated, he shot himself.) A café in the castle ballroom serves Devonshire teas and light snacks. *Camp Rd., tel. 03/476–1302. Admission: $9.50 adults, $3.50 children 5–15. Open daily 9–5.*

❽ **Taiaroa Head,** the eastern tip of the Otago Peninsula, is the site of a breeding colony of royal albatrosses. Among the largest birds in the world, with a wingspan of 11 feet, the albatrosses can take off only from steep slopes with the help of a strong breeze. Outside of Taiaroa Head and the Chatham Islands to the east, they are found only on windswept islands deep in southern latitudes, remote from human habitation. The colony is open for viewing from October through August, with the greatest number of birds present shortly after the young hatch around the end of January. Between March and September the parents leave the fledglings in their nests while they gather food for them. In September the young birds fly away, returning about eight years later to start their own breeding cycle. From the visitor center, groups follow a steep trail up to the Albatross Observatory, from which the birds may be seen through narrow windows. They are only rarely seen in flight. Access to the colony is strictly controlled, and visitors must book in advance. The tour takes about an hour. *Taiaroa Head, Dunedin, tel. 03/478–0499. Admission: $18 adults, $9 children 5–16. Open mid-Nov.–Aug., daily 10:30–4.*

❾ In the same area as the colony is the **"Disappearing" Gun,** a six-inch artillery piece installed during the Russian Scare of 1888. When fired, the recoil would propel the gun back into its pit, where it could be reloaded out of the line of enemy fire. The gun has been used in anger only once, when it was fired across the bow of a fishing boat that had failed to observe correct procedures before entering the harbor during World War II. *Admission: $8 adults, $4 children 5–15. Combined albatross colony/gun admission: $18 adults, $9 children. Open 10:30–4.*

Dining **Bell Pepper Blues.** One of the country's most respected chefs,
$$$$ Michael Clydesdale, combines esoteric ingredients with recipes drawn from both the Pacific and the Mediterranean to produce food with flair. Blue cod comes baked in a parcel of rice paper, venison is roasted with an onion and orange bourbon *jus*, and steak tournedos come with wasabi and sesame seed butter. The setting, inside a converted pub, is casual and attractive. *474 Princes St., Dunedin, tel. 03/474–0973. Reservations advised. Dress: casual. AE, DC, MC, V. No lunch Mon., Tues., and Sat. Closed Sun.*

$$$$ **95 Filleul.** New owner Adrienne Molloy has breathed new life into one of Dunedin's long-standing favorites with an imaginative menu that makes the most of the local game and seafood. The modern, international menu includes grilled cervena venison with a tangy blueberry sauce, as well as lamb fillets with a kumera (sweet potato) and polenta timbale. *95 Filleul St., Dunedin, tel. 03/477–7233. Reservations advised. Dress: casual. AE, DC, MC, V. No lunch. Closed Sun.*

$$$ **Harbour Lights.** Poised on the shores of the Otago Peninsula
★ overlooking the harbor, this restaurant is an exception to the rule that good food and good views don't usually coincide. Fish and game dishes are prominent on a menu that features such main courses as smoked South Island salmon with fresh herbs, wild boar schnitzel, and grilled grouper steak with a béarnaise sauce. The balcony is a favorite spot for summer dining. *494 Portobello Rd., MacAndrew Bay, tel. 03/476–1604. Reservations advised. Dress: casual but neat. AE, DC, MC, V. No lunch Mon. and Tues.*

$$ **Palms Cafe.** Vegetarians are especially well served at this casual, popular restaurant. The menu sometimes includes a casserole of olives, feta cheese, mushrooms, and tomatoes, and a Greek pastry roll filled with spinach and feta. Nonvegetarian mains may include lamb kebabs with peanut sauce, a whole sole with garlic sauce, and fillet of lamb with a green peppercorn glaze. The restaurant has a no-smoking policy. *84 Lower High St., Dunedin, tel. 03/477–6534. Reservations advised. Dress: casual but neat. AE, DC, MC, V. BYOB. No lunch.*

Lodging **Cargills Motor Inn.** In a convenient location close to the city cen-
$$ ter, this motor inn offers superior motel-style rooms as well as

two-bedroom family suites. Reduced rates apply Friday to Sunday nights. *670 George St., Dunedin, tel. 03/477–7983, fax 03/ 477–8098. 51 rooms with bath. Facilities: bar, restaurant. AE, DC, MC, V.*

$ **Larnach Lodge.** A modern timber building on the grounds of Larnach Castle, 19 kilometers (12 miles) from Dunedin, the lodge offers comfortable motel suites with marvelous views. Dinners are available in the castle by arrangement; otherwise the nearest restaurant is a 10-minute drive away. Budget rooms with shared facilities are available in the converted coach house. *Camp Rd., Otago Peninsula, Dunedin, tel. 03/476–1302. 27 rooms with bath. AE, DC, MC, V.*

$ **Magnolia House.** Overlooking the city of Dunedin in a prestige suburb, this gracious B&B offers atmospheric accommodations. The spacious guest rooms are furnished with antiques, and the house is surrounded by a pretty garden that includes native bushland. The house has a no-smoking policy. Dinners are available by arrangement, and children are welcome. *18 Grendon St., Maori Hill, Dunedin, tel. 03/467–5999. 3 rooms share 1 bathroom. Tariff includes breakfast. No credit cards.*

Stewart Island

Tourist Information Stewart Island Visitor Information Centre. *Halfmoon Bay, tel. 03/219–1218. Open weekdays 8–4:30.*

Emergencies Dial 111 for **fire, police,** and **ambulance** services.

Arriving and Departing **By Plane: Southern Air** (tel. 03/218–9129) operates several flights daily between Invercargill and Halfmoon Bay. The round-trip fare for the 20-minute flight is $118 for adults. One child under 14 is allowed to fly free of charge with each adult. For unaccompanied children under 14, the fare is $59. The free baggage allowance is 15 kilograms (33 pounds) per passenger.

By Boat: Stewart Island Marine (tel. 03/212–7660) operates a ferry service between the island and the port of Bluff, the port for Invercargill. The one-way fare is $37 for adults, $18.50 for children under 15. Ferries depart Bluff on Monday, Wednesday, and Friday at 9:30 and 3:30 between May and November, daily at 9:30 and 5 during the rest of the year.

Guided Tours For information on fishing trips, bird-watching trips to Ulva Island, and boat trips around Paterson Inlet, contact **Stewart Island Travel** (Box 26, Stewart Island, tel. 03/219–1269).

Exploring *Numbers in the margin correspond to points of interest on the Southland, Otago, and Stewart Island map.*

The third and most southerly of New Zealand's main islands, Stewart Island is separated from the South Island by the 24-kilometer (15-mile) Foveaux Strait. Even by New Zealand standards, Stewart Island is remote, raw, and untouched. Electricity is a recent innovation, roads total about 20 kilometers (13 miles), and apart from the settlement of **Halfmoon Bay** on Paterson Inlet, the place is practically uninhabited. For most visitors, the attractions are its seclusion, its relaxed way of life, and—despite a once-busy sawmilling industry—its untouched quality.

The island, which covers some 1,700 square kilometers (650 square miles) and measures about 64 kilometers (40 miles) from north to south and about the same distance across at its widest point, forms a rough triangle, with a deep indentation, Paterson Inlet, on its eastern flank. On the coastline, sharp cliffs rise from a succession of sheltered bays and beaches; in the interior, forested hills rise gradually toward the western side of the island. Seals and penguins frequent the coast, and the island's prolific birdlife includes a number of species rarely seen in any other part of the country. One of the best spots for bird-watching is **Ulva Island,** a one-hour launch trip from Halfmoon Bay (*see* Guided Tours, *above*).

Outdoor Activities A network of walking trails has been established on the northern half of the island, leaving the south as a wilderness area. A

Hiking popular trek is the **Northern Circuit,** a 10-day walk from Halfmoon Bay that circles the north coast and then cuts through the interior to return to its starting point. The island's climate is notoriously changeable, and walkers should be prepared for rain and mud. For information on walks, contact the **Department of Conservation** (Main Rd., Halfmoon Bay, tel. 03/219–1218).

Hunting Another major activity for visitors to the island is hunting. Red deer and Virginia or whitetail deer were introduced earlier this century and may be hunted all year round. Hunting permits are available from the Department of Conservation office at Halfmoon Bay (*see* Hiking, *above*).

Dining and Lodging **Stewart Island Lodge.** The most luxurious accommodation on the island offers comfortable, centrally heated suites with private

$$$$ baths. The focal points of life at the lodge are the guest lounge and the dining room, both of which offer expansive views across the bay. The owners have a game fishing launch and can arrange scenic tours of the island. Local seafood is a specialty on the dinner menu. *Halfmoon Bay, Nichol Rd., Stewart Island, tel. and fax 03/219–1085. Tariff includes all meals. 4 rooms with bath. AE, DC, MC, V.*

$ **Rakiura Motel.** Within easy walking distance of Halfmoon Bay, the Rakiura offers standard motel units that sleep up to six. *Horseshoe Bay Rd., Halfmoon Bay, tel. 03/219–1096. 5 rooms with bath. MC.*

6 Adventure Vacations

By David McGonigal

Visitors miss an important element of New Zealand if they do▮ get away from the cities to explore the magnificient outdoo▮ The mountains in this green, clean land are made for hiking a▮ climbing; the sparsely populated roads for bicycling; the rive▮ for rafting. The rugged coastline looks wonderful from the de▮ of a small vessel or, even closer to the water, a sea kayak. A▮ this is the country that invented jet-boating.

Adventure vacations are commonly split into soft and hard a▮ ventures. A hard adventure requires a substantial degree▮ physical participation, although you usually don't have to▮ perfectly fit; in a few cases, prior experience is a prerequisite.▮ soft adventures the destination rather than the means of trav▮ is often what makes it an adventure. With most companies, t▮ adventure guides' knowledge of flora and fauna—and love of t▮ bush—is matched by a level of competence that ensures yo▮ safety even in dangerous situations. The safety record of adve▮ ture operators is very good. Visitors should be aware, howeve▮ that most adventure-tour operators require participants to si▮ waiver forms absolving the company of responsibility in t▮ event of an accident or a problem. Courts normally uphold su▮ waivers except in cases of significant negligence.

Far more adventure-tour operators exist than can be listed▮ this chapter. Most are small and receive little publicity outsi▮ their local areas, so contact the relevant tourist office if you ha▮ a specific area of interest. Here are the addresses of the maj▮ adventure-tour operators mentioned in the following pages:

Abel Tasman National Park Enterprises (Old Cederman Hous▮ Main Rd., Riwaka, Motueka R. D. 3, Nelson, tel. 03/528–780▮ **Adventure Center** (1311 63rd St., #200, Emeryville, CA 946▮ USA, tel. 510/654–1879); **Alpine Guides** (Box 20, Mt. Cook, t▮ 03/435–1834); **Alpine Recreation Canterbury** (Box 75, La▮ Tekapo, tel. 03/680–6736); **Danes Shotover Rafts** (Corn▮ Shotover and Camp Sts., Queenstown, tel. 03/442–731▮ **Hollyford Tourist and Travel Company** (Box 205, Waikaitip▮ Central Otago, tel. 03/442–3760); **Karavan Adventure Treks** (1▮ Harris Crescent, Christchurch, tel. 03/352–2177); **Lan▮ borough River Expeditions** (Box 410, Queenstown, tel. 03/44▮ 3630); **New Zealand Pedaltours** (Box 37-575, Parnell, Aucklar▮ tel. 09/302–0968); **New Zealand Travel Professionals** (Box 2▮ Auckland, tel. 09/377–0761); **Ocean River Adventure Compa▮** (Main Rd., Marahau Beach, R. D. 2, Motueka, tel. 03/527–826▮ **The Rafting Company** (Box 2392, Rotorua, tel. 073/480–23▮ **Routeburn Walk Ltd.** (Box 568, Queenstown, tel. 03/442–820▮ **Southern Heritage Expeditions** (Box 22, Waikari, North Cant▮ bury, tel. 03/314–4393); **Te Anau Travelodge** (Box 185, Te Ana▮ tel. 03/249–7411); **Wilderness Expeditions** (3rd Floor, 441 Ke▮ St., Sydney, NSW 2000, tel. 02/264–3721).

Bicycling

Bicycles may seem an impractical way to travel, but cycling▮ actually an excellent way to explore a small region, allowing y▮

to cover more ground than on foot and observe far more than from the window of a car or bus. And while a bike may not be much fun in the fumes of city traffic, riding down quiet country lanes is a great way to relax and get fit at the same time. Cycling rates as a hard adventure because of the level of exercise.

Season: October–March.
Locations: Both islands.
Cost: From $1,600 for eight days to $4,500 for 19 days, including accommodations, meals, and support vehicle. Bikes can be rented for about $15 a day.
Tour Operators: Adventure Center, New Zealand Pedaltours.

The combination of spectacular scenery and quiet roads is ideal for cycle holidays. Traditionally the South Island, with its central alpine spine, has been more popular, but Auckland is where most people arrive, and the North Island has enough curiosities—the hot mud pools of sulfurous Rotorua, the Waitaimo Caves, and the old gold-mining area of the Coromandel Peninsula—to fill each day. The average daily riding distance is about 60 kilometers (37 miles), and the support vehicle is large enough to accommodate all riders and bikes if circumstances so demand. The rides on the South Island extend from the ferry port of Picton to picturesque Queenstown, the center of a thriving adventure day-trip industry.

Canoeing and Sea Kayaking

Unlike rafting, where much of the thrill comes from negotiating white water, canoeing involves paddling down these gentle stretches of river. The enjoyment comes from the relaxing pace, the passing scenery, and the constant, comforting murmur of the river. Canoeing is soft adventure—and so is sea kayaking, its oceanic equivalent.

Season: December–May.
Location: Abel Tasman National Park, South Island.
Cost: From $85 for one day to $370 for four days, including kayaks, tents, cooking and camping equipment, and park permits.
Tour Operator: Ocean River Adventure Company.

This tour along the sheltered waters of the Abel Tasman National Park provides a waterline view of a beautiful coastline. It allows you to explore otherwise inaccessible golden-sand beaches and remote islands and to meet fur seals on their home surf. When wind conditions permit, paddles give way to small sails, and the kayaks are propelled home by an onshore breeze.

Cross-Country Skiing

Although cross-country skiing doesn't offer the same adrenaline rush as downhill skiing, there are no expensive lift tickets to buy—your legs must do the work. While the crowds build up on the groomed slopes, cross-country skiers have a chance to get away from the hordes and experience the unforgettable sensation of skiing through forests of eucalyptus trees, with their spreading branches, pale leaves, and impressionistic bark patterns. Cross-country skiing is hard adventure, even though many tours are arranged so that skiers stay in lodges every night. The joy of leaving the first tracks across new snow and the pleasure afforded by the unique scenery of the snowfields is tempered by the remarkable fatigue that your arms and legs feel at the end of the day.

Season: June–September.
Location: Mt. Cook.
Cost: $1,550 for seven days, including guide fees, accommodations, food, transport, and aircraft access.
Tour Operator: Alpine Guides.

Mt. Cook and its attendant Murchison and Tasman glaciers offer wonderful ski touring, with terrains to suit all levels of skiers. The tour commences with a flight to the alpine hut that becomes your base; from here the group sets out each day for skiing and instruction.

Hiking

Season: October–March for high-altitude walks, year-round for others.
Location: South Island.
Cost: From $425 for four days to $2,500 for 13 days. The climbing school costs $1,525 for seven days (including aircraft access, meals, accommodation, and transport).
Tour Operators: Abel Tasman National Park Enterprises, Adventure Center, Alpine Guides, Alpine Recreation Canterbury, Hollyford Tourist and Travel Company, Karavan Adventure Treks, New Zealand Travel Professionals, Routeburn Walk Ltd., Te Anau Travelodge, Wilderness Expeditions.

If it seems from the list above that every New Zealand company is involved in trekking, wait till you see the trails—particularly in the peak months of January and February; they can be crowded enough to detract from the nature experience. An advantage of a guided walk is that companies have their own tent camps or huts, with such luxuries as hot showers—and cooks. For the phobic, it's worth mentioning one very positive feature: New Zealand has no snakes or predatory animals.

The most famous New Zealand walk, the Milford Track—a four-day trek through Fiordland National Park—covers a wide variety of terrains, from forests to high passes, lakes, a glowworm grotto, and the spectacle of Milford Sound itself. There are other walks in the same area: the Greenstone Valley (three days) and the Routeburn Track (three days)—combined they form the Grand Traverse—and the Hollyford Valley (five days). For something different, the three- to six-day walks along the beaches of Queen Charlotte Sound and through forests in the Abel Tasman National Park (northwest South Island) are very popular, relatively easy, and well suited to family groups; your pack is carried for you, and you stay in lodges. Karavan Adventure Treks has a series of unusual walks throughout the South

Island. One of the most appealing is a four-day trip in Nelson Lakes National Park, near the top of the island; for two nights your base is the Angelus Basin Hut, spectacularly located beside a beautiful mountain lake beneath towering crags. Another option is the Alpine Recreation Canterbury 13-day minibus tour of the South Island, with one-day walks along the way; it provides an extensive and scenic cross section, but it misses the magic of completing a long single walk.

For the very enthusiastic, Alpine Guides has a world-renowned seven-day course on the basics of mountain climbing, in the area of Mt. Cook, the highest point in the New Zealand Alps. There is also a 10-day technical course for experienced climbers. New Zealand is the home of Sir Edmund Hillary, who, with Tenzing Norgay, made the first ascent of Mt. Everest; clearly the country has a fine mountaineering tradition, and Alpine Guides is the nation's foremost training school.

Rafting

The exhilaration of sweeping down into the foam-filled jaws of a rapid is always tinged with fear—white-water rafting is, after all, rather like being tossed into a washing machine. While this sort of excitement appeals to many people, the attraction of rafting in New Zealand encompasses much more. As you drift downriver during the lulls between the white water, it's wonderful to sit back and watch the wilderness unfold, whether it's stately river gums overhanging the stream, towering cliffs, or forests of eucalyptus on the surrounding slopes. Rafting means camping by the river at night, drinking billy tea brewed over the campfire, going to sleep with the sound of the stream in the background, or sighting an elusive platypus at dawn. The juxtaposition of action and serenity gives rafting an enduring appeal that leads most who try it to seek out more rivers with more challenges. Rivers here are smaller and trickier than the ones used for commercial rafting in North America, and rafts usually hold only four to six people. The rafting companies provide all rafting and camping equipment— you only need clothing that won't be damaged by water (cameras are carried in waterproof barrels), a sleeping bag (in some cases), and sunscreen. Rafting qualifies as a hard adventure.

Season: Mainly October–May.
Location: North and South Islands.
Cost: From $70 for one day to $675 for three days (with helicopter set-down), including all equipment (wetsuits, helmets, footwear).
Tour Operators: Danes Shotover Rafts, Landsborough River Expeditions, The Rafting Company.

There are several rafting rivers on both islands of New Zealand. Near Rotorua, the Rangitaiki offers exciting grade-4 rapids and some good scenery. Nearby, the Kaituna River has the highest raftable waterfall in the world: a 7-meter (21-foot) free fall. On the South Island, the great majority of activity centers on

Queenstown; the most popular spot here is the upper reaches of the Shotover beyond the tortuous Skippers Canyon. In winter the put-in site for the Shotover is accessible only by helicopter, and wet suits are essential year-round, as the water is very cold. Some of the rapids are grade 5—the highest before a river becomes unraftable.

To combine the thrill of white water with a wilderness experience, take a two-day trip down the Landsborough River, which rises in Mt. Cook National Park and flows past miles of virgin forest and into some very exciting rapids.

Sailing

Sailing is an excellent way to take in the varied coastline of New Zealand. While the image of beautiful people sipping gin slings and watching the sunsets in the tropics may be a little exaggerated, your role as a passenger on a commercial sailing vessel can hardly be described as strenuous. You are likely to participate in the sailing of the vessel more than you would on a regular cruise line, but for all intents and purposes this is a soft adventure in paradise.

Season: Year-round.
Location: South Island
Cost: From $1,240 for five days in the Doubtful Sound area to $2,000 for eight days in Fiordland National Park to $3,850–$10,350 for 11–18 days cruising the sub-Antarctic islands of Australia and New Zealand.
Tour Operators: New Zealand Travel Professionals, Southern Heritage Expeditions.

Southern Heritage Expeditions uses the eight-cabin, 65-foot MV *Affinity*, a diesel-powered New Zealand–built vessel, to take visitors to otherwise inaccessible parts of the coastline. From June to August it explores the deeply indented shores of Fiordland National Park. In September and October it heads for the top of the South Island and the warmer waters of Marlborough Sounds—a maze of waterways and islands of incredible beauty. Throughout the summer months (December–January), Southern Heritage Expeditions operates a 140-foot vessel, the MV *Pacific Ruby*, down to the sub-Antarctic islands of Australia and New Zealand. On these stark, rocky outcrops can be seen the ruins of early attempts at settlement and animals such as the royal albatross, Hookers sea lion, elephant seal, and penguins.

New Zealand Travel Professionals offers two cruises along the shores of the South Island aboard the 15-meter (50-foot) *Waverley*. Accommodations for eight passengers are on a twin-share basis. A five-day cruise goes around Doubtful Sound.

Index

Personal Itinerary

Departure *Date*

Time

Transportation

Arrival *Date*   *Time*

Departure *Date*   *Time*

Transportation

Accommodations

Arrival *Date*   *Time*

Departure *Date*   *Time*

Transportation

Accommodations

Arrival *Date*   *Time*

Departure *Date*   *Time*

Transportation

Accommodations

Personal Itinerary

Arrival *Date*   *Time*

Departure *Date*   *Time*

Transportation

Accommodations

Arrival *Date*   *Time*

Departure *Date*   *Time*

Transportation

Accommodations

Arrival *Date*   *Time*

Departure *Date*   *Time*

Transportation

Accommodations

Arrival *Date*   *Time*

Departure *Date*   *Time*

Transportation

Accommodations

Personal Itinerary

Arrival *Date*   *Time*

Departure *Date*   *Time*

Transportation

Accommodations

Arrival *Date*   *Time*

Departure *Date*   *Time*

Transportation

Accommodations

Arrival *Date*   *Time*

Departure *Date*   *Time*

Transportation

Accommodations

Arrival *Date*   *Time*

Departure *Date*   *Time*

Transportation

Accommodations

Personal Itinerary

Arrival *Date*   *Time*

Departure *Date*   *Time*

Transportation

Accommodations

Arrival *Date*   *Time*

Departure *Date*   *Time*

Transportation

Accommodations

Arrival *Date*   *Time*

Departure *Date*   *Time*

Transportation

Accommodations

Arrival *Date*   *Time*

Departure *Date*   *Time*

Transportation

Accommodations

Addresses

Name	*Name*
Address	*Address*
Telephone	*Telephone*
Name	*Name*
Address	*Address*
Telephone	*Telephone*
Name	*Name*
Address	*Address*
Telephone	*Telephone*
Name	*Name*
Address	*Address*
Telephone	*Telephone*
Name	*Name*
Address	*Address*
Telephone	*Telephone*
Name	*Name*
Address	*Address*
Telephone	*Telephone*
Name	*Name*
Address	*Address*
Telephone	*Telephone*
Name	*Name*
Address	*Address*
Telephone	*Telephone*

Addresses

Name	*Name*
Address	*Address*
Telephone	*Telephone*
Name	*Name*
Address	*Address*
Telephone	*Telephone*
Name	*Name*
Address	*Address*
Telephone	*Telephone*
Name	*Name*
Address	*Address*
Telephone	*Telephone*
Name	*Name*
Address	*Address*
Telephone	*Telephone*
Name	*Name*
Address	*Address*
Telephone	*Telephone*
Name	*Name*
Address	*Address*
Telephone	*Telephone*
Name	*Name*
Address	*Address*
Telephone	*Telephone*

Addresses

Name _____ | *Name* _____

Address _____ | *Address* _____

_____ | _____

Telephone _____ | *Telephone* _____

Name _____ | *Name* _____

Address _____ | *Address* _____

_____ | _____

Telephone _____ | *Telephone* _____

Name _____ | *Name* _____

Address _____ | *Address* _____

_____ | _____

Telephone _____ | *Telephone* _____

Name _____ | *Name* _____

Address _____ | *Address* _____

_____ | _____

Telephone _____ | *Telephone* _____

Name _____ | *Name* _____

Address _____ | *Address* _____

_____ | _____

Telephone _____ | *Telephone* _____

Name _____ | *Name* _____

Address _____ | *Address* _____

_____ | _____

Telephone _____ | *Telephone* _____

Name _____ | *Name* _____

Address _____ | *Address* _____

_____ | _____

Telephone _____ | *Telephone* _____

Name _____ | *Name* _____

Address _____ | *Address* _____

_____ | _____

Telephone _____ | *Telephone* _____

Notes

Notes

Escape to ancient cities and exotic

islands *with CNN Travel Guide, a*

wealth of valuable advice. Host Valerie Voss will take you

to all of your favorite destinations,

including those off the beaten path.

Tune into your passport to the world.

CNN TRAVEL GUIDE
SATURDAY 10:00 PMpt   SUNDAY 8:30 AMet

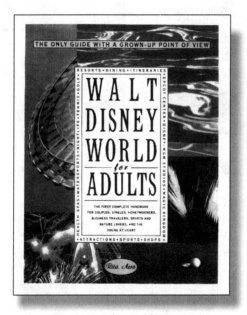

Fodor's Travel Guides

Available at bookstores everywhere, or call 1–800–533–6478, 24 hours a day.

U.S. Guides

Alaska

Arizona

Boston

California

Cape Cod, Martha's Vineyard, Nantucket

The Carolinas & the Georgia Coast

Chicago

Colorado

Florida

Hawaii

Las Vegas, Reno, Tahoe

Los Angeles

Maine, Vermont, New Hampshire

Maui

Miami & the Keys

New England

New Orleans

New York City

Pacific North Coast

Philadelphia & the Pennsylvania Dutch Country

The Rockies

San Diego

San Francisco

Santa Fe, Taos, Albuquerque

Seattle & Vancouver

The South

The U.S. & British Virgin Islands

USA

The Upper Great Lakes Region

Virginia & Maryland

Waikiki

Walt Disney World and the Orlando Area

Washington, D.C.

Foreign Guides

Acapulco, Ixtapa, Zihuatanejo

Australia & New Zealand

Austria

The Bahamas

Baja & Mexico's Pacific Coast Resorts

Barbados

Berlin

Bermuda

Brittany & Normandy

Budapest

Canada

Cancún, Cozumel, Yucatán Peninsula

Caribbean

China

Costa Rica, Belize, Guatemala

The Czech Republic & Slovakia

Eastern Europe

Egypt

Euro Disney

Europe

Florence, Tuscany & Umbria

France

Germany

Great Britain

Greece

Hong Kong

India

Ireland

Israel

Italy

Japan

Kenya & Tanzania

Korea

London

Madrid & Barcelona

Mexico

Montréal & Québec City

Morocco

Moscow & St. Petersburg

The Netherlands, Belgium & Luxembourg

New Zealand

Norway

Nova Scotia, Prince Edward Island & New Brunswick

Paris

Portugal

Provence & the Riviera

Rome

Russia & the Baltic Countries

Scandinavia

Scotland

Singapore

South America

Southeast Asia

Spain

Sweden

Switzerland

Thailand

Tokyo

Toronto

Turkey

Vienna & the Danube Valley

Special Series

Fodor's Affordables
Caribbean

Europe

Florida

France

Germany

Great Britain

Italy

London

Paris

Fodor's Bed & Breakfast and Country Inns Guides
America's Best B&Bs

California

Canada's Great Country Inns

Cottages, B&Bs and Country Inns of England and Wales

Mid-Atlantic Region

New England

The Pacific Northwest

The South

The Southwest

The Upper Great Lakes Region

The Berkeley Guides
California

Central America

Eastern Europe

Europe

France

Germany & Austria

Great Britain & Ireland

Italy

London

Mexico

Pacific Northwest & Alaska

Paris

San Francisco

Fodor's Exploring Guides
Australia

Boston & New England

Britain

California

The Caribbean

Florence & Tuscany

Florida

France

Germany

Ireland

Italy

London

Mexico

New York City

Paris

Prague

Rome

Scotland

Singapore & Malaysia

Spain

Thailand

Turkey

Fodor's Flashmaps
Boston

New York

Washington, D.C.

Fodor's Pocket Guides
Acapulco

Bahamas

Barbados

Jamaica

London

New York City

Paris

Puerto Rico

San Francisco

Washington, D.C.

Fodor's Sports
Cycling

Golf Digest's Best Places to Play

Hiking

The Insider's Guide to the Best Canadian Skiing

Running

Sailing

Skiing in the USA & Canada

USA Today's Complete Four Sports Stadium Guide

Fodor's Three-In-Ones (guidebook, language cassette, and phrase book)
France

Germany

Italy

Mexico

Spain

Fodor's Special-Interest Guides
Complete Guide to America's National Parks

Condé Nast Traveler Caribbean Resort and Cruise Ship Finder

Cruises and Ports of Call

Euro Disney

France by Train

Halliday's New England Food Explorer

Healthy Escapes

Italy by Train

London Companion

Shadow Traffic's New York Shortcuts and Traffic Tips

Sunday in New York

Sunday in San Francisco

Touring Europe

Touring USA: Eastern Edition

Walt Disney World and the Orlando Area

Walt Disney World for Adults

Fodor's Vacation Planners
Great American Learning Vacations

Great American Sports & Adventure Vacations

Great American Vacations

Great American Vacations for Travelers with Disabilities

National Parks and Seashores of the East

National Parks of the West

The Wall Street Journal Guides to Business Travel

At last — a guide for Americans with disabilities that makes traveling a delight

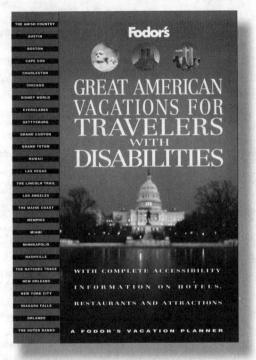

0-679-02591-X $18.00 ($24.00 Can)

This is the first and only complete guide to great American vacations for the 35 million North Americans with disabilities, as well as for those who care for them or for aging parents and relatives. Provides:

- Essential trip-planning information for travelers with mobility, vision, and hearing impairments
- Specific details on a huge array of facilities, along with solid descriptions of attractions, hotels, restaurants, and other destinations
- Up-to-date information on ISA-designated parking, level entranceways, and accessibility to pools, lounges, and bathrooms

AT LAST

YOUR OWN PERSONALIZED LIST
OF WHAT'S GOING ON IN THE
CITIES YOU'RE VISITING.

KEYED TO THE DAYS WHEN
YOU'LL BE THERE, CUSTOMIZED
FOR YOUR INTERESTS,
AND SENT TO YOU BEFORE YOU
LEAVE HOME.

GET THE INSIDER'S
PERSPECTIVE. . .

UP-TO-THE-MINUTE
ACCURATE
EASY TO ORDER
DELIVERED WHEN YOU NEED IT

Fodor's WORLDVIEW
TRAVEL UPDATE

Now there is a revolutionary way to get customized, time-sensitive travel information just before your trip.

Now you can obtain detailed information about what's going on in each city you'll be visiting <u>before</u> you leave home—up-to-the-minute, objective information about the events and activities that interest you most.

Your Itinerary:
Customized reports available for 160 destinations

Travel Updates contain the kind of time-sensitive insider information you can get only from local contacts – or from city magazines and newspapers once you arrive. But now you can have the same information before you leave for your trip.

The choice is yours: current art exhibits, theater, music festivals and special concerts, sporting events, antiques and flower shows, shopping, fitness, and more.

The information comes from hundreds of correspondents and thousands of sources worldwide. Updated continuously, it's like having your own personal concierge or friend in the city.

You specify the cities and when you'll be there. We'll do the rest — personalizing the information for you the way no guidebook can.

It's the perfect extension to your Fodor's guide and the best way to make the most of your valuable travel time.

Use Order Form on back or call 1-800-799-9609

Re
Tr
in t
doma
tion as
worthwl
the perfo.
Tickets are
venue. Alte
mances are ca
given. For more
Open-Air Theatre,
NW1 4NP Open A
Tel: 935-5756. Ends:
International Air Tattoo
Held biennially, the world
military air display in
d e m o s t r a -
tions, milit
bands

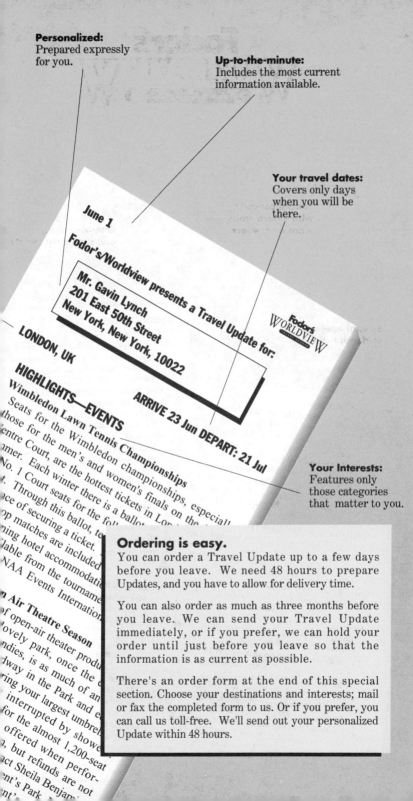

Personalized:
Prepared expressly for you.

Up-to-the-minute:
Includes the most current information available.

Your travel dates:
Covers only days when you will be there.

June 1

Fodor's/Worldview presents a Travel Update for:

Mr. Gavin Lynch
201 East 50th Street
New York, New York, 10022

Fodor's
WORLDVIEW

LONDON, UK

ARRIVE 23 Jun DEPART: 21 Jul

Your Interests:
Features only those categories that matter to you.

HIGHLIGHTS—EVENTS

Wimbledon Lawn Tennis Championships

Seats for the Wimbledon championships, especiall
those for the men's and women's finals on the
entre Court, are the hottest tickets in Lon
mer. Each winter there is a ballot
No. 1 Court seats for the foll
. Through this ballot, te
ace of securing a ticket.
op matches are included
ning hotel accommodati
lable from the tourname
NAA Events Internatio

n Air Theatre Season
of open-air theater produ
ovely park, once the e
ndies, is as much of an
dway in the Park and e
ring your largest umbrel
interrupted by showe
for the almost 1,200-seat
offered when perfor-
, but refunds are not
ct Sheila Benjam
nt's Park
nt'

Ordering is easy.

You can order a Travel Update up to a few days before you leave. We need 48 hours to prepare Updates, and you have to allow for delivery time.

You can also order as much as three months before you leave. We can send your Travel Update immediately, or if you prefer, we can hold your order until just before you leave so that the information is as current as possible.

There's an order form at the end of this special section. Choose your destinations and interests; mail or fax the completed form to us. Or if you prefer, you can call us toll-free. We'll send out your personalized Update within 48 hours.

Fodor's WORLDVIEW
TRAVEL UPDATE

**Special interest,
in-depth listings**

**Special concerts—
who's performing
what and where**

**One-of-a-kind,
one-time-only events**

Children — Events

Angel Canal Festival
The festivities include a children's fu
entertainers, a boat rally and displays o
water. Regent's Canal. Islington. N1.
Angel. Tel: 267 9100. 11:30am-5:30pm.

Blackheath Summer Kite Festival
Stunt kite displays with parachuting t
bears and trade stands. Free admission.
BR: Blackheath. 10am. 6/27.

Megabugs
Children will delight in this infestatio
giant robotic insects, including a pra
mantis 60 times life size. Mon-Sat 10
6pm; Sun 11am-6pm. Admission 4
pounds. Natural History Museum, Crom
Road. SW7. Tube: South Kensington.
938 9123. Ends 10/01.

Childminders
This establishment employs only won
providing nurses and qualified nannies to

Music — Jazz & Blues

Tito Puente's Golden Men of Latin Jazz
The father of mambo and Cuban rumba king
comes to town. Royal Festival Hall. South Bank.
SE1. Tube: Waterloo. Tel: 928 8800. 8pm. 7/15.

Georgie Fame and The New York Band
Riding a popular tide with his latest album, the
smoky-voiced Fame and his keyboard are on a
tour yet again. The Grand. Clapham Junction.
SW11. BR: Clapham Junction. Tel: 738 9000
7:30pm. 7/07.

Jacques Loussier Play Bach Trio
The French jazz classicist and colleagues.
Kenwood Lakeside. Hampstead Lane.
Kenwood. NW3. Tube: Golders Green, then bus
210. Tel: 413 1443. 7pm. 7/10.

Tony Bennett and Ronnie Scott
Royal Festival Hall. South Bank. SE1. Tube:
Waterloo. Tel: 928 8800. 8pm. 7/11.

Santana
Royal Festival Hall. South Bank. SE1. Tube:
Waterloo. Tel: 928 8800. 8pm. 7/12.

Count Basie Orchestra and Nancy Wilson Trio
Royal Festival Hall. South Bank. SE1. Tube
Waterloo. Tel: 928 8800. 8pm. 7/14.

King Pleasure and the Biscuit Boys
Royal Festival Hall. South Bank. SE1. Tube
Waterloo. Tel: 928 8800. 6:30 and 9pm. 7/16.

Al Green and the London Community Gospel Choir
Royal Festival Hall. South Bank. SE1. Tube
Waterloo. Tel: 928 8800. 8pm. 7/13.

BB King and Linda Hopkins
Mother of the blues and successor to Bessi
Smith, Hopkins meets up with "Blues Boy
Royal Festival Hall. South Bank. SE

Music — Classical

Marylebone Sinfonia
Kenneth Gowen conducts music b
and Rossini. Queen Elizabeth Ha
Bank. SE1. Tube: Waterloo. Tel:
7:45pm. 7/16.

London Philharmonic
Franz Welser-Moest and George
conduct selections by Alexand
Messiaen, and some of Benjamin's
positions. Queen Elizabeth Hall. S
SE1. Tube: Waterloo. Tel: 928 880

London Pro Arte Orchestra and Fo
Murray Stewart conducts sele
Rossini, Haydn and Jonathan Wille
Queen Elizabeth Hall. South E
Tube: Waterloo. Tel: 928 8800. 7:

Kensington Symphony Orchestra
Russell Keable conducts Dvora

Here's what you get . . .

Detailed information about what's going on — precisely when you'll be there.

Show openings during your visit

Handy pocket-size booklet

Reviews by local critics

Exhibitions & Shows—Antique & Flower

Westminster Antiques Fair

Over 50 stands with pre-1830 furniture and other Victorian and earlier items. Thu-Fri 11am-8pm; Sat-Sun 11am-6pm. Admission 4 pounds, children free. Old Royal Horticultural Hall. Vincent Square. SW1. Tel: 0444/48 25 14. 6-24 thru 6/27.

Royal Horticultural Society Flower Show

The show includes displays of carnations, summer fruit and vegetables. Tue 11am-7pm; Wed 10am-5pm. Admission Tue 4 pounds, Wed 2 pounds. Royal Horticultural Halls. Greycoat Street and Vincent Square. SW1. Tube: Victoria. 7/20 thru 7/21.

...mpton Court Palace International Flower Show

...ajor international garden and flower show taking place in conjunction with

...ter — Musical

...unset Boulevard

In June, the four Andrew Lloyd Webber musicals which dominated London's stages in the 1980s (Cats, Starlight Express, Phantom of the Opera and Aspects of Love) are joined by the composer's latest work, a show rumored to have his best music to date. The 1950 Billy Wilder film about a helpless young writer who is drawn into the world of a possessive, aging silent screen star offers rich opportunities for Webber's evolving style. Soaring, aching melodies, lush technical effects and psychological thrills are all expected. Patti Lupone stars. Mon-Sat at 8pm; matinee Thu-Sat at 3pm. In-person sales only at the box office; credit card bookings, Tel: 344 0055. Admission 15-32.50 pounds. Adelphi Theatre. The Strand. WC2. Tube: Charing Cross. Tel: 836 7611. Starts: 6/21.

Leonardo A Portrait of Love

A new musical about the great Renaissance artist and inventor comes in for a London pre-... tested by a ... The work explores

...ector Sports — Other Sports

Greyhound Racing: Wembley Stadium

This dog racing track offers good views of greyhound racing held on Mon, Wed and Fri. No credit cards. Stadium Way. Wembley. HA9. Tube: Wembley Park. Tel: 902 8833.

Benson & Hedges Cricket Cup Final

Lord's Cricket Ground. St. John's Wood Road. NW8. Tube: St. John's Wood. Tel: 289 1611. 11am. 7/10.

...ess-Fax & Overnight Mail

...ost Office, Trafalgar Square Branch

Offers a network of fax services, the Intelpost system, throughout the country and abroad. Mon-Sat 8am-8pm, Sun 9am-5pm. William IV Street. WC2. Tube: Charing Cross. Tel: 930 9580.

Fodor's WORLDVIEW
TRAVEL UPDATE

London, England
Arriving: June 23
Departing: July 21

Interest Categories

For <u>your</u> personalized Travel Update, choose the categories you're most interested in from this list. Every Travel Update automatically provides you with *Event Highlights* - the best of what's happening during the dates of your trip.

1.	**Business Services**	Fax & Overnight Mail, Computer Rentals, Photocopying, Protocol, Secretarial, Messenger, Translation Services

Dining

2.	**All Day Dining**	Breakfast & Brunch, Cafes & Tea Rooms, Late-Night Dining
3.	**Local Cuisine**	In Every Price Range—from Budget Restaurants to the Special Splurge
4.	**European Cuisine**	Continental, French, Italian
5.	**Asian Cuisine**	Chinese, Far Eastern, Japanese, Other
6.	**Americas Cuisine**	American, Mexican & Latin
7.	**Nightlife**	Bars, Dance Clubs, Casinos, Comedy Clubs, Ethnic, Pubs & Beer Halls
8.	**Entertainment**	Theater—Comedy, Drama, English Language, Musicals, Dance, Ticket Agencies
9.	**Music**	Country/Western/Folk, Classical, Traditional & Ethnic, Opera, Jazz & Blues, Pop, Rock
10.	**Children's Activities**	Events, Attractions
11.	**Tours**	Local Tours, Day Trips, Overnight Excursions, Cruises
12.	**Exhibitions, Festivals & Shows**	Antiques & Flower, History & Cultural, Art Exhibitions, Fairs & Craft Shows, Music & Art Festivals
13.	**Shopping**	Districts & Malls, Markets, Regional Specialities
14.	**Fitness**	Bicycling, Health Clubs, Hiking, Jogging
15.	**Recreational Sports**	Boating/Sailing, Fishing, Golf, Ice Skating, Skiing, Snorkeling/Scuba, Swimming, Tennis & Racquet
16.	**Spectator Sports**	Auto Racing, Baseball, Basketball, Boating & Sailing, Football, Golf, Horse Racing, Ice Hockey, Rugby, Soccer, Tennis, Track & Field, Other Sports

Please note that interest category content will vary by season, destination, and length of stay.

Destinations

The Fodor's/Worldview Travel Update covers more than 160 destinations world-wide. Choose the destinations that match your itinerary from this list. (Choose bulleted destinations only.)

Europe
- Amsterdam
- Athens
- Barcelona
- Berlin
- Brussels
- Budapest
- Copenhagen
- Dublin
- Edinburgh
- Florence
- Frankfurt
- French Riviera
- Geneva
- Glasgow
- Istanbul
- Lausanne
- Lisbon
- London
- Madrid
- Milan
- Moscow
- Munich
- Oslo
- Paris
- Prague
- Provence
- Rome
- Salzburg
* Seville
- St. Petersburg
- Stockholm
- Venice
- Vienna
- Zurich

United States (Mainland)
- Albuquerque
- Atlanta
- Atlantic City
- Baltimore
- Boston
* Branson, MO
* Charleston, SC
- Chicago
- Cincinnati
- Cleveland
- Dallas/Ft. Worth
- Denver
- Detroit
- Houston
* Indianapolis
- Kansas City
- Las Vegas
- Los Angeles
- Memphis
- Miami
- Milwaukee
- Minneapolis/ St. Paul
* Nashville
- New Orleans
- New York City
- Orlando
- Palm Springs
- Philadelphia
- Phoenix
- Pittsburgh
- Portland
* Reno/ Lake Tahoe
- St. Louis
- Salt Lake City
- San Antonio
- San Diego
- San Francisco
* Santa Fe
- Seattle
- Tampa
- Washington, DC

Alaska
- Alaskan Destinations

Hawaii
- Honolulu
- Island of Hawaii
- Kauai
- Maui

Canada
- Quebec City
- Montreal
- Ottawa
- Toronto
- Vancouver

Bahamas
- Abaco
- Eleuthera/ Harbour Island
- Exuma
- Freeport
- Nassau & Paradise Island

Bermuda
- Bermuda Countryside
- Hamilton

British Leeward Islands
- Anguilla
- Antigua & Barbuda
- St. Kitts & Nevis

British Virgin Islands
- Tortola & Virgin Gorda

British Windward Islands
- Barbados
- Dominica
- Grenada
- St. Lucia
- St. Vincent
- Trinidad & Tobago

Cayman Islands
- The Caymans

Dominican Republic
- Santo Domingo

Dutch Leeward Islands
- Aruba
- Bonaire
- Curacao

Dutch Windward Island
- St. Maarten/ St. Martin

French West Indies
- Guadeloupe
- Martinique
- St. Barthelemy

Jamaica
- Kingston
- Montego Bay
- Negril
- Ocho Rios

Puerto Rico
- Ponce
- San Juan

Turks & Caicos
- Grand Turk/ Providenciales

U.S. Virgin Islands
- St. Croix
- St. John
- St. Thomas

Mexico
- Acapulco
- Cancun & Isla Mujeres
- Cozumel
- Guadalajara
- Ixtapa & Zihuatanejo
- Los Cabos
- Mazatlan
- Mexico City
- Monterrey
- Oaxaca
- Puerto Vallarta

South/Central America
* Buenos Aires
* Caracas
* Rio de Janeiro
* San Jose, Costa Rica
* Sao Paulo

Middle East
* Jerusalem

Australia & New Zealand
- Auckland
- Melbourne
* South Island
- Sydney

China
- Beijing
- Guangzhou
- Shanghai

Japan
- Kyoto
- Nagoya
- Osaka
- Tokyo
- Yokohama

Pacific Rim/Other
* Bali
- Bangkok
- Hong Kong & Macau
- Manila
- Seoul
- Singapore
- Taipei

* Destinations available by 1/1/95

Order Form

THIS TRAVEL UPDATE IS FOR (Please print):

Name

Address

City	State	Country	ZIP

Tel # (   )   -   Fax # (   )   -

Title of this Fodor's guide:

Store and location where guide was purchased:

INDICATE YOUR DESTINATIONS/DATES: You can order up to three (3) destinations from the previous page. Fill in your arrival and departure dates for each destination. **Your Travel Update itinerary (all destinations selected) cannot exceed 30 days from beginning to end.**

			Month	Day		Month	Day
(Sample) LONDON		From:	6 /	21	To:	6 /	30
1		From:	/		To:	/	
2		From:	/		To:	/	
3		From:	/		To:	/	

CHOOSE YOUR INTERESTS: Select up to eight (8) categories from the list of interest categories shown on the previous page and circle the numbers below:

1 2 3 4 5 6 7 8 9 10 11 12 13 14 15 16

CHOOSE WHEN YOU WANT YOUR TRAVEL UPDATE DELIVERED (Check one):
❑ Please send my Travel Update immediately.
❑ Please hold my order until a few weeks before my trip to include the most up-to-date information.
Completed orders will be sent within 48 hours. Allow 7-10 days for U.S. mail delivery.

ADD UP YOUR ORDER HERE. *SPECIAL OFFER FOR FODOR'S PURCHASERS ONLY!*

	Suggested Retail Price	Your Price	This Order
First destination ordered	$ 9.95	$ 7.95	$ 7.95
Second destination (if applicable)	$ 6.95	$ 4.95	+
Third destination (if applicable)	$ 6.95	$ 4.95	+

DELIVERY CHARGE (Check one and enter amount below)

	Within U.S. & Canada	Outside U.S. & Canada
First Class Mail	❑ $2.50	❑ $5.00
FAX	❑ $5.00	❑ $10.00
Priority Delivery	❑ $15.00	❑ $27.00

ENTER DELIVERY CHARGE FROM ABOVE: +

TOTAL: $

METHOD OF PAYMENT IN U.S. FUNDS ONLY (Check one):
❑ AmEx   ❑ MC   ❑ Visa   ❑ Discover   ❑ Personal Check (U. S. & Canada only)
❑ Money Order/ International Money Order

Make check or money order payable to: Fodor's Worldview Travel Update

Credit Card

Expiration Date:

Authorized Signature

SEND THIS COMPLETED FORM WITH PAYMENT TO:
Fodor's Worldview Travel Update, 114 Sansome Street, Suite 700, San Francisco, CA 94104

OR CALL OR FAX US 24-HOURS A DAY
Telephone **1-800-799-9609** • Fax **1-800-799-9619** (From within the U.S. & Canada)
(Outside the U.S. & Canada: Telephone 415-616-9988 • Fax 415-616-9989)

(Please have this guide in front of you when you call so we can verify purchase.)
Code: FTG   Offer valid until 12/31/95